Sinking Columbus

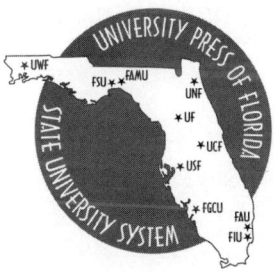

Florida A&M University, Tallahassee
Florida Atlantic University, Boca Raton
Florida Gulf Coast University, Ft. Myers
Florida International University, Miami
Florida State University, Tallahassee
University of Central Florida, Orlando
University of Florida, Gainesville
University of North Florida, Jacksonville
University of South Florida, Tampa
University of West Florida, Pensacola

Stephen J. Summerhill and John Alexander Williams

University Press of Florida
GAINESVILLE
TALLAHASSEE
TAMPA
BOCA RATON
PENSACOLA
ORLANDO
MIAMI
JACKSONVILLE
FT. MYERS

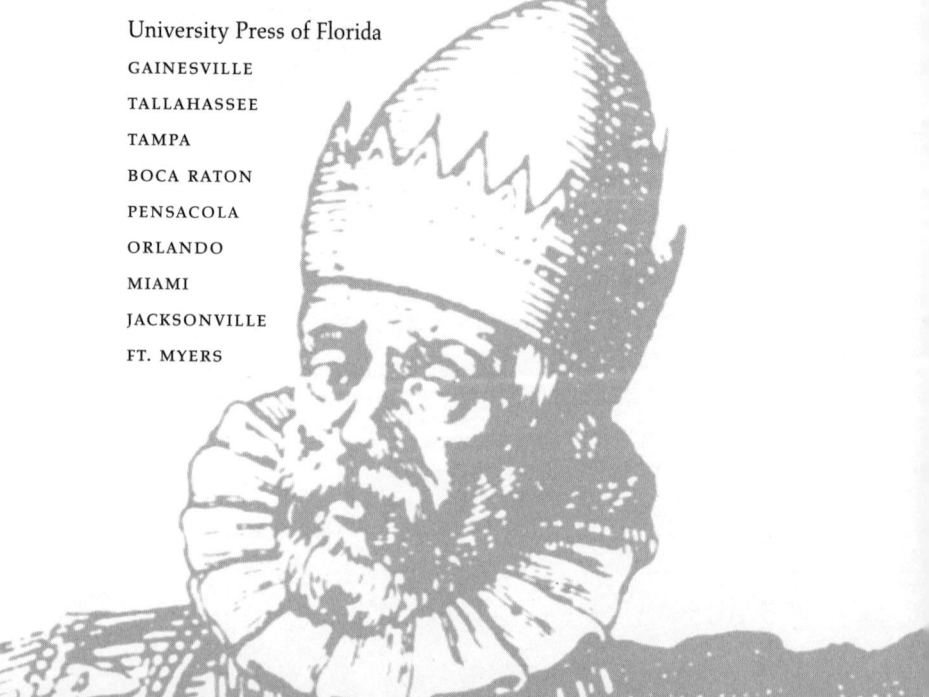

Sinking Columbus

Contested History, Cultural Politics, and Mythmaking during the Quincentenary

Copyright 2000 by the Board of Regents of the State of Florida
Printed in the United States of America on acid-free paper
All rights reserved

Parts of chapters 2 and 4 first appeared in *Encounters* 8 (1992):26–29.
Unpublished material on the Chicago World's Fair in chapter 3 is
published with the permission of The Chicago Historical Society.
Parts of chapters 2 and 7 are reprinted from *The Public Historian*
14, 4 (Fall 1992): 31–56, © 1992 by The Regents of the University
of California.
Parts of chapter 7 appeared in *The Tulanian* (Summer 1992): 19–23.
An earlier version of parts of chapter 4 appeared in *The Torch* 65, 1
(Fall 1992): 24–29.

05 04 03 02 01 00 6 5 4 3 2 1

LIBRARY OF CONGRESS CATALOGING-IN-PUBLICATION DATA
Summerhill, Stephen J., 1944–
Sinking Columbus: contested history, cultural politics, and
mythmaking during the quincentenary / Stephen J. Summerhill
and John Alexander Williams.
p. cm.
Includes bibliographical references (p.) and index.
ISBN 0-8130-1799-8 (alk. paper)
1. Columbus Quincentenary, 1992–1993. 2. Columbus, Christopher.
3. America—Discovery and exploration—Spanish—Historiography.
I. Williams, John Alexander, 1938–. II. Title.
E119.2.S86   2000
970.01'6 21; aa05-01-21—dc00   00-020994

The University Press of Florida is the scholarly publishing agency for
the State University System of Florida, comprising Florida A&M
University, Florida Atlantic University, Florida Gulf Coast University,
Florida International University, Florida State University, University
of Central Florida, University of Florida, University of North Florida,
University of South Florida, and University of West Florida.

University Press of Florida
15 Northwest 15th Street
Gainesville, FL 32611
http://www.upf.com

To Gail and Norma
Compañeras de viaje

> ... I will say at the outset that there is only one world, and although we speak of the Old World and the New, this is because the latter was lately discovered by us, and not because there are two.
>
> Garcilaso de la Vega, El Inca, *Royal Commentaries of the Incas and General History of Peru*, trans. Harold V. Livermore (Austin: University of Texas Press, 1966), 9.

> They go north to get south.
>
> *Juarez by Terry Allen* (Mill Valley, Calif.: Fate Records, 1991), compact sound disk.

Contents

List of Illustrations ix

Acknowledgments xi

Introduction 1

1. Christopher Columbus, the Chicken, and the Egg 7
2. Sailing over the Edge: The U.S. Quincentenary Jubilee Commission 34
3. Cities of Gold 63
4. Ethnos, History, and Myth 107
5. The Quincentenary as Excess: The Case of Spain 127
6. The Same and the Other: Italy and Latin America 150
7. Conclusion: Weeds of Change 179

   Notes 195

   Index 213

Illustrations

"The Columbus Genealogical Tree"   95

The Landing of Columbus by John Vanderlyn   96

A "reenactment" of Columbus's landing, staged annually by San Francisco Italian-Americans, 1989   97

Luis Yáñez Barnuevo, president of the Spanish National Quincentenary Commission, entertaining U.S. Jubilee Commission chairman John Goudie and commission member Jane Lee García   98

Eminent Columbus scholar Paolo Emilio Taviani receiving a Doctorate in Humane Letters from President Edward Jennings, Ohio State University, December 1987   98

AmeriFlora '92, Franklin Park Conservatory, Columbus, Ohio   99

Aerial view of the 535-acre Cartuja Island with the full site of Expo '92, Seville, Spain   100

Aerial view of a portion of Genoa harbor showing one of the most characteristic sights of the Genoa Expo, *Il Bigo*   101

Side view of the Faro a Colón or Columbus Lighthouse, Santo Domingo, Dominican Republic   102

American Indian Movement (AIM) activist Russell Means pouring symbolic animal blood on Denver's Christ-like statue of Columbus   103

AIM protestors forcing Italian-American organizations to cancel the planned Columbus Day parade in Denver in 1992   104

Mounted police escorting costumed Knights of Columbus to a rally   104

Protestors and their slogans at Aquatic Park, San Francisco, October 11, 1992   105

Model Lisa Hayward of Houston posing as "Miss Liberty" in the denouement of Antoni Miralda's "Honeymoon Project" in Red Rock Canyon near Las Vegas, February 14, 1992   106

Acknowledgments

The authors were encouraged in their determination to tell this story by several people, most notably Malcolm Richardson, who first broached the idea of a collaborative book on the Quincentenary and continued to foster it at every opportunity. William H. McNeill also encouraged the project, and William Phillips of the University of Minnesota made valuable suggestions for improving the manuscript for publication. Christian Zacher, the director of Quincentenary programs at Ohio State University, repeatedly supported Summerhill's work in Spain and the Dominican Republic, and he also launched Williams's participation in this project by helping him attend a conference in Santo Domingo in December 1988.

At Appalachian State University, Williams wishes to acknowledge the support of Dean Donald W. Sink and those colleagues who allowed him to talk and teach about Columbus even though his assigned niche was elsewhere. Professor Bettie Bond, now emerita, deserves special thanks, as does John Bond, who first introduced us to the concept of catastrophic sexual transmutation. Williams also wishes to thank family members and friends whose hospitality enabled him to pursue research at widely separated locations; they include Sander Williams and Susan Hockenson in Chicago, Los Angeles, and Las Vegas; Matt Williams and Hilary Hibel in San Francisco; Jared Williams in New York; David Taylor in Washington; and Paola Tavarelli in Italy. Finally, Norma Colyer was every bit a companion on this voyage from its outset—proofreader, critic, translator, advisor, provider of comfort and aid. Thank you for letting me use your computer.

At Ohio State University, Summerhill wishes to thank G. Micheal Riley, former dean of humanities, for the encouragement and support that led to his involvement in the Quincentenary. Former president Edward Jennings and former vice provost for international affairs Francille Firebaugh provided important support at many points. Gail Summerhill was a superb Quincentenary program administrator who helped track down countless items. Sara Dickinson provided crucial information about Genoa and the Italian Quincentenary. Outside Ohio State, special thanks are owed Rosario Sevilla, the former director of the Escuela de Estudios Hispano-Americanos in Seville, Spain, whose assistance and insights contributed centrally to many parts of this book. The present director of the Escuela, Consuelo Varela, also provided important help, while Mercedes Rivas of Salamanca, Spain, Adrian Shubert of York University, Toronto, and Richard Maddox of Carnegie-Mellon University, Pittsburgh, gave of their expertise generously and without hesitation.

Perhaps we should also mention the developers of the software and hardware that made it possible to communicate easily and frequently between the middle of Ohio and the middle of the Carolina Blue Ridge. With the possible exception of this last-named group, none of the people mentioned bear responsibility for the flaws of this book.

Introduction

> In fourteen hundred and ninety-two
> Columbus sailed the ocean blue

We know the rest ... or thought we did. During the Columbus Quincentenary of 1992, the significance and reputation of Christopher Columbus were turned upside down in both the United States and other countries as fully as if the Admiral had indeed found monsters swimming in the Ocean Sea. How fully this change took effect may be fathomed by comparing two commemorative events that occurred in June 1992, as the quincentennial year neared its halfway mark. One was the exhibition "Christopher Columbus, Mariner," organized by the Swedish Maritime Museum outside Stockholm. Most of the guests at the opening reception had gray hair, and a number of the men sported naval insignia. On the exhibit walls, they found the Columbus story as it had been learned by Americans since the 1790s: Columbus was a young Genoese dreamer who went to sea and in time washed up on

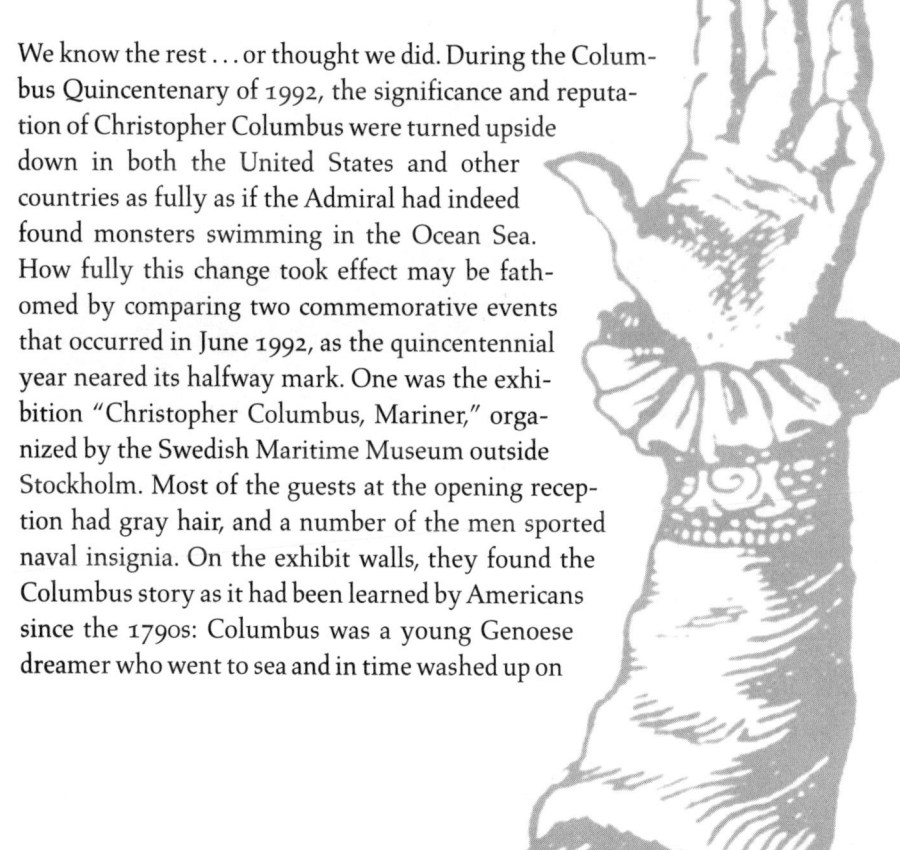

the Iberian peninsula, where inspiration, perseverance, and courage brought him to his destiny—immortality as the "discoverer of America." An audiovisual introduction to the exhibition elaborated on these themes, featuring marine sounds and imagery, tropical islands inhabited by "savages" and "cannibals," and a montage of images from the modern Caribbean featuring West Indian tourist scenes and cheerful calypso music.[1] This exhibition was itself a museum piece and could not have been staged in a major public venue in the United States.

Two weeks later, four thousand miles away, the second event took place at a summer camp in Ohio, where schoolchildren staged a quincentennial pageant based on a new Columbian interpretation advanced by those who were referred to by their critics as the "politically correct." The pageant was entitled "Undoing Columbus." It took place outdoors, around a small lake with an island in the center, where children stood around bearing various cardboard shapes representing trees, flowers, birds and animals, and "an Indian." "Here is our land, our lovely, lovely land," the children sang. The earth, represented by a large cloth disk painted blue, beamed in the background. Then from behind the island, three canoes with square-rigged sails appeared. One of them carried Columbus, bearing a sword. Columbus stepped ashore and, swinging his sword, struck down every living thing. The audience booed and sang, "Mean old Columbus, nasty, nasty Columbus." The narrator appealed to the audience to call to the earth for help. In response to the cries, two large "eyes" on the disk opened wide, and a large, colorful "fish" made of soft foam rubber (inhabited by several children) emerged from behind the "earth" to chase Columbus. Simultaneously, two long cloth arms with large cardboard hands were unfurled from either side of the planet to capture (embrace?) him. Finally, Columbus called out, "I give up." One by one, the slain ones returned to life. Members of the audience were invited to come forward to be embraced in the arms of Mother Earth, while everyone sang "This Land Is Your Land; This Land Is My Land."[2]

A dozen years earlier, when the first stirrings of American interest in the Quincentenary emerged, commemorations like the one staged by the Swedish museum were what most planners envisioned. But by 1992, this heroic, romantic, "Eurocentric" interpretation of Columbus was confined mostly to Italian-American ethnic venues, while the image of Columbus as a genocidal invader of the Americas was being debated throughout Europe and the United States, and was de rigueur in advanced circles. Most quincentennial observances fell between these two extremes, yet—given the impact that previous Columbian anniversaries had had in American life—the most noteworthy aspect of the entire quincentennial enterprise was this shift of understanding about the meaning of Columbus, which emerged during the course of planning for 1992. Equally striking was how little attention the observances ended up commanding from the public at large. In spite of and possibly because of the debates surrounding the meaning of the Quincentenary, the 1992 commemoration failed to stir the public imagination and disappeared from view almost before the anniversary year was under way.

The same or worse occurred in other countries such as Mexico and Italy, where the glare of media attention could not hide the fact that few had cared about the Quincentenary in the first place. And in Spain, which made a major commitment to 1992, the commemoration built up such a large reserve of resentment that many people tried to avoid it and everyone was relieved when it was finally over. How did this shift from heroic celebration to failed public relations venture take place? How did Christopher Columbus go from hero to villain and from icon to false idol in such a short time? Can planners of future commemorations learn anything from this fall of epic into irony? Such are the issues we treat in this book.

Each of us watched the shipwreck of Columbus from a front-row seat. Initially, Williams participated as a federal bureaucrat charged with managing an official program for the Quincentenary. He was in fact the person responsible for the official revival of this awkward word, known in office parlance as the "Q-word," which President Ronald Reagan said would take him another five hundred years to learn how to pronounce. Later, after his official position sank from its lack of political ballast, he watched from the vantage point of a professional historian, detached from but fully absorbed in the spectacle. Summerhill, a professor of Spanish language and literature at Ohio State University, participated in the Quincentenary as a university administrator and academic. Like Williams, he was hopeful of salvaging something of enduring value and intellectual respectability from the wreck, especially from the Quincentenary's international aspects. What follows is our report on the commemoration. We offer it as an account of recent political and cultural history in both the United States and abroad and as an estimate of the ultimate significance of the change in the meaning of Columbus in contemporary life.

No one has yet ventured into this territory, perhaps because things are still too recent or because some of what happened is still felt as too painful. In truth, the story is neither pretty nor inspirational, but the Quincentenary carries many important lessons that we hope will not be lost. Columbus's shipwreck, it is now clear, was an episode in contested history, an event that helped move the interpretation of the past toward the center of a debate about the future that is somewhat glibly known as "the culture wars." The Quincentenary was probably the first major debate to reach the general public wherein contemporary scholarship competed with "public" spokespersons representing official organizations. In the usual skirmishes engaging these groups, public officials defend established historical myths and meanings in the name of the larger public while they also condemn the alleged political and unpatriotic bias of their rivals as "radical" or "extremist." For their part, scholars advance arguments subversive of traditional myths while accusing the officials and bureaucrats who defend the myths of political and/or class bias. The object of the competition—apart from institutional rivalries and generational conflicts—is the legitimacy of a given historical interpretation. One set of experts hurls epithets at the other: "traditional," "Eurocentric," "gender-biased," and "mythical." The other set responds with terms such as "revisionist," "ideological," "politically correct," and "relativistic." With legitimacy comes the validation of the prevailing experts, and this in turn presumably bolsters public confidence in the interpretation they offer, though it is difficult to discern exactly what actual members of actual publics—as opposed to the contestants—really think about such contests. The real prizes for the combatants are institutional approval, peer recognition, and, occasionally, career advancement.

In any case, contested history is, as more than one ironist has pointed out, debate about the future of the past. In this regard, it was particularly appropriate that such debate should focus on the figure of Christopher Columbus. Twice before, in the 1790s and again a century later, the way in which the United States observed the Columbian anniversary forecast with remarkable accuracy the nation's future, first as an expansionist new democracy, and later as an emerging world power. Is there a message about the next century in the way Americans fought over Columbus in 1992? We do not have all the answers to this and similar questions, but the enticement of posing them was what drew us into the often frustrating efforts to participate in the commemoration and it now makes us believe that a report on the Quincentenary is of value.

The importance of our story lies in the fact that the sinking of Columbus and the contested history upon which the official commemorations foundered are what gave the Quincentenary its enduring positive value. One of the arguments we make throughout this book is that *the 1992 Quincentenary succeeded because it failed.* Planners set out to celebrate an imperial past but found themselves confronting difficult questions about the rise of colonialism, the destruction of native American societies, and the disruption of biological habitats throughout the globe. In this way, 1992 contributed to an increased public recognition of the importance of nature, native peoples, and human rights in contemporary society. This was not what organizers had in mind when they launched the "celebration" ten years earlier, but it became the inevitable destiny of a process that was overwhelmed by the demons it unleashed. Of course, marketers do not like a party that stops being fun and they always have difficulty with things that are controversial or complex, so they abandoned the Quincentenary and moved on to whatever other promotional events could sell TV time or newspapers. But this only proved that the Quincentenary as it emerged from controversy and official frustration was no longer trite or superficial. The transformed meaning of 1992 was significant even if official programs now had to struggle to stay in view of the public. The enduring impact of the Quincentenary derives from victory born in the ashes of defeat.

Every year, it seems, we are asked to ponder the meaning of still another commemoration, as if the idea of public anniversaries has become symptomatic of an underlying wish to recall the past and feel ourselves members of an historical community. One might argue that this rage for anniversaries so typical of our time points to a growing need to find meaning in public life beyond the emptiness of television and partisan politics. Whatever the reason, the latest occasion to vie for our attention was the Millennium, the turn of the Gregorian calendar on December 31, 1999, which supposedly launched a new thousand-year period of history. In reality, the millennial turn would not take place until a full year later, but events planners decided to ignore this; the *New York Times*, the so-called newspaper of record in whose eponymous backyard one of the larger celebrations took place, waspishly dismissed those who dwelt on this inconvenient fact as pedants. In Britain, a centrist government, bereft of ideology but awash in cash thanks to a new national lottery, used the occasion to spread projects around the country and to up the ante in its tourism promotion. In the United States, First Lady Hillary Rodham Clinton launched an official Millennium initiative in 1997 as "an opportunity to reflect on the past, on where we've been, on who we are, and what we hope to become."[3] In the end, however, the Millennium disappointed those who expected a moment of profound reflection, not to mention those who looked for the end of time or of civilized life as we know it. Y2K was mainly a huge party, a beguiling combination of rhetoric, spending, and entertainment. Things went on after the hangovers disappeared.

This was not the fate of the Quincentenary, which taught us that good things can happen even when plans go awry and public relations people turn away. It was a moment when habitual categories were challenged and fondly held illusions were disrupted. It was, in short, a moment when things got out of hand. What follows is the story of how that happened.

1

Christopher Columbus, the Chicken, and the Egg

There is no better representation of how we used to view Columbus than a picture that hangs in an Ohio museum, Delacroix's *The Triumph of Columbus*, a portrayal of that day in April 1493 when Columbus presented himself and his American trophies before the Catholic kings of Spain in the city of Barcelona. Surely this was one of the greatest scenes in human history: part Roman triumph, part medieval pageant, above all a supreme moment of personal vindication for Columbus but poignant also because we know that this moment would turn out to be the pinnacle of his glory, that hereafter in his lifetime his triumph would turn to frustration and disappointment.

Delacroix painted the scene in jewel-like colors, with the Admiral in gold, the monarchs bedecked and bejeweled, their dais canopied and carpeted by cloths of velvety red and blue. At Columbus's side the artist placed his American treasures, the objects making a rather puny array at the foot of the thrones, while his human trophies—arrayed in the feathered headgear that would remain for centuries the symbol of the American native—display an attitude at once submissive and dignified. The painting was one of a pair commissioned by a Russian nobleman to hang in a villa he had recently purchased near Florence. The other is painted in somber and contemplative tones and shows the visionary Columbus at the outset of his quest, portraying his arrival at the monastery of La Rábida near Palos, where he would find shelter for his young son Diego and influential support for his quest in the court of Queen Isabella. Neither painting reflects a meticulous concern for historical accuracy: the massing of figures in the *Triumph* is modeled on Titian, and the city portrayed in the background looks more like Florence than Barcelona. Similarly, the monastery portrayed in the companion painting is not the Franciscan La Rábida but is based on Dominican and Cistercian monasteries that Delacroix visited in other parts of Spain. But both pictures are faithful to their inspirational source, the romantic image of Columbus as a lonely and heroic individual presented in the famous biography published in 1828 by the American writer Washington Irving.[1] It thus seems fitting that both paintings now hang in American museums, the first in Toledo, the other in Washington, D.C., for despite their European provenance both reflect the American impact on Columbus's reputation and on the meaning of his life and deeds for the people of the United States.

In fact, in these works by a French artist portraying Spanish scenes and painted for a Russian prince to hang in an Italian villa we have all the essential elements of a thoroughly American creation, an American Columbus enshrined in national myth and popular memory. This is the Columbus for whom cities and children were named in the nineteenth century, whose statue ornaments parks and squares on three continents. This Columbus is the man we learn about in school and remember not for his medieval mysticism or his foundation of a Spanish noble house but for his romantic example of heroic individualism. The American Columbus is a man of unremarkable origins who accomplished remarkable deeds, whose vision, perseverance, and strength of character were enough to change the world. An example for us all.[2]

There were few signs in 1982 that this exemplary Columbus of our schooldays was about to be contested. In fact the earliest stirrings of interest in 1992 harked back to the formats of earlier commemorations, the celebrations that had helped enshrine the Admiral in our national pantheon. American nationalists of the 1790s had made Columbus the central figure in a national origin myth that stressed America's separateness from Europe and the expansive future that seemed open to the "new and rising empire" of the United States. They created the Columbus Day observance, erected the first Columbus monuments, held the first parades, and scattered the Admiral's name in both its latinized and feminized forms across the national map. In this spirit, Columbia, South Carolina, erected a Columbus statue in 1987 on its riverfront, while another namesake city, Columbus, Ohio, began planning to moor a replica Santa María at the edge of its downtown. Fort Lauderdale, Memphis, Mishawaka (Indiana), and Columbus (Wisconsin) were among the other localities that erected new monuments as the Quincentenary approached. The major quincentennial events—such as the parade of tall ships in New York, the AmeriFlora fair in Columbus, Ohio, and the aborted national tour by diesel-powered replicas of the Niña, Pinta, and Santa María—were echoes of the fourth Columbian centenary of 1892–93. In 1892 a parade of ships in New York had included replicas of Columbus's—towed behind Spanish warships, since (as would be the case in 1992) the replicas were unable to make much headway under their own sails. The climax of the quadricentennial celebration was Chicago's World's Columbian Exposition, arguably the greatest of American world fairs, which was postponed until 1893 after its official opening in October 1892. In fact, the earliest official stirrings of interest in the Quincentenary came from those who hoped to replicate in 1992 the achievements and impact of the great Chicago fair.

The man whom these plans were intended to honor was, like Delacroix's icon, a thoroughly American hero. This Columbus was an Italian mariner born in Genoa whom Queen Isabella of Spain provided with ships to sail westward across the Atlantic in 1492. He discovered America and proved that the earth was round. He was robbed of his just rewards by an ungrateful King Ferdinand and of his fame by another Italian, Amerigo Vespucci, who somehow got the Spanish form of his first name affixed to the continents which Columbus found.

These are the "facts" of Columbus's life as most Americans preferred to believe them—an outline confirmed in its essentials in 1985 by no less an authority than Secretary of State George Shultz when he swore into office the presidential commission Congress created to preside over the celebration in 1992.[3] In its wisdom, Congress named this body the Christopher Columbus Quincentenary Jubilee Commission, but most Washington hands who dealt with it quickly shortened this to

"Jubilee Commission," mainly because "jubilee" was the only word in the title that the commission did not share with one or another of the dozens of additional public and private bodies which sprang up to claim a share in planning the Quincentenary program. As it turned out, an awkward name was only one of the commission's many problems. Commissioners soon found out that few of the "facts" about Columbus could be trusted. Almost nothing about his life and deeds is beyond dispute. And disputes about the details of Columbus's life and deeds turned out to be related to other controversies, controversies over the meaning and significance of 1992, about who should celebrate the anniversary, how it should be celebrated, and whether it should have been celebrated at all.

Visitors to the archives of the city of Genoa today can view more than two dozen fifteenth-century documents, mostly notarial records and the like, which testify to the fact that there was born and raised in that city, probably in the year 1451, a person named Cristoforo Colombo. He was the son of a weaver, Domenico Colombo, and of his wife, Susanna Fontanarossa, and had two brothers, Bartolomeo and Diego, and a number of cousins, including one named Amighetto, which translates roughly as "Buddy." Cristoforo Colombo grew to maturity as the Genoese republic reached the apogee of its power as a center of maritime trade linking western Europe with the trading ports of the eastern Mediterranean. He followed a maritime career, natural enough for a Genoese youth although a bit unusual for the son of a weaver, and had ventured as far east as the Genoese-ruled island of Chios in the Aegean and as far west as the Portuguese capital of Lisbon before his name disappears from the records maintained by Genoese magistrates and courts.

When the Jubilee Commission paid an official visit to Genoa in 1987, its members were taken to see yet another document, this one housed in the sixteenth-century palace which serves as the city hall. The document was kept wrapped in casings of velvet and gilt in a safe much like the tabernacle on an altar. This is the famous "Testament" of Christopher Columbus, wherein the Admiral of the Ocean Sea and Discoverer of the Indies testifies to his origins in and love for the city of Genoa and entrusts to its ancient and powerful Bank of St. George the execution of his devises, including the payment of his just debts and the fostering of the considerable inheritance that he left to his heirs. What could be better proof of Columbus's origins than this? Visitors who want to see more can also visit an ancient ruin near the gate of Sant'Andrea in Genoa's medieval walls which is called the "Casa di Colombo" and may or may not be a house in which the future explorer lived as a child. The gate itself is significant, because the city archives demonstrate conclusively that Domenico Colombo served a term in the minor political post of gatekeeper and thus he must have housed his family close by, if not in the structure now called Columbus's house then in one much like it.

This Genoese evidence on Columbus's origins has convinced most historians, and in any event scholars today are not that much interested in such biographical details. They are interested in groups rather than individuals and in social processes rather than events. They regard the arrival of Columbus and his crew in America at best as an "encounter" rather than a discovery—we will see further on the ambiguities attaching to these words—and they would cheerfully have exchanged more definitive data about Columbus's life for a clearer view of how this encounter looked from the native perspective. The scholar's Quincentenary turned on such issues as the numbers and mortality rates of Indians who died from European diseases or the mystery of how the Indian-bred potato made its way into the diets of northwest Europe. The academic response to the Quincentenary initiative of the National Endowment for the Humanities reflects this viewpoint. Although the NEH awarded more than $31 million to some 400 projects between 1984 and 1992, only a handful of the grants actually dealt with Columbus himself.

Paolo Emilio Taviani ran confidently against this academic tide. A Genoese scholar about whom we will see more further on, he was also a politician and emerged in both capacities as Italy's principal spokesman for the Quincentenary: a scholar-participant with no apologies to make for either role. A partisan fighter of World War II, he sat down after the war to write a history of the Genoese insurrection against the Nazis. Later he became a Christian Democratic politico and member of several of the revolving-door cabinets that ruled Italy during the postwar decades. As the Quincentenary approached, he was a senator-for-life of the Italian Republic and a member of the Senate's committee on foreign affairs.

"I can speak from the experience of 44 years," he told the audience at an academic conference held in Santo Domingo in 1988. "I am 76. I can quote de Gasperi of Italy, Jean Monnet the founder of Europe, Marshall from the USA, the creator of that great plan which has given two-thirds of Europe the possibility of life. I can also quote Gromyko."[4] All of which had little to do with the subject that the scholars had gathered to discuss. But it has everything to do with the forcefulness and skill Taviani brought to his task of keeping Christopher Columbus at the center of attention in the international commemoration in 1992. As a biographer of Columbus, Taviani modestly does not count himself the equal of the classic Columbianists, such as the Americans Washington Irving and Samuel Eliot Morison. But he includes himself proudly with Irving and Morison as an admiring biographer. He also sees himself as upholding a tradition of careful scholarship and judicious interpretation in present-day Columbian controversies. Taviani has little patience for writers who take the absence of conclusive evidence on a given point as an invitation to speculate.

Nevertheless, speculation abounds. The Spanish essayist and historian Salvador de Madariaga made it a point in his biography of Columbus published in 1940 to note that the entire corpus of Columbus's known writings contains only a few words of imperfect Italian. Mostly Columbus wrote in Spanish; he also wrote in Portuguese and in a kind of Latin which was probably self-taught. Even his letters to Italians, such as the Testament housed in the Palazzo Tursi in Genoa, were written in Spanish. From this negative evidence, Madariaga concludes that Columbus was probably illiterate in what most Americans today would assume to have been his native tongue. All scholars admit that Columbus would not have been raised speaking the Tuscan dialect that became the basis of written Italian; like all Italians he would have spoken a regional dialect and learned the Tuscan-derived national language—if he learned it at all—in the course of formal schooling. Consequently, most scholars, including Taviani, are prepared to concede that Columbus may not have learned written Italian. But Madariaga goes further than this. On the basis of this and other speculations, he concludes that Columbus and his family were not really Italian at all, but Spanish in origin. Specifically, he argues that they were Spanish Jews, originally from Catalonia or Mallorca, who took up residence in Liguria at the end of the fourteenth century as refugees from persecution and forced conversions in Spain.[5] He is not alone in this assertion. The famous Nazi-hunter Simon Wiesenthal also believes that Columbus's family was Jewish and finds it significant that Columbus's mother, Susanna, bore an Old Testament name. Madariaga speculates that this Jewish Colombo family probably spoke Ladino, the Spanish- and Hebrew-derived language of Sephardic Jews, at home and that, while Columbus may have learned the Genoese dialect in his youth, he acquired fluency in reading and writing only after he settled in Portugal after 1476, which explains why his writings contain only Spanish, Latin, and Portuguese. Taviani bluntly dismisses Madariaga's biography as "a novel."[6] And in fact contemporary novelists do seem to prefer Madariaga to Morison. An American writer who published fictional Columbus "memoirs" in 1987 unambiguously presents the Admiral as a Spanish Jew. The Argentine Abel Posse, in *The Dogs of Paradise* (1989) portrays a Jewish Columbus with a mystic's gift of peering into the future. A ghostly convoy of immigrant ships that only the Admiral can see accompanies the caravels across the Atlantic. Posse's Columbus also has webbed feet. Morison's dictum that more nonsense has been written about Columbus than about any other man in history certainly held up in 1992.[7]

What was at stake in the contemporary version of this controversy? In a word, ethnic and national pride, specifically Italian and Spanish pride and, in the United States, that of Hispanic- and Italian-Americans. But this is a twentieth-century angle, as far as the American Columbus is concerned. Columbus as an American national hero did not start out as an ethnic. As constructed by the patriots and poets of the early American republic, he was as Yankee as they come.

It was writers of the 1780s and 1790s, such as Phillis Wheatley, Joel Barlow, and Noah Webster, who first made Christopher Columbus a symbolic founder of the United States and plastered his name in both its feminized ("Columbia") and Latinized ("Columbus") forms on American places and institutions. For example, the name of the national capital, the city of *Washington* in the District of *Columbia,* received its names from Barlow's friends Thomas Jefferson and James Madison in 1791. Wheatley had linked the name Washington with Columbia in a revolutionary poem of 1775, as had Barlow in his epic "The Vision of Columbus," written in 1784. Both poems were instrumental in establishing Columbus as a sort of official discoverer of the country to complement Washington's role as the official founder.[8] But early American admirers of Columbus paid little attention either to his Italian origins or to his connections with Portugal and Spain. Nor did they emphasize his Catholic piety or speculate about his or his family's possible connections with the persecutions that afflicted the Jews of fifteenth-century Spain. Barlow, a revolutionary war veteran and pious New England Congregationalist at the time he composed "The Vision of Columbus," even made the explorer into a kind of proto-Protestant. In fact, the ambiguity of Columbus's origins suited the propagandistic purposes of these American writers quite nicely, making it easy for them to transform him into a kind of first American, a new man whose very alienation from his European roots and sponsors enhanced his appeal as a hero of the new United States. A favorite American representation during this period was Columbus in chains, a victim of shortsighted and ungrateful monarchs and thus an exemplar of republican virtue. The fact that Columbus was from Italy, which was during the revolutionary era a collection of duchies and papal states that posed no threat to the fledgling American republic, served only to distance the discoverer further from the Spanish empire, a traditional enemy of English-speaking Protestants and an obstacle to the visions of an expansive American destiny that Barlow and others like him entertained.

Washington Irving, the first modern biographer of Columbus in any language and the writer who more than anyone else codified his nineteenth-century image as a romantic and tragic hero, accepted the explorer's Genoese origins, following the sixteenth-century biography written by Columbus's second son, Ferdinand. The question of ethnicity became important only in the later years of the century. In 1882, a fledgling Irish Catholic fraternal association based in New Haven, Connecticut, renamed itself the Knights of Columbus. On one level, the K of C was simply an insurance operation, as it still is, set up to provide benefits for its members that, in the early days at least, they were unable to find anywhere else. But as a social order, the Knights soon emerged as the vanguard of the "American Catholic" movement promoted by the Roman Catholic hierarchy of the United States, a movement designed both to gather the burgeoning multiethnic population of Catholic immigrants to a unified church under Irish leadership and to defend the Catholic community against demands by militant Protestant and nativist organizations which pressed for the restriction of immigration and state control of Catholic schools. Since Columbus was already enshrined in art, literature, and monuments as a hero of America's national origins—and since he had also been a pious Catholic—he provided an ideal symbol for Catholics who denied that their religious duties imposed any impediment to responsible American citizenship. Under the Knights' leadership, Columbus Day parades became an annual event in many northeastern cities. The order also played an important role in an international movement to canonize Columbus as a saint of the Roman Catholic Church, a movement which came to grief over the fact that Columbus's private life did not comport with Victorian ideas of how saints should behave.[9] It was one of Paolo Emilio

Taviani's proudest boasts that his grandfather played a role in derailing this movement by proving beyond question that Columbus had never married Ferdinand's mother, Beatriz Enríquez, even though he instructed the Bank of St. George to provide for her in his will.[10] While Italian immigrants accepted Irish leadership of the American hierarchy and of lay organizations such as the Knights, they did not leave Columbus in Irish hands for very long. Italians began immigrating to America in large numbers during the formative years of the modern Italian nation. Very few arrived here thinking of themselves as Italian. Rather their loyalties, like the dialects they spoke, were regional, even local in character. *Campanilismo*, the suspicion of strangers who were not born within the shadow of the *campanile* or bell tower of the village church in the old country, became the organizing principle for Italian immigrant communities in America. In one well-known study, Rudolph Vecoli found more than seventy distinct communities of Italians in late-nineteenth-century Chicago.[11] But while fragmentation was the rule among Italian communities, attempts to overcome this disunity emerged from several quarters as the numbers of Italians in America grew. Columbus proved an ideal symbol for these unifying efforts.

Mostly it was the children of immigrants, second-generation Italian-Americans unable or unwilling to live within the bounds of *campanilismo*, who attempted to construct a unifying identity which embraced the entire ethnic community. They were generally unsuccessful in emulating Irish achievements in creating political blocs or umbrella organizations such as the Knights of Columbus. But Columbus and Columbus Day proved to be useful unifying symbols that, at least once a year, rallied Italian-American communities across the many fissures that divided them. The annual Columbus Day parades and the once-in-a-lifetime drive to raise money to place a statue of Columbus in a prominent local spot became fixtures of life in Italian-American communities. Italians wrested control of Columbus Day parades from Irish Catholics in New England cities and inaugurated new celebrations, such as Baltimore's parade, which claims the longest unbroken run in the country, beginning in 1890. Italians in Philadelphia erected the first statue, at the time of the American Revolution centennial and exposition in that city in 1876, while New York's Italian-American community erected the most spectacular monument, the column and statue in Columbus Circle which was dedicated in 1892. Subsequently Italian-Americans erected statues in cities across the country, from Walla Walla to Boston, from Fort Lauderdale to St. Paul. The long list of sponsoring organizations that are inscribed on some of the statues, such as those erected in recent years in Torrington, Connecticut, or on the waterfront in Boston's North End, testify to the tenuous nature of the unity that statues and parades achieved. But there can be no denying that, thanks to Italian-American efforts, Columbus became an ethnic hero. By the time that Italian-American efforts achieved the first legislation making Columbus Day an official holiday, in Colorado in 1907, red-green-and-white banners waving over marching Italians had displaced Yankee speeches and Spanish red-and-gold bunting as the most visible manifestations of America's Columbian tradition.[12]

As the Quincentenary approached, however, Spanish nationalists and American leaders of Hispanic descent prepared to change this tradition again. The creation of the Jubilee Commission came about only after a long period of confrontation and negotiation between Italian-American and Latino congressmen and spokesmen, and when Italian-Americans appointed to the commission outnumbered Latino appointments, one influential national Hispanic organization—the National Council of La Raza—set up a rival private group, the National Hispanic Quincentennial Commission, to create alternative programs. Meanwhile the Spanish embassy in Washington provided copies of Madariaga's biography to members of the Jubilee Commission, while its cultural attaché worked to prevent the commission from adopting, in its official report to Congress, recommendations at odds with Spanish viewpoints. Thus when the commission staff proposed a scholarship program emphasizing grants to students who were bilingual in English and in "one of the languages which Christopher Columbus spoke," Spanish and Hispanic representatives argued to have Italian stricken from the list of such languages. The official Spanish position was that Christopher Columbus deserved no more credit for Spain's achievements in the New World than does that other "foreign mercenary," Wernher von Braun, for the achievements of the United States in space.

On the scholarly circuit, Taviani confronted a more sophisticated version of the same point of view. Spanish scholars and American Hispanists complained that his emphasis on Columbus and his Genoese origins was outdated and boring. "I love him but I'm sick of him, too," a leading Spanish scholar complained during the Santo Domingo conference. "It's too much. He's got to learn to revise his paper, at least once a year." At the same conference, another Spanish historian, Luis Arranz

Márquez, directly challenged Taviani's approach as a throwback to the nineteenth century. Spain suffers from the beatification of Columbus, Arranz argues, "because if he is such a good guy, then we have to be the bad guys." The emphasis on "Genoese genius" obscures the contributions of the Spanish monarchs, statesmen, and seamen to the 1492 voyage. Without the Pinzón brothers especially (the captains of the smaller caravels, Niña and Pinta), Columbus "would have ended up as shark food, hung from the back of his ship."[13]

Taviani cut an imposing figure in such gatherings, especially as his status as an Italian national hero allowed him to travel first class, surrounded by aides and welcoming dignitaries. Hooded eyes, a fringe of bristly white hair, and a wide slit mouth gave him a vaguely exotic look when his features relaxed in thoughtful scholarly repose—a kind of mandarin in well-cut Italian clothes. Confronted by a critic like Arranz, however, he turned to his audience with the sunny countenance of a veteran politico. Of course he was an admirer of Columbus, he explained. What Genoese, growing up in the same ancient city as Columbus, sniffing the same sea air, could not be? There was no need for Arranz's sarcasm; he understood that the Spanish had their viewpoint as he had his. There was room for both. But in the course of formulating this disarming riposte, Taviani casually brought up several subjects which cut to the quick of Spanish pride in their country's imperial history: the fate of the native Americans in Spanish hands, the origins of American slavery, the importance of Italian financiers and experts in Isabelline Spain, the "medieval" character of Spanish institutions, the glories of the Italian Renaissance. Then he was out the door to a meeting with the president of the Dominican Republic and a luncheon by the Italian ambassador's pool. Later he presided at the opening of an art exhibit in one of Santo Domingo's colonial museums. The exhibit was entitled "Christopher Columbus, Genoese." Taviani called this his exhibit of 100 cities and planned to accompany it to each and every one. As of late 1988, it had been to Buenos Aires, Miami, Baltimore, and Columbus, Ohio. At the opening reception in Santo Domingo, he gave a shorter version of his standard talk while the Spaniards and their American friends rolled their eyes and muttered into their drinks.

When during the 1830s Ralph Waldo Emerson compiled his list of history's greatest men, Christopher Columbus and William Shakespeare were the only two men included who came from relatively humble origins.[14] So it is probably to be expected that Columbus's achievements, like Shakespeare's, have sparked controversy as to whether or not Columbus really deserves the credit for what he did. This is part of what was at issue when Senator Taviani debated Spaniards about the individual versus the collective responsibility for the breakthrough of 1492. No one has argued that Columbus did not make his famous voyage. Rather this debate centered on more complex issues: first, was Columbus really the first to "discover" America? Secondly, how much of the credit we give to him really belongs to others who provided the ideas, money, or manpower that made his success possible?

As with most Columbian debates, the facts on these questions are much more complicated than the stories that people would rather believe. Take, for example, the popular belief that Queen Isabella pawned her jewels to finance the voyage. The story is not true, but the director of the 1947 British film *Christopher Columbus* found it too good to give up entirely, and so at the appropriate time Isabella proffers her jewels, only to be told "that won't be necessary, Your Majesty."

Evidence of another compromise on these issues can be found on the grounds of the Minnesota state capitol in St. Paul in the form of two statues erected during the decade after World War I. One statue is of Christopher Columbus, the other of Leif Eriksson. Columbus faces toward St. Paul, whose Roman Catholic archbishop, John Ireland, was one of the leaders of the American Catholic movement in the late nineteenth century. Eriksson is nearer to Minneapolis, the Athens of Scandinavian-American culture in the United States. Both statues bear the same simple legend: "Discoverer of America."

Theodore Blegen, a Norwegian-American historian at the University of Minnesota and the state historical society, helped lead the drive to raise funds for the Leif Eriksson statue, but the Kensington rune stone was more than he could take. This was a spurious archaeological find that purportedly demonstrated that a party of Norse explorers had visited Minnesota during the thirteenth century. Blegen and other scholars regarded the rune stone as a hoax and refused to certify its authenticity despite the political pressure brought to bear on the Minnesota Historical Society by Blegen's ethnic compatriots.[15] Today his view prevails everywhere but in Kensington, Minnesota, where merchants do a brisk trade in miniature rune stones, and in nearby Lake Wobegon, whose historian Garrison Keillor insists on a Norse visit to his district in 1381. "Every Columbus Day, the [Lake Wobegon] runestone is carried up to the school and put on a card-table in the lunchroom for the children to see, so that they can know their true heritage."[16] Good stories die hard.

Not all writers take this as lightheartedly as Keillor or insist on solid evidence as seriously as did Blegen. Take, for example, Ivan van Sertima, an anthropologist from Surinam who now teaches at Rutgers University. Van Sertima's book *They Came Before Columbus* argues that African contact with the Americas predated Columbus's voyages by several centuries. His evidence is entirely circumstantial—parallels in African and pre-Columbian American cultures; the Negroid features found on some Mesoamerican sculptures; reports of American trade items and foods that reminded Europeans of things they had seen or heard of in Africa; modern experimental journeys across the Atlantic in Egyptian or African ships.[17]

If van Sertima were an Irishman writing about St. Brendan (an Irish monk who is said to have led a legendary expedition to America from Ireland during the sixth century), most scholars would dismiss him. But because he is a black scholar who claims to have rescued an aspect of Afro-American history from Euro-American neglect, he gets a respectful hearing, since we have learned all too well during recent decades that much *has* been neglected in the history of African and African American cultures. And so in 1991 the Smithsonian hosted a scholarly conference wherein van Sertima's thesis was discussed, though not debated, since no one who disagreed with him took the floor.[18] But even after acknowledging the plausibility of his scenario, and forswearing the Eurocentric premises that govern most traditional accounts of overseas exploration, we still confront the question of the ultimate significance of such contacts. As Morison wrote of assorted hypothesized pre-Columbian European voyages, they "left not one footprint on the sands of time."[19]

So what if Africans visited Mexico or Brazil or Irishmen or Basques visited Newfoundland or Chinese or Japanese drifted over to California? Clearly the true discoverers of America were those paleo-Indian peoples who found and used the land bridge from Siberia to Alaska 30,000 years ago. After that land bridge submerged, nothing really happened to change the isolation of the Americas from Eurasia and Africa until a bridge of ships was thrown across the Atlantic after 1492. Incidental contacts may have taken place before that year—in fact, they certainly did take place in the case of the Norsemen in Greenland and Newfoundland and possibly also in the cases of African traders in Brazil or of fishermen from northwest Europe who may have visited the islands off Canada. But these contacts led to no demonstrable impact on the destinies of either hemisphere, whereas Columbus's voyage of 1492 and its aftermath transformed both forever. In the view of one historian who has considered both the ecological and human dimensions of the "Columbian exchange" of peoples, plants, products, diseases, and ideas that the Columbus voyages inaugurated, 1492 represents the most significant event in human history since the end of the Ice Age and in natural history since the end of the Pleistocene era.[20]

In the face of conclusions like this, why do people still want to argue about who was first? For some, like Bob Power, the pleasure of the argument itself is sufficient reward. A California businessman and armchair historian and geographer, Power is a regular participant in debates about Columbus and about other explorers, such as the English navigator and corsair Francis Drake. Power was one of the organizers of California's celebration of the "Drake Quadricentennial" in 1979, the 400th anniversary of Drake's visit to the California coast during his circumnavigation of the earth. Power also has a theory about Columbus's first landfall in the Bahamas which is at odds with most other scholars. During the 1980s, he worked to refurbish the scholarly reputation of the celebrated "Vinland Map." This is a purported medieval map showing land to the west of Greenland, originally published in Basel in 1440, lost for centuries, found and republished by Yale University Press on Columbus Day of 1965 (a choice of dates that did not go unnoticed among the Italian-American politicians who govern New Haven, Yale's hometown and also that of the Knights of Columbus). Initially welcomed by many scholars as the first proof that Europeans apart from Icelanders and Norsemen knew of the Viking discoveries in North America, the Vinland map was subsequently denounced as a fraud on the basis of a chemical analysis of its ink. Power obtained a new and more complex analysis by University of California physicists, which he along with many other scholars believes to have superseded the earlier one. Power also offered a new interpretation of the map which argues for pre-Columbian European knowledge of the entire east coast of North America, from Florida to Cape Cod, and of the islands of Cuba, Hispaniola, and Jamaica as well. Maybe Columbus knew where he was going because he had a map.[21]

Most participants in the discovery debate approach it on a level that is both more and less serious than Bob Power's detective work. They are less serious because most of them are impatient with the evidentiary caution of scholarship; they are wary of facts that could interfere with belief. They are more serious because of the nature of their beliefs about history. The issue of who was really America's first discoverer is grounded in the linear theories of history that have prevailed in western culture since the eighteenth century. Joel Barlow revised his "The Vision of Columbus" of 1784 as "The Columbiad" in 1805, turning it into a secular vision of America's destiny with Columbus as that destiny's prophet. His prophecy was nothing less than Anglo-American domination of the entire American continent. The Columbian celebrations of 1892–93 were an unabashed tribute to America's progress. Native American symbols were appropriated and their artifacts exhibited at Chicago in 1893, but as a primitive counterpoint to the industrial might and expansive destiny that the fair's other exhibits asserted for the United States. At the Panama-Pacific Exposition in San Francisco in 1915, the contrast between the vanishing Indian and Euro-American progress was made even more explicit in the famous sculpture "The End of the Trail," which portrayed a slumping Indian horseman facing dejectedly toward the west, having been pushed to the continent's limit by the vigorous and successful industrial culture whose achievements were the focus of the fair.[22]

If history is a linear process whose end is known and welcomed, then it becomes important to know how and where the trajectory began and who started it. This is the role which Columbus came to play in the mythic view of the origins and destiny of the United States, and this role thus became worth contesting for partisans of other individuals or groups for whom a share in Columbus's glory could plausibly be asserted. But what if history is not linear, after all? While the progressive tradition in American historical thought is by no means dead, it certainly has been shaken by the fears and doubts of the twentieth century. Dejected Indians now appear in television ads as ironic commentators on the cost of progress, weeping over littered roadsides and polluted air. A more ambiguous destiny now appears to await the beneficiaries of modern industrialism, and so the question of who was or was not first to inaugurate the progressive trajectory becomes less relevant than other questions about the meaning and significance of 1492. Among historians and other scholars, attention has shifted from men and events to those whose deeds were overshadowed by the traditional emphasis on dead white males and even more so to the study of aggregate social change wherein the actions of individuals are submerged in those of the mass.

Post-structuralism has endowed these shifts in the scholar's gaze with ideological significance. The argument that all matters of interpretation are ultimately grounded in ideology paradoxically makes the facts of Columbus's life not more, but less important. If knowledge is inherently political, then groups exercising new political authority, or the spokespersons who claim to speak in their name, plausibly argue that the facts put forward by earlier generations of Columbianists are weighed and found wanting in comparison to other questions that went unanswered or that were not even asked. A Smithsonian official, asked to explain the institution's showcasing of van Sertima's opinions, argued that the facts of his arguments were unimportant: Africans may or may not have found the New World; the important thing is that they *could* have done so, and acknowledging this fact figured in contemporary arguments about group identity and self-esteem.[23]

In this context, the Jubilee Commission decided to dodge the issue of who was first and concentrate on honoring Columbus as the founding venturer in today's modern global network of communications and trade. Or as the official manifesto of the commission phrased it, "Columbus' joining of the New World to the Old was the decisive event in the discovery of our planet, and it began the modern era of human history." Yet the manifesto also affirmed the progressive tradition by touting 1992 as "both the culmination of an epoch of achievement and the beginning of a new and more promising age."[24]

If we accept the centrality of Columbus's role, whether as discoverer of America or the initiator of global change, it becomes important to figure out where he got the inspiration and funding for his voyage. There is plenty of ethnic pride and national rivalry at stake in these issues as well. Senator Taviani, following Morison, argues that Columbus as a master mariner figured out the wind and sea currents of the eastern half of the Atlantic over the course of his career between 1465 and 1483. Sailing out of Genoa and, after 1476, Lisbon, Columbus visited the remotest outposts of western European trade, reaching south to the Bight of Africa, west to the Portuguese offshore settlements in Madeira and the Azores, and north to England and possibly also Ireland and Iceland. This experience could have allowed Columbus to intuit the other, western, half of the Atlantic's circular wind and current patterns; having formed the idea of sailing west to find the East in this practical manner, he then ransacked the Bible and the best available writers on history and geography to find arguments supporting his theory that the ocean could be crossed.[25]

The arguments Columbus marshaled failed to convince the committees of experts that both the Portuguese and Spanish monarchs appointed to hear the case, giving rise to one of the most durable and wrongheaded tales in the Columbus legend—that Columbus was turned down because official opinion held that the earth was flat and that it was the 1492 voyage which proved definitively that the earth was round. Where this story came from is not clear, but it clearly appealed to Protestant writers who liked to contrast Columbus's enlightened modern views with the medieval ignorance of his interlocutors, who were mostly Catholic churchmen.[26] In fact, the issue was not the earth's sphericity—which all educated persons accepted in Columbus's day—but its circumference. Columbus calculated the circumference of the earth incorrectly but the error allowed him to calculate that the ocean fronting the Iberian peninsula—the Ocean Sea, as it was called to differentiate it from the Mediterranean Sea—could be crossed and recrossed safely in the ocean-going vessels of the day. In other words, he more or less correctly calculated the width of the Atlantic, except that neither he nor his critics knew that the Atlantic was not the only ocean between Europe and Japan. The Talavera Commission, which heard his arguments on behalf of Isabella's court, correctly calculated that the circumference of the earth was much larger, and so it naturally declined to accept Columbus's erroneous figures on this point. The commission was of course incorrect about the width of the Ocean Sea and thus wrongly concluded that the journey which Columbus proposed was not practical. He was right about the practicality of the journey even if his geographical arguments were flawed.

Columbus was right for the wrong reasons, in other words, and his admirers have tended to endow his success with the logic of genius. There remains, however, the question of whether Columbus formulated his enterprise solely on the strength of his intuitive seamanship and cockeyed geography. Apart from the Vinland Map issue, could there not have been some other sort of "pre-discovery"? Columbus kicked around most of the major waterfronts of Europe's coastal Atlantic trade. Did he encounter someone there—in Lisbon or the Azores or Bristol or Iceland—who had been across the Atlantic and who could tell him how to "find the East by sailing West"? A Spanish historian, Juan Manzano Manzano, is the latest and most formidable proponent of this view. Portuguese scholars and patriots are also partial to this theory, since otherwise Portugal, whose monarchs and seafarers inaugurated systematic exploration of the Atlantic sea routes, gets no credit for Columbus's achievements and fame.

Two things lend plausibility to the notion of a "pre-discovery." One is a trail marked out by Columbus himself when he spoke and wrote of his "secrets." Apparently he had something—which he was willing to show or say to the right people—which he regarded as the clincher for his arguments. His son and first biographer, Don Hernando Colón, listed ten such clues, most of them having to do with stone-chiseled driftwood found on Atlantic beaches, land sighted but never found by mariners sailing west of the Azores, and non-European corpses found adrift in the ocean in bark or cane boats. In the absence of certain knowledge about what the rest of Columbus's secrets might have been, writers inclined to speculate have had a field day.

The more interesting issue derives from the fact that Columbus's journey across the ocean was so easy and that the journey back, while far from easy, followed precisely the right track to bring him back safely to Europe across the wintry Atlantic. The route that Columbus established—sailing south and west utilizing the east-to-west trade winds blowing between the Canaries and the Caribbean, then sailing north and east following roughly the clockwise winds and currents of the North Atlantic—remained the principal Atlantic trading route throughout the age of sail. How did he find it so unerringly the first time out? Doesn't this mean that someone had to have shown him the way?

One can accept the scholarly answers to this question patiently assembled by writers like Taviani. Or you can accept the iconographic message conveyed in William Hogarth's engraving, "Columbus Breaking the Egg." In this 1752 work, Hogarth portrayed an apocryphal story originally told about the Florentine artist-architect Brunelleschi in Vasari's *Lives of the Painters*. The Vasari version had to do with Brunelleschi's design of the dome of the Florence *duomo*. The Columbus version portrayed the Admiral and some of his critics arguing during a meal of hard-cooked eggs and eels. The critics challenge the significance of Columbus's breakthrough; the route is so obvious that someone sooner or later would have found it if he had not. By way of answering, Columbus invites them to take an egg and make it stand on its smaller end. None of the critics can do this. Whereupon he takes the egg and mashes it down gently, enabling it to stand on its flattened base. The critics are confounded and the moral is clear: Anything is easy after a genius shows you how.

Hogarth chose to illustrate this scene for reasons which had nothing to do with Columbus. He created it as the subscription ticket to a series of engravings called "The Analysis of Beauty." For him, the key visual element in the scene was the two eels arranged in intersecting serpentine curves around a single egg on the serving plate in the foreground.

The curving lines they establish are repeated in the arrangement of Columbus and the other figures seated at the table around him. The whole composition makes a point about the role of figure and line in the aesthetics of drawing. But the American artists who copied Hogarth's engraving and made Columbus and the Egg into one of the icons of the Columbian tradition in the United States neglected or missed this point. Michele Felice Corne, an Italian painter who settled in Salem, Massachusetts, and painted a "Columbus Breaking the Egg" for the East India Marine Society of that city in 1805, showed no eels at all, just eggs on the platter. Three other Columbus and Egg paintings done in Salem during the nineteenth century either follow Corne or show the eels in a slithery pile, with no thought to Hogarth's essay on figure and line.[27] In the same vein, other American paintings show Columbus on the deck of the Santa María, distinguished by demeanor and by dress from the cowering seamen who grovel before him, begging him to turn back. In fact one frequently copied scene, still to be found in college textbooks today, shows Columbus dressed in the black-and-white garb associated with New England's founders, while his crewmen are depicted in colored but decidedly less splendid clothes. A different version of this scene ornamented a five-dollar bill issued by the U.S. Treasury during the early twentieth century.[28]

When Emerson wrote in his essay on "Self-Reliance" that "Columbus found the New World in an undecked boat," the implication is that he did it more or less on his own.[29] Similarly, the focus in American history paintings, done by or for Yankees for whom the discoverer was a national hero and genius, is strictly on Columbus. In these icons there is no room for scholarly quibbles about who else may deserve a share of the credit. The American Columbus is a hero not only of progress but of individualism, a personal embodiment of the nation's democratic hopes.

The indomitable genius celebrated in the Salem paintings grew into the American Columbus still enshrined in statues and schoolbooks. In 1988 Scott Redmond of San Francisco wanted to make sure that Columbus remained enshrined in American hearts. At that time, Redmond was an accomplished practitioner in the rising and lucrative field of "special events" and as such was deeply involved in planning for 1992 in the Bay Area. He was also a licensed private investigator and a volunteer counselor on a suicide prevention hotline in San Francisco. Calls on the hotline since he joined it in 1980 had mushroomed from 10,000 to more than 70,000 a year. Redmond figured that in the life of Columbus there was a message that could heal the feelings of futility that afflicted so many of the people whose calls he took.

Redmond and John Williams met in the lobby of a San Francisco hotel in November 1988. He impressed Williams as thirty-something, with a blandly handsome face, sincere and talkative but cautious. In the course of a three-hour conversation, he ordered only a glass of ginger ale. Williams wondered if he was a Mormon, especially after Redmond began to describe the moral purposes of the people he had assembled in his Events America Foundation to work on the Columbus celebration. The foundation was legally separate from his events production company and was not intended to generate business for his firm. His detective-work sideline had familiarized him thoroughly with some of the seamier arrangements that events like this can generate among promoters: kickbacks, side deals, and the like. Determined to prevent this in 1992, he assembled a foundation board of "achievers" in the advertising, public relations, and nonprofit organization fields. The foundation was also committed to promoting an "International Code of Ethics" for events producers. And no, in response to a question, the group was not bound together by membership in a particular cult or church. Most, however, had some connection or other with the Exploratorium, San Francisco's influential reinvention of the science museum. The group hoped to connect the ideas of discovery and exploration which the public naturally associate with Columbus with concepts of personal growth for ordinary people.

Like most people in the field of special events, Redmond more or less backed into it. He began by producing "Footstock," the music and arts festival of the *San Francisco Examiner's* annual "Bay to Breakers" run. Later he did a little of everything, from the annual Coyote Ball of Margo St. James's San Francisco–based hookers' union to a Native American arts festival to special effects for the San Francisco Giants. When Williams first talked with him, his production company was putting on Christmas extravaganzas. The next day he would make it snow inside the Crocker Galleria for the building's annual tree-lighting ceremony. The previous week he provided the special effects that welcomed Santa Claus to San Jose. Santa came in a giant silver/gilt package like a stripper in a cake. The package exploded as he emerged. There were more than $3,000 of lighting effects alone, Redmond commented. There were sound effects, lasers, animal characters like the reindeer, a duck, and a chicken.

"The San Diego Chicken?" Williams interrupted. "I think it was the Chicken," he replied. "At least it looked like the Chicken."

Williams hoped it *was* the San Diego Chicken. That would bring things full circle from the afternoon in Columbus, Ohio, six months earlier when he shared the platform at a press conference with another events producer named Rick Liebert, whose resumé's proudest boast was that he was the man who thought up the San Diego Chicken, one of the greatest radio promotions in history. For those who don't know or remember, the Chicken was the first and best known of the feathered mascots that multiplied in baseball stadia during the 1970s. Originally a promotion for a local radio station, the Chicken quickly outgrew its temporary status and eventually outgrew San Diego. Even today it can be found in summertime wandering from one minor league town to another, the star attraction at promotional events. It so happened that Williams had visited San Diego during the Chicken's heyday and had gone to a Padres baseball game with his children. They loved the Chicken and it was obvious that the mimetic talent of the young man in the costume was impressive. But the man at the Columbus press conference was neither the Chicken nor the radio station manager nor any of the baseball team owners who had sponsored the Chicken. Rather, he was the father of the Chicken concept, and from this conceptual breakthrough his career as a producer of special events had taken off.

Williams was at the press conference in what he had until then thought of as a position of some dignity: the director of a presidential commission sanctioned by the highest authority in the United States. But from the standpoint of the reporters and public relations people in the room, there was little if any difference between the Chicken and the Columbus Quincentenary. Both were promotions, both came at them in the artificially excited prose of press releases, neither engaged them seriously, and they were lured to such occasions as this one only by the food and booze that awaited them when the speechmaking was over. It was at this precise moment, as the reporters and flacks sat there listening with a polite but distracted air, like winos at a mission waiting for the sermon to be over so they could eat, that Williams realized that the Quincentenary was something he could understand only by writing about.

And so when he got home to Washington, he went out and bought a copy of Daniel Boorstin's *The Image*. This is a reissue of an astonishingly prescient 1962 essay on the impact of mass media in American public life. According to Boorstin, that impact is carried out largely through what he calls "pseudo-events." The pseudo-event is arranged rather than spontaneous. It is designed to be reproduced—that is, to have its principal impact through reportage in the media rather than on the persons who happen to be present, even if they are present in large numbers. And the event in question has an ambiguous relation to reality, that is, to authenticity; a pseudo-event is staged, but it should not appear to be.[30]

As the Quincentenary approached, there was something like a boom going on in special events, many of which differ little in their essentials from the features that Boorstin ascribed to pseudo-events. The reason for the boom was that commercial sponsors of special events could target advertising dollars much more precisely to intended audiences than is usually the case with mass media. Thus beer makers sponsor sports events that attract audiences of young males, Cadillac and BMW sponsor polo matches, and banks or conglomerates which wish to enhance their prestige and reputation for civic virtue sponsor "blockbuster" art exhibits or visits by ballet troupes. The Statue of Liberty Centennial in 1986 demonstrated the commercial possibilities in historical commemorations, and even the Bicentennial of the U.S. Constitution—considered alike by most scholars and most events producers to have been a flop—stimulated a 67 percent rise in tourism in Philadelphia. The Washington State Centennial Commission raised at least $4 million in commercial sponsorships for its events in 1989. With stats like these, how could Columbus fail to miss?[31]

Special Events Report, "The International Newsletter of Events Sponsorship and Lifestyle Marketing," is the bible of this new and lucrative business. In 1988, its editor believed that the Quincentenary could be the greatest special event of the century, Redmond commented, but Williams knew from uncomfortable experience that the newsletter had also been highly critical thus far of attempts by the Jubilee Commission and others to exploit this promise. The problem had to do with focus. The same multiplicity of meanings and controversies that made the Quincentenary so fruitful for academic debate was no blessing but a curse for an events promoter. If we could not say with assurance those three famous words—"Columbus Discovered America"—then where was the message that could be packed into a TV sound bite or a logo or a tag line or the grabber sentence of a press release? If we didn't know exactly where Columbus landed, where could we send the cameras and dignitaries on October 12?

Redmond thought he had an answer of sorts. "Maybe I shouldn't say this, but in some ways I hate my work." Most special events are meaningless, he explained, but the Quincentenary was different. He discoursed at length on the universal, quasi-religious appeal of Columbus, articulating more or less the same view of genius that got Senator Taviani an occasional roasting from his Spanish critics, but expressing it in a kind of California newspeak whose intensity is hard to capture in print. He talked about a "Columbus Myth-Icon" which offers "hope and opportunity to each person by saying that great discoveries can be made on your own notepad or in your own backyard." "Columbus was an ordinary man, who responded to an extraordinary challenge. He can serve as an inspiration to anyone," even to the people Redmond met on the hotline whose feelings of futility and insignificance had driven them to the brink.[32] Redmond saw the Columbian myth as having power to motivate and ennoble such people, as well as the rest of us who are coping more successfully. That is why he planned to invest so much of his time and energy in 1992. He and his friends set sail with Columbus, hoping that by their extraordinary efforts they too could change the world.

If Scott Redmond thought that Columbus gives the special event a moral dimension, Antoni Miralda thinks that the special event *is* the moral dimension. Like Liebert or Redmond, Miralda deals in promotions, but his events are sanctioned by Art. Take the time he built a wall of 4,000 loaves of dye-splashed bread in the Contemporary Art Museum in Houston. Of course, Miralda did not actually build the wall himself; it was his concept. He conceived also of the idea to enliven the exhibit by incorporating an appearance by the Kilgore Rangerettes, the all-girl drill team that entertains crowds at Texas football games. The Rangerettes were not there, of course, but there was a documentary about them on a TV monitor not far from the waist-high wall of colored bread. One could think that the dye was a clever way of prolonging the life of the wall after the bread started molding, but what about when it started to smell? Still what stuck in one's mind longest was the Concept: majorettes and Wonder Bread in a cathedral of Art.

Little did one imagine that a decade later there would be Miralda again, this time fully loaded for the Quincentenary. This one he called the Honeymoon Project, a symbolic wedding of the statue of Christopher Columbus in Barcelona with the Statue of Liberty in New York. Miralda is a native of Catalonia and manages to combine a fervent Catalan nationalism with the postmodern cool of the avant-garde. The

Catalan angle in the Honeymoon Project was Miss Liberty's trousseau, a closetful of gargantuan garments representing the traditional crafts of Catalan needlework. The clothes were mostly made from polyester, however. For example, the engagement dress was made from more than 4,000 yards of turquoise fabric, trimmed in pink and blue. The project's publicity brochure contained a 1986 photo of the dress hanging from the rafters of the Javits Convention Center and draped over a reviewing stand where Mayor Edward Koch and the mayor of Barcelona toasted the happy couple. Columbus was present on a TV monitor which served as the stone in a huge engagement ring, placed under the dress for the engagement ceremony. Miralda was well-known in New York at this time for the decor he designed for a trendy downtown Spanish restaurant, El Internacional. Later he brought other elements of the trousseau to other cities—stockings to Philadelphia, lingerie to Miami (including a huge brassiere with a map of the Old World embroidered on one cup, the New World on the other). He planned to stage suitable symbolic events at the sites of other monuments, such as the Sphinx, St. Peter's in Rome, and the Corn Palace in Mitchell, South Dakota. These ceremonies were to have represented the statues' honeymoon tour, after which there would be a birth of at least two new monuments in 1992 at locations yet to be chosen. The implementation of these plans depended upon fund-raising, of course, but aided by another conceptual artist, Cristo, and a cadre of international glitterati, Miralda claimed to have raised about $3 million at the end of 1988. He also got an official endorsement from the Spanish National Commission for the Celebration of the Fifth Centenary of the Discovery of America.

Special Events Report considered the Honeymoon Project to be "the dumbest idea" of the Quincentenary when the editors first heard about it.[33] Initially, most were inclined to agree. The National Park Service made it clear from the start that the Statue of Liberty was not available for wearing the trousseau. In October of 1986 the Copley News Service and two CBS-Radio affiliates got hold of one of Miralda's press releases and, instead of calling the Jubilee Commission office, called one of the commissioners, an Illinois state senator who had never heard of the project and who proceeded to dig himself into a deeper hole with a wisecrack about the relative size of the two statues. Williams was able to calm the budding controversy by telling the reporters that the project was "a New York art thing" that had no official standing with the commission or the Park Service. They seemed to accept this. Later, in the summer of 1988, a Miami philanthropist and art collector introduced

Miralda to the commission chairman, who was thoroughly charmed. Eventually Honeymoon became an official project of the Jubilee Commission.

Wacky though it sounded, the Honeymoon Project was certainly the most original project to take shape as the Quincentenary approached. Miralda's audacity in proposing it and in charming his way into official support was certainly appropriate to the occasion, especially if we consider the likelihood that Christopher Columbus must have seemed to his soberer contemporaries to be a bit off the wall. Miralda himself explained his objectives in his publicist's loftiest terms: "Honeymoon is an intriguing public arts project interpreting civilization, spiritual guests, and cross-cultural exchange in today's technological world.... [It] explores the power of ritual to transform consciousness ... reaffirm[ing] powerful traditions in the visual arts while reflecting new directions." It was also, he claimed, a nifty candidate for corporate sponsorship because of the "high visibility" the project would likely receive in the media.[34]

Faced with such logic, even *Special Events Report* softened a little. After reading Miralda's press kit, the editors no longer considered Honeymoon to be the wackiest Quincentenary project, only the most esoteric one. Its originality was highlighted by the fact that all of the other major projects under discussion during the 1980s were mostly updated versions of what was done in 1892–93. There is something to be said for originality—or is it, to borrow from Edward Gibbon's catalogue of symptoms of decline in another empire, merely freakishness masking as originality? Only time would tell.

It is tempting to equate special events with Boorstin's notion of pseudo-events, but the equation is not always precise. Take the Statue of Liberty, for example: one might argue that the refurbishing of the statue needed no grand finale; the authorities might simply have declared the restoration completed and reopened the doors. But this argument ignores the human urge to commemorate achievement and to observe anniversaries as ceremonial occasions. These habits predate the media age by many generations. For example, as Chicago's Art Institute planned its Quincentenary program in 1986, it mounted an exhibition of Japanese paintings, several of which commemorated the refurbishing of the historic shrine at Nara during the seventeenth century and the festival that was held at the project's completion. Though each manifested some of the extravagances of their respective ages, the festival at Nara and the Statue of Liberty celebration each embodied a core of authentic meaning that was shared both by those who participated and those who looked on.

Boorstin recognized such distinctions when he identified pseudo-events as events designed specifically for media, primarily intended to be reproduced rather than experienced. In this regard, he would have appreciated the remark of an events producer who held up the Super Bowl as the model for events such as the Quincentenary. The Super Bowl, the producer explained, had been created by and for television. But its ability to attract enormous audiences, not to mention the thousands who traveled at great expense each year to attend the game in person, depended upon the all-but-universal belief that the event would have occurred even if the cameras weren't present.[35] The success of the event as special event—or mega-event as happenings on the Super Bowl scale have come to be known among promoters—therefore depends upon its authenticity. The very name, Super Bowl, said it all—the first word embodying its megabucks scope, the second a tenuous but deeply believed-in connection with American football championship games going back nearly a century.

In addition to invented mega-events like the Super Bowl, ours is an age of reinvention. Consider what happened to Wimbledon, once the stodgy old distinction between amateur and professional had been eliminated in tennis. Or to the America's Cup, once a minor event scarcely on the margins of public consciousness except among individuals who owned or raced yachts, transformed since the 1980s into a global media spectacle. After political controversies, terrorist attacks, and cost overruns in Munich (1972), Montreal (1976), and Moscow (1980), Los Angeles organizers had reinvented the Olympics as a commercial spectacle in 1984. In each case, the traditional event was transformed radically, but the connection with an authentic past reassured the public that these events were still in all essentials *real*, not pseudo.

The Columbian Quincentenary seemed during the 1980s to offer that germ of authenticity, that bedrock of reality that served to distinguish mega-events such as Wimbledon or the Super Bowl from pseudo-events, such as the pseudo-sports with which the TV networks filled their off-season Saturday afternoons. Columbus was, after all, a real person, whose story was known to every schoolchild and adult. In the 1790s and again a century later, the commemoration of his landfall had had a major impact on the nation. The Statue of Liberty Centennial had demonstrated the commercial possibilities in historical commemorations. No wonder events promoters large and small thought of Columbus's 500th anniversary as a sure thing.

But what if the Quincentenary's meaning were contested? What then for the bedrock of authenticity that was needed to erect a megaevent? How could a focus for the celebration be provided if the celebrants had no single point of view? The task of confronting such issues, of reconciling the assorted claims of ethnic pride and national aspirations, of accommodating events promoters and learned controversialists, fell to those involved in planning Quincentenary events. Two of the most important groups were the members of the U.S. Jubilee Commission and the organizers of the ill-fated Chicago World's Fair.

2

Sailing over the Edge

The U.S. Quincentenary Jubilee Commission

Something about the Quincentenary summoned the idea of commissions. Maybe it was the superficiality of the occasion, or precedence, or simply the bureaucratic habits of the late twentieth century. For whatever reason, the Quincentenary was full of commissions—international, national, state, local, ethnic—some of them official, others self-appointed, all busily dedicated to developing plans and carrying out programs, and most beset by typical commission problems such as conflicting egos, differing political agendas, insufficient funding, changing priorities, and other predicaments. None of these bodies encountered problems more serious, petty, and ultimately intractable as those suffered by the national commission of the United States, the Christopher Columbus Quincentenary Jubilee Commission. Perhaps because it is still too close or maybe too sordid, the full story of the Jubilee Commission has yet to be told. We offer the story here not as a cautionary tale intended to help the organizers of future mega-events, nor as a critique of (mostly) well-meaning persons whose (sometimes) heroic labors led to such meager results, but as a record of the way unintended consequences flowed from official indifference to cultural and historical concerns. The irony is that the commission might actually have accomplished something positive had its official sponsors taken it seriously. Instead neither Congress nor the White House paid much attention to the commission until scandal forced them to do so. Even then the official response was confined chiefly to identifying a culprit and then pulling the plug.

The Jubilee Commission's difficulties began at birth. There was first of all the matter of the law that established it. Public Law 98–375, the commission's enabling legislation, had a checkered history. Its legislative antecedents reached back to May 1982, when Senator Charles "Mac" Mathias of Maryland introduced the first version of the Christopher Columbus Quincentenary Jubilee Act. The idea behind Mathias's bill was nothing new, of course. The Columbus anniversary had been observed before, and there were ample recent precedents in the cases of other anniversaries, most recently the American Revolution bicentennial, which had called forth a similar federal commission. But the 1980s were different from the 1970s. For one thing, legislative issues were dogged by concern about the huge federal budget deficit, and this inevitably made discussion of new initiatives a struggle among priorities. It was hard to imagine any member of Congress—or anyone else in official Washington, where six years (the length of a senator's term) is generally the most distant horizon for nonmilitary planning—placing a high priority on a commemoration ten years off of an historical event 500 years past. Then too, control of Congress was divided between a Republican Senate and a Democratic House, each of which in the summer of 1982 was maneuvering for advantage in an upcoming election that would mark the first electoral test of the popularity of Ronald Reagan since his election as president two years earlier.

In such circumstances, for any measure to sail smoothly through Congress would have required broad agreement. Mathias thought that he had just that. Soon after his bill was introduced, it picked up a sextet of cosponsors, two Republicans and four Democrats, while the venerable Democratic congressman Peter Rodino introduced an identical companion measure in the House with a Republican cosponsor, Silvio Conte. Mathias's bill passed the Senate on October 1, 1982, and later the same day was referred to the House Committee on Post Office and Civil Service. It went to this committee because it had to do with a federal holiday and thus a day of closed post offices and civil servants' time off. Following a similar logic, it had been reviewed by the Senate Judiciary Committee, which looked after legislation affecting the federal courts. Rodino's bill was referred to the same committee. If bipartisan backing had been all that was needed, the sponsors might have had the Quincentenary bill through both houses of Congress and up to the White House for the president's signature in time for Columbus Day. Instead both Mathias's and Rodino's bill perished in the post office committee.

The culprit was not partisanship, but that other unruly issue we see throughout the Quincentenary, ethnicity. Of course, Mathias was no ethnic, at least insofar as that term was then understood. He was a Marylander whose patrician bearing advertised blue blood and colonial stock. Like many WASPs, he thought of himself as a custodian of American history, of what is good and proper in the nation's past. He embodied this high-minded approach in his bill, which required the commission to call into existence (but not to pay for) books and bibliographies, symposia and films. It is not irrelevant to mention also that Baltimore has a significant Italian-American vote which, as in other northeastern cities, had traditionally broken toward Republican nominees in state and local elections.

Thus, whatever Mathias's personal motives, his bill, like Rodino's, had been drafted by a lobbyist representing the National Italian-American Foundation (NIAF). Four of the Mathias bill's six Senate cosponsors were Italian-American, as were Rodino and Conte, the sponsors in the House. But the head of the subcommittee of the House Committee on Post Office and Civil Service to which the bills were referred was Representative Robert García, then a little-known congressman from the South Bronx. First elected to Congress in 1978, García was the first native New Yorker of Hispanic descent to win election to Congress. His Puerto Rican constituents along with other Latino New Yorkers had taken to celebrating October 12 with the rest of Latin America as *El Día de la Raza*. Columbus Day in New York had in fact become a weekend of rival celebrations, with Latinos parading one day and Italians the next.

In 1982, García marched in both parades, and beside him was his new wife, Jane Lee García, whom he had married in 1980. Unlike Robert García, who grew up in the Bronx in an immigrant household, Jane García was from the island of Puerto Rico. And unlike the majority of

Puerto Ricans in New York who came from poor farming or working-class backgrounds, Jane García's antecedents are Puerto Rico's social elite, an anachronistic upper class that is archaic in both its social position and outlook. It is "a ruling class that does not rule" and more than other Latin American elites, which after all still seek power and control, has ended up preoccupying itself almost exclusively with issues of status and form. No issue more concerns its members than the matter of Puerto Rico's ambiguous status vis-à-vis American colonialism. Divided within itself between advocates of statehood and defenders of the present Commonwealth status (which is a halfway house between full independence and direct American rule), the Puerto Rican elite had already in 1982 embraced the Quincentenary as a rare opportunity to heal the psychic discomfort of its politics.

For spokespersons of Commonwealth status (affiliated on the mainland with Democrats), 1992 presented a chance to declare a certain independence from the United States in terms of cultural identity while also expressing pride in Hispanic heritage. It also offered an opportunity to express solidarity with Spain and other Latin American countries, thereby reinforcing the image of independence and celebrating *hispanidad*. The appeal of the Quincentenary was not essentially different for the advocates of Puerto Rican statehood (a nominally Republican group that included Jane García), since it allowed one to express pride in one's Spanish heritage while also showing patriotism toward the United States. Power in La Fortaleza, the historic governor's palace in Old San Juan, had oscillated between the two elite factions in recent years, but both were united in preparing to celebrate a double anniversary, the quincentenaries of the discoveries of America in 1992 and of Puerto Rico in 1993. Most of all, neither group had in mind a celebration that would be led by Italian-Americans. Thus, while the significance of the celebration's approach may not have been a pressing issue among Robert García's constituents in the impoverished South Bronx of 1982, it was not likely to have been lost on his wife. In these circumstances, the Mathias and Rodino bills disappeared into García's subcommittee just before Columbus Day and were heard of no more.

García had killed the Italian bills, but he and his staff knew that Italian congressmen could make equally short work of a purely Hispanic approach to the Quincentenary. So his and Mathias's staffs constructed a compromise during the early weeks of the 98th Congress that bore fruit in the forms of S[enate bill] 500 and H[ouse of] R[epresentatives bill] 1492. These identical proposals committed the nation to a commemoration which honored both Columbus and his crew and instructed the commission to "particularly examine the historic role of the government and people of Spain in order to promote a greater public awareness, understanding, and appreciation of the contributions made by Spain with respect to [his] voyages." Both bills also provided for nonvoting representatives on the commission from the governments of Italy and Spain. The García-Mathias compromise thus built into the commission's foundations a fault line that expressed the competition between Spain and Italy, Hispanics and Italian-Americans. It would only become worse as 1992 approached.

The language of S. 500 and H.R. 1492 eventually became the basis of Public Law 98–375, but there were two more gauntlets to run before the legislation was passed. One was created by senatorial supporters of the Chicago World's Fair, the other by conservative Republican budget cutters. The Chicago problem will be discussed in more detail in chapter 3. Essentially, it involved an amendment to S. 500 which enjoined the commission from interfering with the World's Fair or duplicating its programs. It also required recognizing the fair as "a major highlight of the Quincentenary celebration." It was proposed by Senator Charles Percy of Illinois, who was facing a difficult reelection campaign in 1984, and then supported by Senator J. Strom Thurmond, the chair of the Senate Judiciary Committee, which as noted had jurisdiction over S. 500. Thurmond was known as an enemy of Mathias and was therefore only too happy to oblige Senator Percy. As for the funding restrictions, the commission's federal appropriation was limited to $2 million over the next nine years, and a $50,000 cap was imposed on corporate and other private donations. The point of this was to reduce the likelihood that the commission would be able to interfere with Chicago's plans.

Meanwhile, H.R. 1492 sailed through García's subcommittee and passed the House in the spring of 1983. When it reached Thurmond's committee in the Senate, however, it was discarded in favor of S. 500, which passed the Senate in February 1984. Another round of negotiations ensued before the two bills were reconciled in a House-Senate conference held on June 26. Finally H.R. 1492 with the Senate amendments passed the Senate on June 27 and the House on July 25. President Reagan signed the bill into law on August 7, 1984—492 years and three days after Columbus's departure from Palos in 1492.

The law establishing the Jubilee Commission prescribed the manner and time of making appointments. The appointing power remained with the president, but seven of the twenty-four public members of the commission were to come from the recommendation of the majority leader of the Senate and seven others on recommendation of the Speaker of the House. Both the majority leader and the Speaker were required in turn to consult with the minority leaders of the two houses. Six additional members of the commission were to serve ex officio: the secretaries of State and Commerce, the Archivist of the United States, the Librarian of Congress, and the chairmen of the two endowments, arts and humanities. All appointments were to be completed within ninety days of the enactment of the law, but this coincided almost exactly with the elections of November 1984, which of course gave Ronald Reagan an even greater margin of victory than in 1980. Therefore, it was not until February 1985 that President Reagan made his first appointment, and not until the following August, a year after enactment, that the roster was complete. The commissioners were sworn into office and held their first meeting at the State Department on September 12, 1985.

It is important to recognize that no one in Ronald Reagan's Washington took the Quincentenary very seriously. "If anyone had come to me with this matter in 1984 or 1985," a high-ranking presidential advisor admitted later, "I would have shown him the door."[1] The same mix of general indifference and ethnic infighting that had afflicted the legislation characterized the appointment process. With the upper echelons of the Reagan White House preoccupied by weightier matters, the question of finding commissioners was left to junior personnel, who usually have charge of presidential boards and commissions in any administration. The key personnel officer was Susan Borchard, a Californian of acerbic wit and fiercely conservative views who cheerfully applied the "litmus test" developed by Presidential Personnel Director Robert H. Tuttle: barring more pressing concerns, presidential appointees must have been not only Reagan supporters in 1980 and 1984 but in 1976 as well. Only three of the ten commissioners appointed directly by President Reagan were exempted from Tuttle's test: James O'Connor, representing the civic elite behind the Chicago World's Fair; Virgil Dechant, the Supreme Knight of the Knights of Columbus; and William H. McNeill, a prominent historian whose candidacy was backed by the National Endowment for the Humanities. Even McNeill, whose name was selected by NEH Chairman William E. Bennett following staff recommendations, did not get by Borchard and Tuttle without a fight because of his lack of political credentials.

The result, as numerous observers later complained, was a list of commissioners devoid of "heavy hitters" and celebrities with name recognition, a serious flaw if the commission were to live up to the promises its congressional backers had made about raising private funds, a requirement within the environment created by Reaganism. Speaker Tip O'Neill nominated Governor Mario M. Cuomo, the country's most prominent Italian-American officeholder and the only figure on the list who might qualify as a celebrity. The Speaker also nominated Jane García and Arthur Decio, the nephew of another congressman, Representative Frank Annunzio of Illinois. Most of the appointees were persons of considerable accomplishment, but they were little known outside their own communities and business or professional circles.

So constituted, the Jubilee Commission presented a sharp contrast to the federal commissions created to deal with matters of serious public concern or of substantive interest to Washington policymakers. Such "old-boy commissions" are a commonly recognized Washington phenomenon. "The Chairman is a wise old lawyer, grown rich from corporate clients with Big Problems in Washington," writes a veteran observer. "The members are picked for their predictability" and their eminence.[2] The Challenger Commission, impaneled by the Reagan administration to look into the explosion of the space shuttle Challenger early in 1986, was an example. Chaired by a "wise old lawyer" in the person of a former secretary of state, all but one of its remaining members were eminent scientists. The Quadrennial Commission, which handled the ticklish issue of salary levels for judges, congressmen, and high-ranking federal officials, was chaired by a veteran Washington lawyer and included five corporate chief executives and three former congressmen in its membership. Similar profiles could be drawn from other "blue ribbon" commissions of the 1980s which tackled matters pertaining to Social Security, the Iran-Contra scandal, or government ethics.

The budgets of such commissions formed an equally illuminating contrast with the Jubilee Commission. When there is broad bipartisan agreement about the importance of a commission's mandate, somehow money is found even in tight budgetary circumstances to ensure that the commission's work can be done. By contrast, the Jubilee Commission's budget was small and hedged with restrictions, reflecting the fact that no consensus had emerged in Congress or the nation about either the significance or meaning of the anniversary in 1992.

The contrasts between the Jubilee Commission and its more august counterparts also grew out of the culture of official Washington, a culture that makes habitual and firm distinctions between matters of current policy interest and just about everything else. Washington residents get a daily reminder of this distinction in the pages of the *Washington Post*, which prints anything having to do with the arts, history, and culture in what used to be the women's pages, now called the "Style Section." Subjects having to do with current politics or policy debates go up front with the men's news. Thus, while arts news or cultural institutions, even minor ones such as the Jubilee Commission, might occasionally be featured on page one of New York or Los Angeles newspapers, in Washington such matters are strictly soft news. Journalists whose chief claim to fame may have been that they once rode on Gary Hart's campaign bus would find their eyes glazing over at the mention of historical or cultural subjects. The topic of the Quincentenary was simply not the sort of thing that typically interested official Washington. Therefore, it was not surprising that the politicians charged with making appointments to the Jubilee Commission did not want to use experts, celebrities, or wise old men but considered the whole a kind of throwaway for the purpose of canceling minor political debts. The idea was to accommodate loyal constituents and different ethnic groups. It was not until scandal threatened to overwhelm the commission at the end of 1990 that it made it into the pages of the *Post*'s Section A.[3]

The process of naming commissioners was hardly a thoughtful one at either end of Pennsylvania Avenue. Besides McNeill, the only commissioners with any expert knowledge or interest in the historical aspects of the Quincentenary were an historian, Charles Polzer of Arizona, and a retired Washington journalist, Henry Raymont, who specializes in Latin American affairs. Each had strenuously and successfully lobbied congressional Democrats for the job. But other congressional nominees got the nod almost casually. We were told of one Democratic nominee who was approached with the following words: "Hey—you're Italian. Wanna serve on this commission?" Another nominee, this one from the Senate, showed his understanding of the process when he said: "Look, I know I'm on here because I'm a Republican whose name ends in a vowel."

This was also the context of the ethnic infighting around the chairmanship of the Jubilee Commission. Public Law 98–375 confined the chairmanship to one of the ten commissioners named directly by the president. Cuomo was thus ineligible as well as unacceptable on partisan grounds, and neither of the presidential appointees with national reputations in their chosen fields—McNeill and Dechant—wanted the job or met the Tuttle litmus test. The leading candidate for the chairmanship in these circumstances was Frederick W. Guardabassi, a conservative Fort Lauderdale businessman and Republican contributor who spent most of 1985 under the illusion that he had in fact been promised the job. Perhaps he had been, in a way. His was the first appointment announced, in February 1985, a full six months ahead of the others. The son of an upper-class Italian artist-musician who married into a New England mill-owning clan, Guardabassi had been a sailing enthusiast since prep school, had graduated from Harvard, studied diplomacy at Georgetown, and spoke fluent standard Italian (as opposed to an immigrant dialect) as well as passable Spanish. Tall, silver-haired, and distinguished in bearing, he even looked the part of a commission chairman. His affable personality and refined manners coexisted uneasily with intensely held conservative views, but in face-to-face encounters his congeniality usually prevailed. He had wanted to be ambassador to Italy but had been offered (and declined) two less appealing diplomatic posts. The Jubilee Commission seemed just right in that it offered status in places that mattered and did not appear to involve much work. He seems to have spent much of the autumn of 1984 and most of 1985 convinced that the chairmanship was his, even going to the extent of joining what must have been the distastefully liberal company of Cuomo, Walter Mondale, and Geraldine Ferraro in the 1984 New York Columbus Day parade.

But ethnic issues interfered, and Guardabassi's chairmanship never materialized. Someone in the White House started toting up the slots. Of the twenty-three public members designated by August 1985, eleven were Italian-American, only three Hispanic. Of the presidential appointees eligible to serve as chairman, only one was a Latino. This was John N. Goudie, whose name had been brought to Susan Borchard's attention by her family physician and former boss, a Cuban-born Los Angeles surgeon and Republican Party activist named Tirso del Junco. The problem was that Italian-Americans produced more wealthy Republican campaign contributors but Latino communities held more votes, particularly if the Republicans' future hopes for dominance in states such as Florida, Texas, and California were taken into account. After an internal struggle which "came right down to the wire," according to one White House insider, and during which the idea was briefly floated of giving the chairmanship to the commission's only African American member, a conservative Miami lawyer named Arthur Teele, the presidential nod went to Goudie. He was elected chairman unanimously at the Jubilee Commission's first meeting on September 12, 1985.

The process of Goudie's election was a lesson for those commissioners who did not know how things worked in Washington. Goudie's name was placed in nomination by Dechant and seconded by Peter Secchia, the Republican national committeeman from Michigan (to whom President Bush would later give the job that Guardabassi had wanted, the ambassadorship in Rome). Raymont and Polzer attempted to call a recess in order to discuss Goudie's qualifications and canvass the interests of other commissioners. However, Edward Derwinski, a former congressman who as a State Department counselor chaired the meeting on behalf of Secretary of State George Shultz, maneuvered around the objections and brought the election to a close within a few minutes. The chairmen of the arts and humanities endowments, although loyal to the White House designation of Goudie as chairman, had held an earlier caucus to promote the election of McNeill as vice-chairman. This gave credibility to the overall situation. Otherwise, the objectors received assurances that they could vote again on Goudie's continuance as chairman after he had been in office a year.[4]

Henry Raymont was one of the first commissioners to attempt to generate serious public interest in the Quincentenary. His position was important because it expressed a view supported by many during the period leading up to 1992. A former *New York Times* correspondent in Latin America, he was well connected on both continents to molders of opinion and culture. His was the classic lament of the Latin Americanist: we know too little, pay too little attention, presume too much of our neighbors to the South. He believed it important not to squander the Quincentenary on superficial ceremonies that flattered American ethnics, or in tributes to and reenactments of Columbus's navigational skill. Here was "a unique opportunity to develop [in the United States] a more balanced view, a sense of proportion, and an appreciation of the place of Spain, Italy, Portugal, and Latin America in the history of the Western world." He wrote in the *Times* in 1983 that "we need to again grasp and take pride in what might be called the storybook truth about the New World: That the Americas were settled by peoples seeking new frontiers and status in a hemisphere free of the oppressiveness of the old European order. The fact that the New World's two hemispheres are physically far apart and were developed by two predominant cultures—Iberian Roman Catholicism and Northwest European Protestantism—should not obscure, as it frequently does, the common striving for freedom, democracy and justice that is the miracle of the new American man."[5]

Echoes of this view would be found later in Carlos Fuentes's *The Buried Mirror* and also in many aspects of Spain's quincentennial commemoration, which as we will see in a later chapter also aimed to overcome what it saw as centuries of prejudice and neglect in the United States toward the Hispanic cultures. As Raymont saw it, the Quincentenary was a chance to remedy a long and unfortunate tradition of postcolonial abuse that had fostered distrust between Anglo-American and Latin American cultures. His great hope was that this once-in-a-lifetime chance not be wasted.

Of course, such views gave little weight to the 1,200 Italian-American organizations around the country which did not feel an immediate interest in Latino issues and believed that the Quincentenary was *their* civics lesson, not Raymont's. Indeed, even congressmen who belonged to the Hispanic Caucus knew they were greatly outnumbered by their Italian-American colleagues. Most of them were average men, just glad to be there, and unlikely to lead—or fund—a drive to educate Americans about Latino culture. Beyond this, it must be admitted that Raymont was not especially tactful or organized in his approach. Inquisitive and disputatious by nature, he tended to prefer argument to persuasion. These habits blunted his impact and undercut the ideas he sought to advance.

It was Henry Raymont who first suggested that John Williams, one of this book's coauthors, apply for the commission directorship. "You know how to get things done," he said, which Williams admits was just the right phrase to seduce an intellectual-turned-bureaucrat. An historian by training, he had been serving since 1980 on the staff of the National Endowment for the Humanities, where he had worked with NEH colleagues Malcolm Richardson and Eugene Sterud to encourage interest in and planning for the Quincentenary. The three had organized five NEH-sponsored conferences in 1982–83 in different parts of the country for humanities scholars and professionals in museums, research libraries, and public broadcasting, and these had made it clear that the scholarly community and major cultural institutions were deeply divided over how to approach the Quincentenary. At this early date, the most that could be said was that while 1992 meant something to nearly everybody, it did not mean the same thing to any of them. Moreover, it was one thing to organize scholarly conferences, quite another to direct a divided and underfunded presidential commission. Anyone with a little knowledge of Washington knew that presidential commissions, whether chaired by a Washington wise man or not, are usually staffed by political appointees, not experts. Williams's political credentials included working in the presidential campaigns of Gene McCarthy in 1968 and Jimmy Carter in 1976, hardly the kind of experience to earn points with the Republican commission chairman, John Goudie, much less with Tuttle or Borchard. He submitted an application to Goudie and underwent an interview late in 1985, but he was not hired; nor was he particularly surprised or disappointed at this result.

Instead, Williams represented the Endowment at meetings of the Jubilee Commission, beginning at Miami Beach in January 1986. This encouraged ongoing contact with Polzer, Raymont, and McNeill, who had also served as a keynote speaker at one of the NEH conferences. Along with representatives of other cultural agencies such as the National Archives and Library of Congress, the historians gradually formed a nucleus of persons bound by educational interest in the Quincentenary tempered by skepticism concerning the means. Part of the problem was the continuing absence of an overall vision for the commission. For example, Goudie chose as his first director a young Miami businessman named Armen Cruz. Cruz had been the first Cuban-American to graduate from West Point, but he had left the military in favor of civilian life, most recently as the director of Miami's unsuccessful 1992 world's fair effort. He managed commission affairs for no more than a few months but left a file full of flow charts and diagrams of authority regarding the commission's two-person Washington staff. No progress was made during his tenure toward determining the ends to which these elaborate means would be put.

Similarly, the Miami Beach meeting was dedicated mostly to socializing and a search for precedents which might guide the commission in its work. The Statue of Liberty Centennial celebration, then nearing its climax, was an obvious model, except that the commission lacked both a symbol with the universal appeal of the Statue of Liberty or a chairman who could command the kind of attention in fund-raising and public relations as the Statue's spokesman, Lee Iacocca. The idea of a single Quincentenary spokesman immediately provoked the divisions of ethnicity again. Moreover, even if a polyethnic Iacocca substitute could have been found, the very idea of searching for one required the members of the commission to confront their own limitations, something that few of them were prepared to do. The fourth Columbian centenary had centered on the great Chicago world's fair, but the chances of this happening again in 1992 were already starting to appear remote; the proposed Chicago fair was floundering and it was too late for Miami or any other city to win the federal and international sanctions which were needed for an event of this sort. The Los Angeles Olympics of 1984 remained the most beguiling model in its demonstration of the power of corporate sponsorship to underwrite special events for which taxpayer rebellions had cut or limited public support. The L.A. model also held a special appeal for chairman Goudie in the person of the Olympics Coordinating Committee's dynamic leader, Peter Ueberroth. Whatever other factors may have contributed to the success of the L.A. Olympics, Goudie tended to place the greatest weight on Ueberroth's personal skill and renown. Like Ueberroth in 1984, Goudie in 1986 was young, smart, attractive, energetic, and unknown; why couldn't he score a like success with the Quincentenary?

Goudie's history, experience, and cultural background reinforced the idea of attributing success to personality. He had enjoyed considerable business success in Miami not only through hard work but also because of his personal skill as a salesman and promoter. He was charming and good looking and possessed of a distinctly "un-Cuban" name which he believed appealed to Anglos. He also ascribed his prominence among Cuban Republicans to personal relationships with Anglo politicos such as George Bush's son Jeb and to his success in raising campaign funds among his fellow YUCAs (Young Upwardly Mobile Cuban Americans). Personal connections had of course won him the commission appointment and chairmanship, and he tended to look upon the job as an opportunity to expand his personal contacts, first in Miami and ultimately in the Caribbean/Latin American economic sphere. Toward this end, he was in many respects successful. While traveling for the Jubilee Commission to places such as Spain, Venezuela, Costa Rica, and the Dominican Republic, he acquired a certain prominence among Miami Cubans as well as a new visibility among influential segments of the Anglo business community. The problem was whether this was adequate for the Quincentenary. Enhancing one's local reputation fell far short of what was needed in Washington or the nation at large, and in the long run the failure of the chairman to pursue his goals beyond local circles ended up limiting the Jubilee Commission's reputation and prospects. In addition, like many outsiders Goudie had difficulty making the right bureaucratic connections in Washington, which always remained to him an impenetrable labyrinth.

On the other hand, it can also be said that in the short term, John Goudie's personal attributes made up for some of the commission's weaknesses. His good-humored charm was helpful in reassuring the leading Italian-American members of the commission and avoiding most ethnic infighting, although Guardabassi remained unconvinced. His energy also established the commission's presence internationally when he visited Spain and Italy. In Costa Rica, for example, he brashly intruded into an international meeting of "Ibero-American" Quincentenary Commissions organized by Spain and demanded membership for the United States on the grounds of his own Hispanic heritage.[6] The group was not amused but did offer observer status to the Americans.

The Jubilee Commission's third meeting took place even farther offshore in Puerto Rico, in the heart of San Juan's colonial district. Jane García helped make the personal contacts that secured support for the meeting from the Puerto Rican authorities. "Bob and I have an excellent relationship with him," Jane García wrote the governor of Puerto Rico about Goudie. "He is charming, articulate, organized and effective. In short, someone we can be proud of to represent Hispanics everywhere in the world."[7] The Puerto Rican hosts provided the commission with an even more glittering social reception than in Miami Beach, but, again, little business was accomplished. There were skirmishes between Republican and Democratic commissioners and there were tours of the island, but several of the businessmen commissioners either skipped the meeting or complained about one aspect or another of the local arrangements. Goudie himself left the meeting early to attend to business matters in Miami, a sign that problems were brewing. When Director Cruz returned home a few days later, Goudie fired him. In the absence of a coherent plan for the commission, Goudie now set about composing a mission statement by himself.

It is important to note also that during 1985–86, John Goudie was facing other kinds of problems. For example, shortly after he took over as chairman, his White House patron, Susan Borchard, suffered a near-fatal illness and was eventually forced to resign her post and return to California. He also faced family emergencies at this time, and the collapse of Miami's real estate boom led to a series of lawsuits in which creditors tried to force him to liquidate some of his real estate holdings. Dozens of civil suits were filed against him between 1985 and 1987, with more to follow in subsequent years. Creditors also foreclosed on a new office building he had built and forced him into Chapter 11 bankruptcy in order to save other holdings.[8] To make matters worse, his erstwhile sponsor and mentor, Tirso del Junco, was named by President Reagan to fill a vacant spot on the commission in June 1986. Del Junco had hoped for a cabinet post; failing that, he wanted Goudie to turn over to him the commission chairmanship and hinted on several occasions that this step would save Goudie from future embarrassment, since he might be forced to step down if the full extent of his financial woes became known to the White House. At the time, Goudie dismissed del Junco's pressure as the reaction of an out-of-date old man who did not know how to adjust to the success of his juniors. In time, however, del Junco would be proven correct.

Still, in spite of his difficulties, Goudie remained optimistic and worked energetically for the commission. Perhaps he *could* become a new Ueberroth, some persons suggested, especially if offered help in developing the commission's program and in piloting it through Washington's bureaucratic shoals. In these circumstances, John Williams again emerged as a candidate for commission director. Coming to an agreement with Goudie in June 1986, Williams arranged to be "detailed" from the NEH to the commission directorship. If he and Goudie liked working together and if Goudie won confirmation as chairman at the commission's next meeting, scheduled for Chicago in September, they further agreed to make the arrangement permanent.

Upon assuming the directorship, Williams had to deal with several urgent issues. First of all, a sense of purpose and momentum had to be created. This required securing Goudie's reelection as chairman so as to stabilize the leadership. Then too, the commission's credibility had to be established and contacts abroad had to be firmed up. Mostly, the task of creating a viable and focused Quincentenary program had to be accomplished along with developing the financial capacity to realize it.

The main obstacle to Goudie's reelection was Commissioner Guardabassi, who still held aspirations to become chairman, although by this time the other Italian-American commissioners had accepted Goudie's leadership. In San Juan, Goudie had tried to reach out to Guardabassi by making him chairman of a "Maritime Committee," but that was of limited appeal because many committees had been appointed and there was nothing pressing for any of them to do. Williams, however, thought that if this Maritime Committee could be made more meaningful, things might improve. Guardabassi could bring real expertise and credibility to an enhanced committee because he was genuinely interested in maritime affairs, was well-informed by a lifetime of sailing, and possessed wide contacts among yachtsmen, retired naval personnel, and others who formed the natural public for a maritime celebration. Columbus holds a special place in the hearts of mariners everywhere, and maritime programs was one area where ethnic issues were literally submerged in the undeniably Italo-Spanish character of the 1492 voyage.

In addition, two important quincentennial programs were primarily maritime in orientation and needed careful attention. One was the creation of replicas of Columbus's three ships, or caravels. Actually not all three ships were caravels. The Santa María was probably a type of ship known as a *nao*, though the experts were not sure of this any more than they were agreed on any of a dozen other questions, such as how the ships were constructed, what they looked like, how many masts they had, or how they were rigged. There was also disagreement over whether to build ships with concealed modern navigational and convenience elements or to rebuild and sail them as the rather primitive and uncomfortable vessels they actually were. No fewer than six different groups had approached or would soon approach the commission with plans to replicate the ships, but none had any money to speak of and all wanted an exclusive sanction from the commission before they would proceed. The ships would provide an undeniably dramatic program element, and the fact that the rival groups looked to the commission to sort out their claims offered a chance to strengthen the commission's credibility. Here was where Guardabassi could provide needed leadership, though all recognized that sorting out the different claims would not be easy. From another point of view Spain was going to win the contest hands down.

The second maritime program faced by the commission involved the use of traditional sailing vessels or tall ships as the photogenic symbols of historic occasions. Such ships had been used to spectacular effect on two recent commemorations, the Statue of Liberty centennial on the July 4 weekend in 1986 and the American Revolution Bicentennial ten years earlier. On both occasions the parades of tall ships into New York Harbor had captured the public's imagination. Efforts were already under way to do it again in 1992, something that seemed all the more appropriate because the first such parade of ships had taken place in honor of Columbus in 1892, and it seemed almost obligatory to recapture an event that "belonged" to the Admiral. At the same time, if New York occupied July 4, where might the ships be on the actual anniversary, October 12? California seemed like a good idea, and thus was born the idea of upstaging the New York parades of 1976 and 1986 by having two regattas in 1992, one commemorating Columbus's crossing the Atlantic, and a second in California, commemorating the world-transforming impact of Columbus's feat as well as a pair of regional anniversaries, the Cabrillo expedition of 1542 and the Malaspina expedition of 1791–93. This would emphasize the links between Columbian explorations and the European advance into what is now U.S. territory.

Guardabassi pursued the idea of twin regattas as his own and he also accepted suggestions for dealing with a related issue, the designation of official host ports for the 1992 transatlantic regatta, which British and Portuguese yachtsmen and Spanish government officials were already eager to pin down. Rather than ratify the initial European suggestions, which called for the 1992 regatta to avoid New York in favor of preferred yachting harbors such as Norfolk and Newport, the commission appointed Guardabassi head of a delegation to attend a meeting called by the Europeans in late September 1986, in Lisbon. As he threw himself enthusiastically into the enriched agenda of his committee, he lost interest in contesting Goudie's reelection and gradually developed a more positive working relationship with the chairman, who was reconfirmed at the Chicago meeting. At the same time, by pursuing these maritime programs, Guardabassi was contributing centrally to the commission's need for a meaningful quincentennial plan.

The Jubilee Commission's credibility in Washington was further strengthened by what Williams later described as his "Blue Room Strategy." The Blue Room is a small parlor decorated with Chinese antiques on the second floor of the DACOR Bacon House, a restored federalist mansion on the corner of 18th and F streets in Washington, a block from the White House. A private residence until 1980, it was renovated in 1985–86 as the headquarters and club rooms of an association of retired diplomats, with offices rented to outside organizations with international concerns. Through one of Henry Raymont's contacts, Williams was able to rent three-fourths of what had been Mrs. Bacon's back bedroom on the third floor as commission office space and to share a copier and conference room with another organization. And though the Blue Room was not part of the deal, the landlords made it available for occasional use. This permitted the commission to use it for the reception of important visitors who needed to be shown more luxurious facilities than circumstances would otherwise have permitted. Foreign visitors in particular were subjected to this tactic, but it was also used for the events promoters who now started to approach the commission more often once the scope of the promoters' cut of Liberty Weekend's proceeds became known. None of the promoters who visited the Blue Room during this period actually offered cash, and the fundraising restrictions of the commission's enabling legislation would have made it difficult to accept their offers in any case. But it was important to keep such persons interested in planning activities while the commission sought to change the legal restrictions on fund-raising and without revealing how mismatched the commission's mandate was to its means. As long as the visitors did not wander into the cramped and noisy quarters upstairs where the small staff actually worked, the Blue Room answered this need.

Ultimately, the Blue Room symbolized a larger strategy: to endow the commission with the authority of the U.S. government. Congress had given the commission the responsibility of creating a national program without the means or power to call one into being. The next best thing was thus to borrow the reflected authority of other agencies, such as the Smithsonian Institution or the Library of Congress or the two endowments, which were beginning to create Quincentenary programs of their own. The commission had no money, clout, or prestige to offer these agencies, but they had much to offer the commission, especially if Spanish, Italian, and Latin American diplomats bought the idea that the commission and these prestigious cultural institutions were in fact "working together." Williams began to use his contacts and McNeill's prestige among Washington's cultural bureaucrats to establish such relationships and found that in doing so he could sometimes assist Quincentenary program planners among the various agencies in winning more attention and support from their superiors. He also encouraged program developers at prestigious non-federal institutions to apply for the commission's endorsement of their plans, although initial efforts in this direction led to an unfortunate clash with a young Puerto Rican lawyer whom Goudie had hired as his assistant.

One of the organizations encouraged to apply for endorsement was WGBH-Boston, where executive producer Zvi Dor-Ner was beginning work on the documentary series *Columbus and the Age of Discovery*. "What if they take our endorsement and then make a pornographic film?" the lawyer queried in all seriousness. Nothing in the station's long record of journalistic distinction answered this concern. As a result, the lawyer drafted rules to govern the commission's endorsements which contained a clause committing the endorsees to accept all future changes in policy by the commission. Or, as the Library of Congress's representative put it, they were being obliged to follow the commission's "future whims." WGBH's lawyers objected to the future whims clause on First Amendment grounds. Eventually, a compromise was worked out whereby the offending clause remained, but WGBH was allowed to reject it in accepting its project's endorsement. Interestingly, neither the Smithsonian nor any of the academic institutions that applied for endorsement ever objected to the future whims clause.

The Blue Room strategy was applied in other ways as well. The first two meetings of the commission had established a standard of entertainment which the commission's own resources could not sustain. In addition, the wealthier commissioners expected to stay in first-class hotels when they came to meetings, and only one—Arthur Decio—consistently refused to do so at the government's expense. All of them felt, not without justice, that they should get something in the way of a reward for their donated time and labor, but federal regulations meant that the government rate was insufficient to meet their expectations. As a result, director Williams developed a variant of the Blue Room strategy when organizing commission meetings. He called it the posture of the mendicant prophet, holding a lantern in one hand which pointed to great future events, and a tin cup in the other. Beginning with the Chicago meeting in September 1986, the strategy worked. The city's tourism promotion organizations were eager to keep the world's fair alive, while cultural institutions agreed that it would be a shame for the commissioners to see only the promotional aspects of 1992 and not its educational potential. The result was an excellent social program in Chicago as well as a thrifty room rate negotiated by the Convention and Visitor's Bureau at the Hyatt Regency. This then became the standard that helped to wrangle comparable deals from other host cities for subsequent meetings, such as those in Los Angeles, Columbus, Baltimore, and Dallas.

This was strictly a road show operation, however, since Washington hoteliers and tourism authorities were unimpressed by presidential commissions. Still, there were embassies, the State Department, and cultural institutions to fall back on. The luncheons and receptions they put on when the commission met in Washington late in 1986 and again in September 1987 marked the extent to which the Blue Room strategy could be turned to good ends in boosting the commission's morale and prestige without depleting its meager resources. It was an especially useful strategy in dealings with other governments. Government support of cultural and commemorative activities is the rule in Europe and Latin America, as is direct government operation of programs such as the Quincentenary. The absence of a ministry of culture in the United States, with the functions of such a ministry parceled out among a dozen or so cultural agencies, made it difficult for foreign Quincentenary planners to know where to look in Washington for information and support. Thus, when the staff staked out this territory for the commission, foreign representatives generally responded quickly and gratefully to offers of "coordination." And while the commission's actual authority to do this was weak and uncertain, the fact was that commission staff knew more than most about where and how to make cultural contacts.

Meanwhile, the commission debated and adopted an ambitious quincentennial plan that it hoped would reach wide audiences in a culturally sensitive manner. High-profile public events such as the parade of tall ships or caravels were tied to the promotion of educational programs. The idea was that public events underwritten by corporate sponsors would build audiences for the numerous cultural programs then being planned by museums, public broadcasters, and arts organizations. These programs would add to the Quincentenary's cumulative impact and allow a more complex and accurate representation of New World history to displace the now anachronistic "Columbus Discovered America" theme inscribed in the popular imagination. Everyone who came to the observance with certain expectations would find those expectations challenged, but they would also find something of what they were looking for. There would be ethnic pride for Latinos and Italians, for example, but no less importantly, programs would include reconciliation with Native Americans and a deeper understanding of the profound sense of anger, sorrow, and loss with which Indian scholars and spokesmen looked toward 1992. As we discuss in chapter 4, such issues had been building for some time and the commission was forced to acknowledge them. The capstone was to have been the Columbus Scholars program, financed through the sale of commemorative coins to this enlarged and enlightened public. As developed by McNeill with the aid of a blue-ribbon committee of educators, this "living memorial" would have gone beyond the parades, statues, and world's fairs of earlier commemorations to embody in Columbus's name a multicultural, bilingual program that was deliberately constructed to contravene the racist, colonialist values once embodied in Cecil Rhodes's scholarship plan of a century earlier.[9]

In August 1987, Congress amended the 1984 act establishing the commission to permit corporate underwriting adequate to the scope of these ambitions. Shortly afterward, in October 1987, an ambitious strategic plan and fund-raising scheme was adopted by the commission's finance committee in order to seek and deploy the financial wherewithal to make the plan happen. The members of the finance committee were all businessmen, many with experience raising money for one cause or another, and all had contributed to the plan. To launch this effort, the wealthier commissioners contributed some $200,000 of their own funds in addition to perhaps another $100,000 worth of donated services.

However, to everyone's surprise, more than a year passed without success in landing major corporate sponsors. One problem was that corporate sponsors, notwithstanding the success of the Statue of Liberty celebration, were beginning to reevaluate their involvement with so-called mega-events.[10] Another was difficulty in dealing with Spain's official Quincentenary agencies, whose cooperation was essential if an American program focused on maritime events was to be realized but which were uncertain as to how much they were willing to share control of the program with an American commission numerically dominated by Italian-Americans. But the biggest problem was the commission itself. Many commissioners had the potential for opening doors to corporate underwriters but they remained unconvinced or unwilling to put forward a major effort. Virgil Dechant's Knights of Columbus, a major insurance company as well as a charitable and fraternal organization, was preoccupied with underwriting new political initiatives in the antiabortion campaign. Arthur Decio, who had raised millions for Notre Dame and the Special Olympics, or James O'Connor, a powerhouse in raising money for Chicago charities, chose not to put their time into the commission. Commissioner Gene D'Angelo devoted most of his considerable energies to promoting the quincentennial programs of Columbus, Ohio, and Ohio State University.

Goudie too was finding obstacles in his fund-raising activities. He was ill-prepared to deal with leaders of multinational corporations, and fissures had begun to appear within his Miami base of support. The nation's most prominent Cuban-American businessman at that time, Coca-Cola president Robert Goizueta, refused to see Goudie or to acknowledge his numerous letters and calls. In 1988, he would add injury to insult when Coke launched a quincentennial advertising campaign of its own. It was targeted to Spanish-speaking consumers while completely disregarding the Jubilee Commission and its programs. Meanwhile, an individual by the name of Alberto Cárdenas, a former partner of Goudie in real estate dealings, entered into a complicated series of lawsuits and countersuits, the depositions of which contained charges and countercharges about Goudie which in due course found their way into the files of business credit-reporting services and law enforcement agencies. Apparently some of the businessmen on the commission had access to these reports but did not share them with the White House or with commission staff. "They trust you, but they don't trust him," Peter Secchia later told Williams; failing to support the commission's fund-raising initiatives was one way of keeping Goudie on a short leash. Only during the latter half of 1988, when Goudie began to cut back visibly on his personal spending and to insist on full reimbursement for his phone calls and trips on commission business, did others begin to glimpse the seriousness of the problem. Even then, everyone was unprepared for the revelations that would eventually come out.

Further complicating the commission's financial prospects was the fact that Goudie did not personally subscribe to his finance committee's plan. Hurricane Floyd, which briefly threatened Miami in October 1987 (and reminded everyone of how lucky Columbus had been as he poked around the Bahamas and Cuba in the autumn of 1492), forced Goudie to miss the committee meeting in Chicago where the plan had been hammered out. Thus he was free to regard the plan as something Williams had foisted on the committee rather than the product of the businessmen commissioners whom Goudie most admired. Two issues in particular caused friction. First was the plan's call for restraint in seeking minor sponsorships for Quincentenary activities—licenses to reproduce the commission's logo on T-shirts and comparable souvenirs and in promoting minor pre-1992 events. The conventional wisdom among special events organizers was that these should be the last sponsorships to be sold, after major corporate underwriters had signed up to sponsor big-ticket items such as the Grand Columbus Regatta and the American tour of the replica caravels. Signing up T-shirt vendors first cheapened the event in the eyes of prospective major underwriters and also amounted to discounting the minor sponsorships since these would become much more valuable once the big sponsors were on board. For reasons that became all too clear much later, Goudie was eager to press forward with these sign-ups. For example, when a West Coast branch of a Procter & Gamble marketing division offered $10,000 for a one-shot endorsement of a Columbus Day Chicano music festival in the San Jose area in 1988, he jumped at it with alacrity, notwithstanding the resulting conflict with the plan.

The second and ultimately more crucial disagreement concerned the hiring of a professional fund-raiser, something that the finance committee members had insisted was absolutely essential. During the summer of 1988, a headhunter whose services were underwritten by one of the finance committee members turned up several candidates for the job, one of whom, Paula Jellinghaus, a woman with solid business credentials and the requisite accounting experience, was willing to work on a semi-contingency basis, with the commission putting up her first six months' salary and expenses, with all else being contingent on meeting specified fund-raising goals. At the commission's eleventh meeting in Baltimore in September, several of the wealthier commissioners agreed to contribute $10,000 apiece to a pool to get the ball rolling. Although Williams insists that Goudie gave verbal authorization to proceed, Goudie stated that the director overstepped his authority in issuing a contract to Jellinghaus. As a result, he dismissed both the director and the fund-raiser.[11] This took place on the day after George Bush's election, November 9, 1988.

Behind the disagreement over fund-raising, other differences had been developing. Goudie had come to believe that Williams failed to provide effective guidance through the Washington bureaucracy. Having successfully exploited personal networks in Miami and the Caribbean, he thought that the commission's failure to raise funds was simply a matter of not yet making the right contacts. Following Bush's election, Goudie believed that things would undoubtedly fall into place because of his personal contacts with the president-elect's son. For his part, Williams made the mistake of overlooking the personalistic ties so important to Goudie and pressing instead for a bureaucratic solution to solve the commission's financial woes. Thus, he proposed hiring an expert whom nobody *knew* in personal terms and whose authority derived from impersonal certifications such as those provided by executive search firms and professional fund-raising councils. In the eyes of chairman Goudie, such references were not likely to appear as important as personal recommendations from someone he knew.

After Williams's departure, Goudie personally took over the commission's direction. At the twelfth meeting in Miami in December 1988, Jeb Bush was introduced to the commissioners and all were given a tour of the Goudie company's new rented quarters in a Coral Gables penthouse. In March 1989, the commission met in Washington, where Goudie posed in the center of his colleagues holding a $1 million check, from the Quincentenary's first corporate sponsor, Texaco. The check was turned over to the Spanish Commission's delegate as a down payment on the much-anticipated American tour of the Columbus caravels. At this and subsequent meetings there were glowing reports of progress, with assurances that other major sponsors were about to sign up.

In May 1989, the commission staged a gala New York luncheon to showcase its maritime program and to impress potential Japanese investors in the caravel tour. Governor Cuomo was not invited until the last minute, but other prominent New Yorkers came, including Mrs. Donald Trump and Jane García. Notwithstanding the fact that García and her husband had recently been indicted in connection with the Wedtech scandal, she "out Evita[d] Evita," in the words of one observer. But there were also signs of trouble. The commission's finances necessitated reducing the number of meetings from four annually to three, and there was also the problem of finding a new director. The retired diplomat who was thought to have the inside track remained in limbo through the first half of 1989; finally, in September, Goudie appointed Raúl de Quesada, a fellow Cuban-American from Miami.

In spite of these portents, there was no stinting on travel. Commission meetings were held in the Bahamas, Dallas, and Santa Fe. Quesada lived out of his suitcase, commuting from Miami to Washington; and Goudie visited places as far flung as Japan, Argentina, and Spain, as well as more customary haunts such as Washington and New York. Occasionally he traveled with Jana Joustra, the commission's "public relations director," whom he later made "deputy director" under Quesada. Joustra was a law school graduate with Republican credentials whose White House patrons arranged for another agency to pay her salary while she worked for the commission. The General Accounting Office investigators who would later be called in found that some $125,000 was spent on travel during the last fifteen months of Goudie's chairmanship, $45,000 of it on staff trips, $60,000 for commissioners (including Goudie), and $15,000 for "guests."[12] This was travel on a truly Columbian scale, and like the Admiral on his later voyages, Goudie's luck was about to run out.

At the Jubilee Commission's September 12, 1990, meeting in Washington, following an acrimonious session of the finance committee the night before, someone circulated to each commissioner a document denouncing Goudie's tight control of the commission and calling for more openness in its finances.[13] During a hastily called executive session, Goudie defended his record and denounced the document and its anonymous means of distribution. Several commissioners agreed, notably Mary Jane Checchi, a former Capitol Hill staffer turned lobbyist, who termed the circular "too sneaky" to take seriously. The anonymous critic presumably wished to open up questions about Goudie's leadership, but his or her method instead led to a resounding endorsement.

Meanwhile, the same or a like-minded person placed near the public phones outside the meeting room a stack of copies of an article from *Special Events Report* entitled "A Sponsor's Guide to the Columbus Quincentenary." The article reported that "sponsors are wary" of the Jubilee Commission and relayed criticisms by Columbus buffs and state and local Quincentenary planners. But it also quoted Joustra's assurances that she had "letters of intent" for an additional $10 million beyond the $5 million already pledged by Texaco.[14] Apparently, a member of the commission staff scooped up the copies before most commissioners spotted them, and so another opportunity to open up the commission's operations to scrutiny went by the boards.

Still, trouble continued to build. On September 30, 1990, Texaco suspended its payments to the commission after only two installments on its $5 million pledge.[15] Then in October, Quesada abruptly resigned. Reports began to circulate about possible illegalities concerning those minor sponsorships that had earlier caused tension between Goudie and former director Williams. In July 1989, the commission had recognized a "Christopher Columbus Licensing Group" (CCLG) as its sole licensee for the purpose of arranging minor sponsorships. Several individuals had invested sums in excess of $500,000 each into CCLG, but when they subsequently became concerned about their investment, they were successively reassured, cajoled, stalled, threatened, and eventually "fired" by Goudie as the commission's licensing agent. As the complaints of these investors found their way to Congress and to the press during the latter half of 1990, other complainants came forward and various investigations were launched. As Rep. Thomas Sawyer later summed it up in November 1991, the story was one of "widespread conflict of interest in planning commission activities, inappropriate intrusion into the management of contracted activities, inappropriate use of corporate funds on the part of the Christopher Columbus Licensing Group and the apparent insolvency of that corporation by this point, allegations of bribery and fraud with respect to the awarding of Commission contracts, and possible abuse of authority on the part of the ... chairman."[16]

The shadow thus cast on Goudie was enough to force him to resign the chairmanship on December 17, 1990. The next day, the *New York Times* gave page one coverage to the sponsorship problems as well as the suspension of Texaco's payments. It also revealed that the commission was $600,000 in arrears on payments to the Spanish builders of the Columbus caravels, that a federal audit and possible congressional hearings were in the works, and that Goudie's personal and financial problems in Florida included the suspension of his real estate license, illegal campaign contributions, tax problems, and "Court records [that] show numerous financial judgments against him."[17] The *Washington Post* weighed in the next day with further details, and then on January 6, 1991, the *Miami Herald* published a full and detailed account of Goudie's woes for the delectation of hometown readers. The rumors and accusations that had been circulating turned out to be only the tip of an iceberg. Most of the lawsuits investigated by the *Herald* were for small sums of money, but there were also major judgments and foreclosures. For example, Goudie had lost not only his new office building but three apartment complexes, one of which he was judged to have conveyed fraudulently to his wife. His campaign contributions to Florida Republican causes turned out to have been far more meager than he had led people to believe, and at least one of them was illegal, made with his company's funds, which led to the suspended real estate license. Even his car had been repossessed, the story related, and his lawyer had quit because of unpaid bills.[18]

The newspaper stir that these revelations inspired soon died down, but official investigations continued. In February 1991, agents of the General Accounting Office's special investigations division were dispatched by the commission's oversight committee in the House of Representatives (no longer chaired by Robert García but by Rep. Sawyer) to examine the commission's books. While an independent audit had earlier found everything to be in order shortly before Williams's departure in the fall of 1988, bookkeeping after that point had become shoddy, even derelict. The investigators reported in April 1991 that the commission itself was "insolvent." Further, the investigators found that "over $120,000" of the CCLG's funds had been paid to a Miami friend of Goudie named Manuel Gonzales and that, of this amount, at least $28,000 had been used by Gonzales to make mortgage payments on Goudie's residence. Manny—as Goudie called him—had also employed Jack Goudie, the erstwhile chairman's brother. An additional $46,000 had been used to make mortgage payments on a Florida house shared by still another Goudie associate, and $16,000 was used for travel unrelated to CCLG business. The investigators could not account for additional missing funds.[19] At subsequent House hearings, Gonzales admitted making "undocumented loans to John Goudie" but said that "he was never an agent, representative, stockholder, or officer of the [Christopher Columbus Licensing] Group." Other friends and business associates "declined to provide any information about the details and circumstances of their financial transactions relating to the commission or the Group." Goudie, although invited to testify, failed to appear.[20]

Meanwhile, on the NBC tabloid program *Expose*, viewers were treated to the scene of Goudie walking a floodlit gauntlet at the Miami airport, muttering "no comment" into a microphone thrust in his face. Further hearings revealed additional individuals who had paid large sums for licenses of different kinds. Goudie eventually testified under subpoena, as did Joustra. The latter denied knowing anything about the funding irregularities and indicated that she had never witnessed unethical conduct of any kind at the commission. She also testified that "I can only remember seeing Chairman Goudie three or two times before Director Williams resigned," a statement at odds with one that Goudie subsequently made about his frequent travel to Washington, not to mention an encounter they had had at the 1988 Republican National Convention in New Orleans, which Joustra described to the congressmen in some detail.[21]

When Goudie followed her to the witness chair on November 21, he was not accompanied by an attorney. "I did not have the money to bring one in here," he explained.[22] "I feel it is a great injustice that I have left the commission," he added, complaining that the congressmen would not let him show a promotional video about the Columbus caravels. "Knowingly I have not done anything wrong. I am here to answer any questions that you have." But when questioners got down to the specifics of the commission's licensing operations, Goudie invoked his Fifth Amendment rights thirty-two times.[23]

As the Goudie debacle unfolded, President George Bush appointed Frank Donatelli to become chairman of the Jubilee Commission. Donatelli in turn selected Jim Kuhn, a Republican lawyer and former Bush campaign scheduler, to be the commission director. The White House also dumped Fred Guardabassi unceremoniously over the side with Goudie, even though he had not been implicated in the latter's alleged misdeeds. His removal made room on the commission for Frank Stella, president of the National Italian American Foundation. With these changes, the triumph of Italian-Americans in the ethnic conflicts surrounding the commission was complete. Stella pledged to oppose "those who have elected to engage in revisionist history to try and discredit Columbus."[24] But the victory was empty because it had absolutely no impact on the 1992 commemoration. For while Donatelli assured the congressmen that the commission would now go forward to a scaled-down but worthy observance of the Quincentenary, he also noted "I am a realist and I like to play the hand that is dealt."[25] It is clear that his assignment was to stanch the flow of bad news, keep the commission's name out of further headlines, and give it a decent burial once the Quincentenary was past. As with so much else associated with the Quincentenary, events were over before they even began.

The Jubilee Commission's notoriety inspired more interest than its programs, but it is important to place its troubles in a broader context than simply focusing on John Goudie's misdeeds. A primary reason for the commission's failure was the federal budget mess, which was in turn a product of the American government's willingness to pursue and unwillingness to pay for an aggressive foreign and military policy during the Cold War. While the same can be said of any federal program that needed money during the 1980s and 1990s, such as the war on drugs or educational reform, it applies with special force to cultural initiatives, which always have a low priority in the official political culture. The legislation establishing the commission and defining its mandate is proof that political leaders still wanted such programs; they just didn't want to pay for them. But the legislation also indicates a reluctance to confront the logic of the situation. Both Congress and the White House told the commission to raise funds from corporations, but during 1988 when major corporate underwriters might have been landed with a call from the Reagan White House or a letter from the secretary of state, neither office was willing to provide even this much support. The politicians wanted to sell official history but they also wanted to remain personally above that sort of thing. A similar logic pervaded the appointment process which gave commissionerships to persons lacking credentials either in history or in major fund-raising. If Goudie came to grief partly because he did not know what he was doing, neither did the people who created the Jubilee Commission and put him in charge of it.

The much-decried "inside the Beltway" mentality of Washington, with its myopic focus on the political near term and its indifference to most intellectual and cultural pursuits, was yet another factor in the Jubilee Commission's failures. This was especially apparent with other endeavors, such as U.S. participation in the Seville World's Fair, which with the caravels and the Barcelona Olympics showed the lavish funding that Spain, a nation much less wealthy than the United States, gave its mega-events. The Jubilee Commission staff spent much time in 1987 and 1988 trying to break a bureaucratic logjam in Washington that delayed planning an American pavilion in Seville and then shunted responsibility for funding it primarily to an ill-defined "private sector." The results were predictable. "It's tacky and there's no money in it and it looks like a third world country," exclaimed a New York woman who visited the pavilion in 1992. Architectural critics and fair aficionados found recourse to similar words: "tacky," "a mishmash," "crude," "abominable." The criticism referred to the pavilion's exhibits as well as its design, for the centerpiece was a recycled exhibit left over from the Bicentennial of the Bill of Rights. In theory, the message was about America's most basic values, but it seems mainly to have communicated the idea that, when it comes to history, American talk is cheap.[26]

3

Cities of Gold

Few things are less interesting in history than accounting for something that never happened. Yet the rise and fall of the 1992 Chicago World's Fair involved more than just a nonevent; it actually marked a turning point in the city's history. A past era in which a small elite of prominent businessmen could speak for the entire city gave way to a coalition of citizen activists seeking a livable local environment. Paternalistic modernity was confronted by participatory postmodernity and lost the battle, as indeed has subsequently happened in many cities throughout America.[1] Moreover, other cities shared Chicago's Quincentenary experience—places such as Baltimore, Miami, and Columbus (Ohio)—that likewise struggled with mixed results to use the Columbian commemoration as a launch pad for various kinds of civic enterprises. The Quincentenary thus became a zone of confrontation for many of the forces that shape the struggles and difficulties of all cities. Chicago's approach to 1992 pitted the contemporary city's heterogeneity of political and economic power against the premise of cultural unity that underpins what we have called the mega-event. Large projects such as world's fairs, olympiads, and other civic undertakings have since the late nineteenth century been used as means of galvanizing popular support for a certain style of privately directed urban renewal. In the postmodern city, such activities have come to appear increasingly anachronistic, like vaudeville or the circus, remnants of an earlier era that has lost its appeal. The Chicago World's Fair of 1992 is an instructive case in point.

The history of this stillborn mega-event is well-documented because its organizers confidently assumed that they were making history. In fact, one of their first steps was to hire a historian and create an archive at the Chicago Historical Society. The result is a record that constitutes an exception to the dictum that success has many parents while failure is orphaned. Few nonevents in cultural history have been better documented than the Chicago World's Fair of 1992, though the lesson to be learned is not the one originally intended. On the contrary, it offers an illuminating view of the intertwined fates of global change and American civic life in the late twentieth century. It is also a story whose combination of grand ambitions and petty defeats seems appropriately linked to the name of Christopher Columbus.

Appreciating the story fully requires a brief overview of world's fairs generally. From the moment that the Crystal Palace opened its doors in London in 1851, these events have played an important role in the construction and representation of modern culture. At one level fairs have proclaimed the cultural unity of what today is called the developed (in the nineteenth century, the "civilized") world. At another level they sanction and define modernity's fascination with novelty and change. They present an ordered universe wherein differences among cultures are interesting but not threatening, the future seems inviting and manageable, and novelty is contained. Not the least of their functions, as anthropologist Burton Benedict has observed, has been to teach members of an emerging consumer society what and how to consume.[2] Benedict compares the fairs' competitive displays of products and their prestige contests among nations and cities to the potlatches of Northwest Coast Indians. It seems an apt comparison, considering the extravagant temporary structures of the fairgrounds and lavish displays of objects which are destroyed or dispersed when the fairs close.

Today we remember the greatest fairs by the products they introduced: the dynamo (Vienna 1873), the telephone (Philadelphia 1876), the Ferris wheel and carnival midway (Chicago 1893), ice-cream cones

(St. Louis 1904), long-distance telephone calls (San Francisco 1915), air-conditioning (Chicago 1933), television and nylon (New York 1939). But the organizers of fairs have always insisted that they were much more than trade shows. The amount of space devoted to commercial exhibits at world's fairs has declined steadily since 1851, while the proportion of space devoted to education and amusements has grown. The linkage of world's fairs with the commemoration of great events grew out of this moral dimension. Thus the Philadelphia fair was tied to the centennial of American independence in 1876; Paris in 1889 commemorated the French Revolution, St. Louis (1904) the Louisiana Purchase, Montreal (1967) the anniversary of Canadian nationhood. Chicago's great 1893 exposition established such a link with Columbus, but there had also been an 1892 exposition in his honor in Madrid, which featured among other things a Smithsonian exhibit of Native American artifacts and copies of no fewer than seventy portraits and busts of the Admiral himself.

Another manifestation of cultural unity and moral purpose was the modern Olympics, sustained during the second, third, and fourth olympiads as an annex to world's fairs (Paris 1900, St. Louis 1904, and London 1908). Still another was the effort of fair organizers to create a structure which somehow embodied an exposition's dual expression of present satisfactions and future hopes. Paris's Eiffel Tower is the most enduring structure of this type, but there have been others which have enjoyed comparable if shorter-lived fame, such as New York's Trylon and Perisphere of 1939, Seattle's Space Needle (1962) or Montreal's Habitat (1967). In the case of the pavilion that Mies van der Rohe designed for the Barcelona exposition of 1929, we have an example of a temporary fair structure that turned out to be such an accurate predictor of future taste that it was reconstructed on the same site some sixty years after it had been torn down.

During the nineteenth century, world's fairs were the vehicles for national aspirations, but increasingly toward the century's end they were taken up by civic advocates and builders. In the United States, fairs came to be a means by which provincial cities competed for commercial and cultural recognition from the centers of commerce and fashion in the northeast. Thus New Orleans held its first exposition in 1884–85, celebrating the bicentenary of La Salle's colonizing expedition. Atlanta followed Chicago's success with a Cotton States Exposition in 1895. San Francisco boosters, who had hoped to get a road-show version of the Chicago 1893 fair, instead held a "Mid-Winter Fair" in 1894 to tout the

California climate. Nashville marked Tennessee's centennial with an exposition in 1897. San Diego, San Francisco, and New Orleans launched rival plans for world's fairs early in the twentieth century to commemorate the completion of the Panama Canal. San Francisco's fair had to be postponed because of the 1906 earthquake but was eventually staged in 1915 as a means of announcing to the world the city's triumphant rebirth. In the meantime, Norfolk held a fair in 1907 to commemorate the tercentenary of Jamestown.

Civic leaders pursued two goals in mounting world's fairs. One had to do with promoting their city's identity by making it famous, that is, by "putting it on the map." The other had to do with what today's fair promoters call "residuals," permanent improvements to the city's infrastructure and amenities which grow out of the staging of a fair. In both cases, Chicago's great World's Columbian Exposition of 1893 provided the model. The choice of Chicago (over Washington and Philadelphia) as the locus of the nation's Columbian celebration was a congressional matter. Chicago's victory represented national acceptance of its promoters' argument that their city best embodied the relentless westward surge of empire and progress that Columbus's voyage had launched. The successful staging of the fair literally "brought the world to Chicago," thereby validating the city's resurgence from the ashes of the 1871 fire while also establishing its reputation for decades to come as America's second city. The fair also consolidated the city's position as the national meeting place and left behind a dazzling array of residuals growing directly or indirectly out of the fair. The fair site itself, built on landfill near what was then the southeast edge of the city, became a lakefront park extending inland along the "Midway Plaisance." The University of Chicago, founded in 1892, grew up on either side of the Midway, while farther north the founding of the Chicago Symphony Orchestra (1891) and the Art Institute (1891) embodied the civic cultural aspirations which the fair had sought to promote. The Field Museum of Natural History was founded in 1894 to house the ethnographic materials that the fair had brought to the city. The Chicago Museum of Science and Industry found what turned out to be a permanent home in the only one of the fair's buildings to survive. One of the more unusual residuals was a replica of one of Columbus's ships, which had been towed across the Atlantic in 1892 and ended up in Chicago in 1893 after leading New York's parade of ships on Columbus Day the previous fall. The caravel remained anchored on the city's southern lakeshore as an attraction for tourists and schoolchildren until the vessel caught fire and burned to the waterline in 1934. Some of the older men among the 1992 world's fair promoters could remember visiting the caravel in their youth.

Chicago, moreover, was not alone in reaping such benefits. Audubon Park in New Orleans, Balboa Park in San Diego, Flushing Meadows Park in New York, and Fairmount Park in Philadelphia are residuals left behind on the sites of expositions. Museum buildings in New York, San Antonio, San Francisco, and Seattle once housed world's fair exhibits, as did the headquarters of the historical societies in Buffalo and San Diego. Spokane got its riverfront park and cultural complex around the falls of the Spokane River from its 1974 fair, while Knoxville in 1982 got $450 million worth of federally financed freeways and interchanges, along with the transformation of the fair site, a disused railroad yard in a ravine near the center of town, into a park.[3] Even the second New Orleans fair of 1984, a record money loser, left the city with a waterfront aquarium and a boutique and entertainment complex.

Of course, these residuals were not entirely free, but the theory of world's fair finance was beguilingly simple. The idea is that fairs pay for themselves, or rather that the people they attract do. Commercial enterprises will pay to show off new products or to display or refine new public relations strategies. Nations and cities (and states in federal countries such as the United States) will erect imposing buildings to show off their cultural and commercial attainments. Individuals will flock from near and far and pay hefty admissions fees if the fairgrounds hold forth the promise of a "once in a lifetime" experience, a chance to meet the world's diversity and to greet its common future firsthand. The promoters of most fairs even promise to turn a profit in order to attract the bank loans and government subsidies that are necessary to organize the event and prepare the grounds. In the case of the New York fairs of 1939–40 and 1964–65, the looked-for profits were also supposed to pay for the transformation of the fairgrounds into Flushing Meadow Park, the promised residual. In fact, the profits never materialized in New York, but the fact that both the 1893 and 1933 Chicago fairs made money ensured that the theory remained alive and well in that city in 1981.

The great problem with this theory is that it grew threadbare through frequent use. The proliferation of expositions in the first third of the twentieth century undermined the expectation that fairs would introduce business and the public at large to something truly new and important. Why would Louie meet us in St. Louis if he could expect to find more or less the same exhibits and panoply the next year in Omaha or St. Paul? This issue only intensified with the advent of television and mass marketing, which made travel unnecessary for seeing the new. Moreover, as fairs multiplied, public exhibitors began to resist the repeated strains that fair buildings and programs in distant places put on their treasuries. The benefits to cities hosting the fairs became increasingly speculative. Barcelona, for example, had to share the spotlight in 1929 with another fair in its own country, an "Ibero-American" Exposition held the same year in Seville. Both fairs required heavy subsidies from the Spanish government, though both left behind nice parks and, in the case of Seville, the basis of the modern city's infrastructure. The American consulate in Seville, which the Reagan administration closed in an economy move shortly before the Jubilee Commission visited Spain in 1988, was housed in one of the exhibit buildings left over from the 1929 fair.

The proliferation of fairs and alternative entertainment possibilities threatened both the commercial value and the moral and educational purposes of expositions, not to mention the sense of excitement and novelty which they were expected to generate. To remedy this situation, the United States and thirty-one other countries established the Bureau of International Expositions (BIE) by treaty in 1928. The bureau established rules to protect the vitality and worthiness of the enterprise—thus the requirement that every fair have an educational theme—and also to protect exhibitors' pocketbooks. Exhibitors could no longer be required to build permanent structures or to keep their exhibits open for more than six months; governmental exhibitors could not be charged ground rents for the space they occupied. The distinction was established between specialized expositions, devoted to a single area of endeavor (such as "Energy" in the 1982 fair at Knoxville, or "Rivers" in the ill-fated 1984 fair in New Orleans), and universal expositions which undertook to construct a global vision and address the loftiest themes. An interval of two years was established between the limited expositions, and ten years had to separate universal fairs, with a further provision that only one universal exposition could be held on the same continent within the ten-year frame. All of these rules were subject to "quiet bending" through negotiation—the New York fair of 1939–40, for example, was allowed to run over two seasons and followed Chicago's "Century of Progress" fair of 1933 by only six years. In general, however, the BIE brought order into a confusing situation. When the New York master builder Robert Moses defied the BIE in

1964–65, it not only withheld its sanction but asked its signatory countries to boycott the fair, which most did. As a result there were only seven nations and a handful of states represented by official pavilions in Flushing Meadow. The result was a financial and public relations disaster that put an end to Moses's career (although he had actually lost no more money than had his predecessors of the sanctioned fair of 1939).[4]

In late 1981, the city of Chicago made its first representation to the BIE in Paris to host a world's fair or "universal exposition" on the occasion of the upcoming Columbian Quincentenary of 1992. The delegation was led by Donald Petkus and George Burke, serving respectively as director and secretary of the Chicago 1992 World's Fair Corporation. This entity had been established the previous January under the leadership of several major business leaders, including Petkus's boss, Thomas Ayers, retired chief executive of Commonwealth Edison, Chicago's electric utility company, who served as corporation president. Burke's employer was Stanton Cook, publisher of the *Chicago Tribune*. Petkus continued as Edison's executive vice-president while running the Fair Corporation, though Burke—rather unwisely as it later turned out—gave up his *Tribune* job to work full-time on the fair.

Petkus and Burke were accompanied to Paris by George Pratt, the director of the Office of World's Fairs in the U.S. Department of Commerce. Following the Olympics model, the BIE would consider only one application at a time from a given country, and Commerce was the sanctioning body for applications from the United States. Pratt was a great supporter of Chicago who believed the city had already hosted two of the greatest fairs in history, those of 1893 and 1933. He made no secret of his hope that 1992 would top them both and he had visited the city to help prepare the BIE application.

Using the *Tribune*'s resources and those of other civic-minded ad agencies and PR firms, the Chicago delegation had put together a dazzling audiovisual show employing eighteen projectors and hundreds of slides, to accompany the formal BIE application. "I must say they were very impressive," recalled Marie-Hélène Defrène, the assistant and eventual successor to the director of the BIE, René Chalon.[5] Chalon was a retired French diplomat of about seventy who cautioned the American team not to get their hopes up because many rivals were seeking authorization for a universal exposition, and there was resentment among other BIE nations at the recent problems with American world's fairs such as those of the upcoming 1984 limited fair in New Orleans. Chalon also advised the delegation to persist if they were serious about the project, which they were. The result was a roller coaster ride that eventually exceeded everyone's expectations, though not in the way they would have wished.[6]

The first problem for the Chicago promoters was to contend with rival domestic claimants. Miami was the most serious challenger, but Houston promoters were talking about a fair linking Columbian and space themes, and Columbus, Ohio, was also stirring. "Even Sacramento, California, of all places, out in the bean fields, wanted to do a fair," as Burke put it.[7] In the end, only Miami contested Chicago's claim. From his position in the Commerce Department, Pratt mostly tried to discourage this. He believed that civic leaders in Miami were only half-serious about a 1992 world's fair, and that what they really wanted was federal money to build more causeways to the keys (islands), where most elite Miamians have their homes. He later commented that when it became clear such aid would not be forthcoming under Reagan administration budgets, the city's downtown leadership lost interest.[8]

Other information corroborates this view of the Miami situation. A University of Florida history professor summoned to Miami in 1982 to help strengthen their BIE application later commented that local boosters had no idea what they wanted other than to promote a mega-event. By the time that the Jubilee Commission became involved in world's fair issues in 1986, such interest as there was in Miami was centered in the Cuban community. Unfortunately, according to the *Miami Herald*, the downtown corporate leadership did not include any Cubans at that time.[9] As a result, local leaders considered Columbus and 1992 "an ethnic thing," as a Miami museum director once put it. Joan Didion found that Cuban-Americans considered the downtown banks and other civic institutions such as the *Herald* to be ranged against them and thus against civic events which might bridge the ethnic divides fragmenting the city. The *Herald* confirmed this attitude when it reproduced a *Washington Post* op-ed piece on the Quincentenary written by two Smithsonian Institution staff members. The article was reprinted verbatim except for a single sentence which identified Miamian (and Cuban-American) John Goudie as the national Jubilee Commission's chairman.[10] From the standpoint of the *Herald* editors and those who thought like them, 1992 was less significant than 1995, the centennial year of Miami's founding. Then perhaps they would mobilize for a mega-event.[11]

Still, in their efforts, Miami fair boosters raised enough money to hire an executive director, Armen Cruz, who later became the first director of the Jubilee Commission. They also hired a design firm, Meta-Form of New York, which had worked on the unfortunate New Orleans fair. And they brought strong political pressure to bear on the White House and Congress to support their plans. Notwithstanding Pratt's opposition, the city of Miami filed a BIE application in competition with Chicago that required a pro forma site visit at the prospective fairgrounds on Virginia Key. After a decent interval, the Secretary of Commerce and the White House accepted Pratt's recommendation on behalf of Chicago, and on November 9, 1982, President Reagan proclaimed Chicago the victor, officially certifying its application to the BIE as the only American candidate for a 1992 world's fair. This action not only quieted the aspirations of other American cities but was also the first official federal action relating to the forthcoming Quincentenary.

Domestic competition was only a first problem for Chicago; promoters also had to deal with several international rivals at the BIE. For example, Paris wanted to repeat its greatest nineteenth-century fair with a 1989 exposition commemorating the *bicentenaire* of the French Revolution. In fact, a Paris representative followed the Chicago delegates in addressing the December 1981 meeting of the BIE. He said that he did not have a slide show or a bunch of pretty pictures, but only a map of Paris. However, everyone knew Paris and loved it and wanted to go there, whereas nobody knew anything about Chicago or would care to go there. Some thought that this arrogant tactic backfired with the French press, but a formula lay readily at hand for compromising the two cities' claims. While technically Paris 1989 and Chicago 1992 would violate BIE rules about ten-year intervals between universal expositions, in fact Montreal 1967 and Osaka 1970 had also been held within three years of each other. The trick had been to charge one to the 1960s and the other to the 1970s, thereby making the ten-year rule once-in-a-decade. Since no universal exposition had been held since Osaka, the same rule could work again. But then Paris dropped out of the picture as French plans for 1989 evolved into an array of art shows, academic conferences, and building projects, climaxed by an extravagant parade on July 14.[12]

Another formidable rival appeared in February 1982, however, when the Spanish city of Seville notified the BIE that it too would file a 1992 application. One of the weaknesses of Chicago's application, as Chalon had noted, was "the fact that Columbus had never been to Chicago, not even on the lake."[13] No one could say this about Seville. Columbus had lived and worked in that city and had recruited sponsors and sailors there; he had been buried there, at least for a time, and the city's cathedral is the site of one of his two official tombs (the other is in Santo Domingo). For the better part of three centuries, Seville had been one of the richest cities in Europe, the hinge between peninsular Spain and its American empire. And, as we discuss in a later chapter, the Spanish now wanted a 1992 fair to showcase Spain's new democracy and its links with both the established democracies of western Europe and the emergent democracies of Latin America. The moral urgency of this theme—a fair to consolidate and advance democracy—was hard for the BIE to resist, especially because it was delivered personally by King Juan Carlos I and then reinforced by both the outgoing Conservative and incoming Socialist prime ministers when a BIE delegation visited Madrid in 1982. Seville was thus a serious rival, at least on the surface, and BIE politics made it even more formidable. The bureau had been pleased to gain a number of new signatory nations during recent years, most of them Latin American. In a showdown between the United States and Spain, there was little doubt as to which way these members would vote.[14]

Following what had now become a characteristic pattern, the Chicagoans decided not to press for a choice but sought rather another compromise. Privately, they scoffed at the idea that Spain could pull off a major world's fair in a place like Seville. Clayton Kirkpatrick, chairman of the *Tribune*'s parent company, spoke for many when he stated that "I just don't think the Spaniards can put together a major exposition. . . . Seville is quite a small town."[15] At the time, there was certainly some truth to this, for in 1982 Seville had a small airport, only one first-class hotel, and antiquated rail and highway links with Madrid. However, rather than impressing these facts on the BIE, the Chicagoans decided to let their city and its amenities speak for itself. No holds were barred when the BIE delegation consisting of Defrène and the British, Russian, and Finnish BIE representatives arrived in May 1982 to inspect the city. Mayor Jane Byrne met the delegation at the airport brandishing a newly minted ten-year plan for the city which showcased the 1992 fair as the climax of the decade. The group was given a first-class tour followed by a climactic visit to Orchestra Hall, where each of the delegates and their hosts had a private box and personal greetings after the concert from the Chicago Symphony's renowned conductor, Sir Georg Solti. At this session, the maestro delivered the clincher. His permanent home was in London, he told them, but Chicago is the most magnificent city in the world. In his experience, this was the only place where you could get anything done. Fair Corporation president Ayers later noted that if this had come from the Chamber of Commerce, it would have been considered mere fluff, "but to have the maestro say it, a European, not a canned speech, it was absolutely sensational."[16]

Defrène and her colleagues agreed. Shortly after the Reagan administration certified the Chicago application, the BIE granted the city a "permit" to plan for a universal exposition in 1992. But there was a twist. A compromise worked out with the Spanish meant that the Chicago fair would not stand on its own but would be half of a "twinned" exposition, divided equally between Chicago and Seville. Just what this might mean practically was anyone's guess, but in this way (the Paris 1989 fair being still alive at this point), the BIE could bend its rules without breaking them. Three years later, the bureau granted still another 1992 permit, this one to Columbus's hometown of Genoa, Italy, which also wanted a fair.[17] The Chicagoans received these rulings with equanimity, earning plaudits from a relieved Defrène for their tact toward the Spanish "who are very proud." Privately, the Chicago group felt that in a showdown—in the case, say, of exhibitors who were willing or able to mount only a single 1992 exhibit—their city would surely win out over provincial European towns whose populations scarcely equalled the number of passengers who monthly passed through O'Hare Airport. So, the BIE action made it official. Chicago now had a "site registration" for a 1992 World's Fair. The fair promoters set about securing the site and finances to realize their project.

The initial idea for a 1992 world's fair in Chicago assumed its contemporary form in the fertile mind of architect Harry Weese. His vision was complex and involved a domed stadium partially submerged in Lake Michigan, a divided fairgrounds extending out from the lakeshore in front of the Loop, below-grade pathways linking the Loop and the lakefront via promenades of boutiques and cafes, and an over-water aerial ride between exhibition areas which would give fairgoers a dazzling view of the sight that Chicagoans never grow tired of: the city's skyline seen from the water's edge. "Harry Weese never fails to express his ideas," noted a prominent developer, "and some of them are good."[18]

Weese's interest in fairs dated back to the age of twelve, when he set sail for the 1933 Chicago exposition in a homemade boat from suburban Wilmette. While in college he visited the last great Paris fair (1937) and later visited both New York fairs and the Montreal Expo. While serving as a member of the American Revolution Bicentennial Commission during the early 1970s, he witnessed the squabbling between Boston and Philadelphia boosters over the siting of a 1976 fair and briefly entertained the idea of offering a Chicago site as an alternative. By the end of the decade he was ready to go public, convening a group of Chicago architects under the aegis of the city's American Institute of Architects (AIA) chapter and dividing them into subcommittees on financing, a fair theme, and a site. During 1980, Weese held a series of breakfast meetings with business leaders and by mid-summer a private World's Fair Steering Committee had been launched. Ayers was not the group's first choice for the chairmanship, but he agreed to take it in July after two other executives turned it down. Ayers in turn drafted Petkus while Stanton Cook drafted Burke. Frank Considine, CEO of the Continental Can Company, became the fifth member of the committee, which evolved into the directorate of the 1992 World's Fair Corporation the following January. Meanwhile, the Chicago-based architecture firm of Skidmore, Owings, and Merrill contributed talent to work on the site problem, while another Chicago-based national company, the advertising firm of Foote Cone Belding, undertook to do market research. In August 1980, a Foote Cone Belding report certified that both the Chicago metropolitan and the midwestern regional publics would support such a fair, while the Steering Committee had raised funds to employ a Spokane-based fair planning consultant with the improbable name of King Cole. Cole remained a part of the planning group for nearly a year, until the Chicagoans grew wary of his personal money-making schemes and impatient with his seemingly ineffective Washington connections, mostly bureaucrats who had been involved in the limited Spokane and Knoxville fairs—"church carnival[s] writ large," in Burke's view, and not the kind of extravaganza Chicago was planning.[19] After the Chicago group dropped Cole, he showed up briefly in Miami and then was heard of no more.

By this point, some twelve to eighteen businessmen had been involved in the gestation of the fair. Many were of an older generation that had fond memories of the 1933 fair. They also smarted under the stings of a lifetime of living with Chicago's image as a city of gangsters. Hollywood's first gangster movie, *Underworld* (1927), was scripted by a Chicago newspaperman, Ben Hecht, who with another midwesterner also coauthored the script of *Little Caesar* (1934), based loosely on the life of Al Capone. The latter film was a runaway hit and consolidated Chicago's reputation for crime while making Capone its best-known citizen. "Chicago is a most underappreciated, undervalued, misunderstood city in the world by people who don't live here," exclaimed Arthur Schultz, the head of Foote Cone Belding. The fair offered a chance to change this. Even the tactful Chalon admitted that like most Europeans he thought of Chicago primarily in terms of its gangsters and applauded the fair organizers' effort to displace the stereotype with something more positive.[20]

But the businessmen had practical as well as sentimental reasons for backing the fair. Most of the fair supporters were, like Ayers and Cook, associated with businesses whose health and prospects were directly dependent upon the overall growth of the city. This included newspapers, real estate, construction, banking, and related professions such as architecture and law. Except for Considine, no prominent manufacturer was involved in the planning, nor did executives at McDonald's take much of an interest in the fair, apart from hosting the BIE luncheon. Neither was there much interest at Sears or Playboy, two other famous consumer-oriented companies based in Chicago. And the commodities and option traders who gave La Salle Street its "go-go" reputation during the 1980s were not represented in the Fair Corporation. The world's fair group was, as its critics charged, a distinctly Old Guard, though not all of them were old.[21] They understandably regarded themselves as custodians of the city's future and, in 1980, their contemplation of that future aroused genuine concern.

This concern was best summarized in an article from the *Economist* of London which circulated within the business community during the spring of 1980. Its author was Andrew Neil, a British business reporter who capped a series of dispatches on the city's troubles with a lengthy survey in the issue of March 29. Neil characterized Chicago as "the city that almost works," cataloguing a familiar array of urban ills to which Chicago had long claimed immunity: eroding jobs and tax bases, financially and educationally bankrupt schools, a decaying infrastructure and inadequate city services. He conceded that Chicago, which during the twenty-one-year regime of Mayor Richard J. Daley had claimed to be "the city that works," was still in better shape than many older American cities, but he gave readers little comfort in this. During the 1980s the city would enter an era of accelerating decline unless action was taken. "Chicago will have to start thinking big in new ways" if worse was not to come.[22] The *Economist* survey focused upon three problems in particular: a "political civil war" within Daley's Democratic city hall machine, since he had died in 1976 without naming a successor; racial segregation, which Neil termed with good reason the worst of any big city in the nation; and the failure of the metropolitan economy to generate enough jobs in the service sector to replace the manufacturing jobs it had lost. Significantly, the response of the businessmen who reacted to his article focused almost exclusively on this last problem. They were particularly impressed by the argument that "Chicago needs to drop its parochial obsessions and reinvigorate its economy by selling itself more vigorously on the international market." It needed to build upon existing assets: "a superior business climate, compared with other northern cities," a leadership structure wherein "it is still possible to meet almost everyone who is supposed to matter in Chicago at one cocktail party," a "sophisticated" banking center, diversity in its manufacturing base, a tradition of business-government cooperation, and the advantage of its central location vis-à-vis transportation and American markets. Instead of "trying to fight [the] market forces" that underlay the shift from manufacturing to services, from Rust Belt to Sun Belt, and from developed to developing countries, Chicago needed "to tout" itself as a place for corporate financial and administrative functions and for research facilities. "Chicago has the right credentials," Neil concluded, "but they remain largely unknown in Western Europe and Japan."[23]

To the world's fair promoters, Neil's survey sounded as an authoritative call to arms, though they heard only one of the notes he had sounded. Neil had actually devoted more space to race and politics than to business concerns, and he had urged civic leaders to concentrate their energies on solving these problems as a necessary prelude to turning their gaze outward. However, if the fair promoters ever understood this point, they gave no evidence either in word or deed. As the fair project took shape during the early 1980s, the racial and political problems Neil wrote about merged into a bitter battle for city hall succession between Mayor Jane Byrne, Richard M. Daley (the son of the old boss), and Harold Washington, a former Boss Daley lieutenant who emerged as the standard-bearer of the old machine's African American voters. The businessmen stood on the sideline during these battles, waiting for the air to clear so that, presumably, the reliable business-political alliance of the Boss Daley years could be reestablished.[24] This proved to be a fatal decision as far as the fair's prospects were concerned. Although it is difficult to see how anyone concerned about local government could have known where to lay bets in 1981–82, Harold Washington's eventual victory meant that the fair promoters would be faced with a skeptical and distant presence at city hall just when they needed friends there the most.

It is also significant that the committees of architects charged with developing ideas for the fair's site, theme, and finances failed to come to any conclusions before they turned these issues over to the Fair Corporation.²⁵ The fair site had to be determined before the BIE application could go in, and so the promoters moved swiftly after the corporation was created early in 1981. Only lakefront sites were seriously considered, although pro forma attention was initially given to other parts of the city and again in 1983 after the lakefront site became controversial. The Foote Cone Belding market research assumed a lakefront site. "Did you ask them [members of the market research focus groups] about any other place?" an interviewer asked Schultz. "No, but they liked the idea of the lake." Potential fairgoers also liked the idea of cleanliness, Schultz added. "They want a clean restroom and a clean fair." And a safe one, with no "drunks and druggies coming in." It is not hard to read into these characterizations—assuming that, as Foote Cone Belding claimed, they were the views of a representative sample of Chicagoans—the fears that the city's white and nonwhite people have of each others' neighborhoods. The lakefront was neutral ground, safe and pleasant. As for a suggestion made later that the fair reach out to incorporate sites in the neighborhoods, Ayers had what for him seemed a definitive answer: if St. Louis were having a fair, "would you buy an airplane ticket to go to St. Louis and walk around their neighborhoods?" Despite the controversy that "doing it in the Lake" always aroused in Chicago, the businessmen in the corporation could not imagine doing it anywhere else.²⁶

The choice of a lakefront site meant that the fair, while privately conceived and directed, inevitably became the subject of public discussion, discussion which quickly evolved into heated debate centered primarily on finance, a focus which dismayed architects and others who had been attracted by the visionary promise of the fair. The issue of finance was "a silly question," in the opinion of Bruce Graham of Skidmore, Owings, and Merrill. "If man did not put energy into improving his environment and into living in sympathy with his environment, and energy is the investment or whatever you want to call it, money or exchange or whatever, we'd still be living in the trees. You have to have visions that inspire men and then you go out and figure out how to get the energy to do it."²⁷ But therein lay another rub. Had the fair promoters generated a vision sufficiently compelling to convince others of the value of the fair, the outcome might have been different. But they did not. They provided neither a practical program which explained how such a costly extravaganza might produce solutions to actual problems, such as the city's need for jobs, nor a visionary statement which could plausibly endow the fair with a "once in a lifetime" aura.

Moreover, it was obvious to everyone that a 1992 fair had to compete in a very different market from that of the earlier Chicago fairs. Critics pointed out that the attendance figures on which the Fair Corporation's financial projections were based would require every person in metropolitan Chicago to attend at least four times. The promoters argued that Chicagoans would come out to see the fair's presentation of exotic lands and peoples and new technologies. "Or, on the other hand, they could watch television," as a skeptic commented.[28] Forty percent of the U.S. population lives within a day's drive of Chicago, as the promoters never tired of pointing out. But midwesterners who could afford a four-day trip to the fair could also afford to visit the Black Hills or Tennessee theme parks or even fly down to Orlando, where Epcot Center, the Disney Corporation's permanent world's fair, opened to record crowds in 1983. The Chicago World's Fair of 1992 would celebrate "The Age of Discovery," it was determined in the BIE application. But the promoters were never able to articulate this theme in such a way to convince skeptics that an eager public would forego its other choices to attend the fair or that voters would find in either the fair's theme or its residuals sufficient justification for the investments of public resources which were required.

This is not surprising in view of the almost offhand way in which the fair's theme was developed. George Burke, who left his job at the *Tribune* to head the Fair Corporation's public relations in 1981, explained that the theme was chosen by a process of elimination, starting with two drafts of two pages each prepared by him and Arthur Schultz. Celebrating Columbus himself was uninspiring, or so the inner circle of promoters thought; this was too old-fashioned, too much focused on the past. Thus, 1992 would not be a World's Columbian Exposition II. The promoters wanted a theme that would signify cultural interchange "without getting into the whole idea of one-worldism and . . . universal peace, and all those other big words. . . . It was also important that it would be an acceptable concept to countries all over the World. So New World had to die. The only thing left on this platter after everybody had cut off the parts that they didn't like the taste of, was discovery."[29]

It should be pointed out that the Seville half of the 1992 World's Fair developed a fully articulated program based on the amorphous Age of Discovery theme. But the Seville fair was heavily subsidized by the Spanish government and promoters did not have to woo investors and taxpayers, only potential exhibitors. The Chicago promoters had to start from scratch. They needed up-front funding in the form of cash subsidies or loan guarantees to private investors, and they needed assurances that the city or state government would meet the fair's transportation, crowd-handling, and security requirements. Only when these were met could they turn to the job of recruiting the foreign and domestic exhibitors whose attractions would bring the fair's theme, such as it was, to life.

These requirements ultimately placed the fate of the fair in the hands of the Illinois state government. This was because city hall in Chicago was paralyzed first by the three-way battle over the Democratic mayoral nomination in February 1983 and then, after Harold Washington's victory, by a standoff between the mayor and a hostile majority of the city council, a stalemate that lasted until Washington's supporters won a majority of seats in the council elections of 1985. Nor was the other Washington—the federal capital—ready to play the role that the Spanish government did for Seville. In fact, the Reagan administration, facing record budget deficits and a rising number of demands for federal world's fair expenditures in the specialized fairs of the 1980s (Knoxville 1982; New Orleans 1984; Tsukuba, Japan, 1985; Vancouver 1986; and Brisbane, Australia 1988), agreed with congressional critics of these projects to place a moratorium on new commitments while a special task force studied the value and funding of future U.S. participation. The study was not completed until 1987; predictably it favored increased private participation in the funding of official exhibits. The president did not officially accept the Spanish invitation to the Seville fair until 1988 and then made only a heavily qualified commitment to the funding of a U.S. pavilion. Congressional resistance delayed an appropriation until mid-1990; even then Congress provided less than half of the $30 million needed to build the pavilion, requiring that the rest of the funds be raised from corporate sponsors, even though the national exhibits of the hundred-plus other countries represented at the fair would be government funded.[30] In this climate, it was difficult to be responsible for world's fairs in the Department of Commerce. George Pratt noted that if one Washington or the other (Harold or D.C., in other words) had supported the Chicago fair, things might have turned out differently. "I pissed off the wrong people and the Commerce Department let the Chicago Fair die." Eventually he was forced to move to another agency, dependent upon the patronage of a Republican higher-up who "felt sorry for him."[31]

Thus all roads led to Springfield for the fair promoters during the critical eighteen-month period following the BIE's final approval of the

Chicago-Seville application in December 1982. There had been no difficulty getting a unanimous resolution endorsing the fair from the Illinois legislature while the application was pending; when the BIE committee visited Springfield in May 1982, Governor James Thompson promised similar results when it came to funding.[32] But things turned out differently when it was to back up these promises with cold cash. Legislation creating an Illinois Exposition Authority and authorizing the sale of bonds to finance the fair remained stalled through the first half of 1983 as criticism about the fair's cost and skepticism about its residuals and impact mounted. Mayor Washington created a special commission to study the matter. So did the Illinois House of Representatives. The Fair Corporation created a "Fair Review" committee in an attempt to co-opt or at least appease its critics. Finally Thompson broke the deadlock with a compromise that gave the authority funding for one year, required yet another feasibility study, and delayed all other decisions. He also drafted one of his most trusted and admired aides, John D. Kramer, the thirty-six-year-old secretary of the Illinois Department of Transportation, to be the Exposition Authority's general manager.[33] Directors of the private Fair Corporation moved over to provide a majority of the directors of the new public authority, while the architects and other consultants who had worked previously for the private promoters also signed on.

During 1984, Kramer tried to put together a political coalition that would support permanent funding for the fair. Efforts had to take place in public because critics of the fair forced the reluctant Fair Authority to conduct its business under the state's open meetings and freedom-of-information laws. The process resembled less an undertaking in responsible public planning than a kind of taffy pull wherein the scope and boundaries of the fair were pulled this way and that to accommodate the interests of potential allies in Chicago neighborhoods and communities in downstate Illinois. Nothing seemed to work, and it did not help that the effort took place against the background of a steady flow of bad publicity, the worst of which was the news from New Orleans. The specialized fair there experienced construction delays, poor attendance, management scandals, and eventual bankruptcy, requiring huge subsidies from the Louisiana legislature while angering French Quarter bar and restaurant owners who complained that the fair, far from increasing New Orleans' tourist business, merely diverted it from one part of the city to another. All of this made front-page news in Chicago, notwithstanding Kramer's efforts to generate a more positive "stream of events" to distract from the New Orleans news.[34] The determinedly optimistic way in which the Fair Authority greeted all this only served to further undermine the fair's prospects and its promoters' credibility. Kramer, for example, was known as a "wunderkind" when he began his term with the Fair Authority. By the end, journalists were calling him "hapless." "Kramer's heart was in the right place," an admirer who worked with him during this period later explained, "but he was set up."[35]

In June 1985, the special committee appointed by Illinois House Speaker Michael Madigan advised against further state funding of the fair. Madigan promptly called a press conference to agree with its findings. "It's time to pull the plug," he stated. Governor Thompson rushed with unseemly haste but visible relief to agree. Postmortems began promptly in Chicago newspapers, and critics claimed gleefully that the project collapsed quickly like a punctured balloon.[36] Actually, this was not quite the case. While Kramer resigned and the Fair Authority disbanded, the private 1992 Chicago World's Fair Corporation, still headed by Ayers and Petkus, remained in existence. While the fair certainly seemed moribund in 1985, it lingered on for another two years, until the end of 1987, when the last plug was finally and officially pulled. To understand the reasons for this lingering demise requires us to consider Chicago's social geography.

The city of Chicago is laid out in an unmistakable way for anyone who approaches the Loop by subway from the west. To go north or south, the passenger must change trains, which means walking through one of two tunnels that connect the Dearborn Street subway with the north-south lines under State Street. During rush hours, the crowd of people moving through the tunnel toward State Street sorts itself into two streams, a mostly black stream on the right, a mostly white one on the left. The separation is complete where the tunnel reaches State Street and travelers must choose between passages leading to northbound or southbound trains. White people choose north. Black people choose south. That's Chicago: pure, but never simple.

There are of course exceptions. Whites live in the heavily patrolled enclave of Hyde Park around the University of Chicago on the city's south side, but they never take the subway to get there. Farther north, the Mies van der Rohe-designed Illinois Institute of Technology campus stretches between 31st and 35th Streets, defined by perimeter fencing and also patrolled by Chicago policemen, several of whose squad cars can be found during the wee hours of any given night pulled up next to the 7-11 now housed in IIT's Miesian Commons. West of IIT across the Dan Ryan Expressway lies the white working-class district of

Bridgeport, a bastion of Irish Catholic politicos, including three of the city's modern mayors: the present incumbent Richard M. Daley, his father the legendary "Boss" Richard J. Daley, and the latter's predecessor as mayor and boss, Edward J. Kelly. The concrete ramps and ramparts of the new Comiskey Park baseball stadium rise in the southeast corner of Bridgeport, across the freeway from IIT, while northeast of the campus a string of heavily secured high-rise apartment buildings and low-rise townhouses stretch along Michigan Avenue and Martin Luther King Jr. Drive (formerly South Boulevard). This enclave provides middle-income housing for one of the city's premier medical centers surrounding Michael Reese Hospital. Its northern boundary is defined by the Stevenson Expressway which connects the Dan Ryan to Lake Shore Drive and McCormick Place, the city's mammoth lakeside convention center.

West of McCormick Place and its appurtenances, extending across Michigan Avenue and State Street to an irregular boundary defined by the ganglia of freeways and railroad and elevated subway tracks converging on the southwest corner of the Loop, lies a mixed-use area full of warehouses, small industrial plants, garages and machine shops, low-income housing (including all-black housing projects but also Hispanic and Asian enclaves), plus a sprinkling of nineteenth-century architectural and historical landmarks. At the time of the 1893 and 1933 Chicago world's fairs, this area enjoyed notoriety as the city's First Ward, the home of Chicago's most famous ward heelers, Bathhouse John Coughlin and Hinky Dink Kenna, and its most famous criminals, John Torrio, Frank Nitti, and Al Capone. Its brothels and saloons were particularly well-patronized at the time of the World's Columbian Exposition.[37]

The First Ward also contained the city's first Gold Coast—the homes of Pullmans, Palmers, and Fields—and the first Chinatown, though by 1980 these names had long since been affixed to other parts of the city and redistricting had rendered the name First Ward obsolete. Fragments of all these historic uses remained in the area, yet none in sufficient number to give it a definitive character. Motorists and subway or "El" riders skimmed across this area underground or at rooftop height, but a few thousand poor people called it home. No one else knew quite what to call it. The most commonly used terms are South Loop, which refers to the mostly commercial district immediately south of the business district, and Near South Side, which takes in all the territory between the Loop and IIT.

A comparably sized area stretching north from the Loop embraces much of Chicago's most valuable and desirable real estate, but real estate values on the Near South Side were in 1980 uneven and generally depressed. What to do about this problem had been an item on the city's planning agenda since the age of urban renewal and neighborhood redevelopment began after World War II. The high-rises, freeways, and broad green lawns which characterize the institutional enclaves around Michael Reese Hospital and IIT represent the 1950s and 1960s approach to the problem, just as the elegant new McCormick Place and its dependent annexes and hotels are a legacy of the 1970s. During the 1980s, "gentrification" in the form of rehabilitated turn-of-the-century warehouses and apartment buildings, plus new high-rise and townhouse construction, began to push south from the Loop along Dearborn, Clark, and State Streets. "Just think," Don Petkus once commented without irony while gesturing from his 37th-floor office in the First National Bank building toward the patchwork of South Loop construction below, "You can buy a house there and walk to work in the Loop for only $450,000."[38] Inevitably, the issue of whether—and how—to expand such opportunities to upper-income residents and developers on the Near South Side became entangled in the politics of the Chicago World's Fair. From the standpoint of nonwhite residents and white community organizers and activists in the existing Near South neighborhoods, the fair proposal and the controversy it stirred constituted just another attack by Chicago's rich white north on its poor south.

After 1984, when the lakefront site was in trouble and the Fair Authority was trying to lower costs, recruit friends, and enhance residuals, the focus shifted inland to the Near South. Even then the precise program for redevelopment remained vague. Governor Thompson tied the fair to McCormick Place's expansion and to statewide tourism promotion, but insisted that it be anchored to its original lakefront site.[39] When the Jubilee Commission visited Chicago in September 1986, it was shown a prospective site along the Chicago River's south branch. Moreover, since 1982 architects had been considering the idea of digging a canal between the river and the lake, with fair pavilions clustered at either end. Another idea designed to attract private investors called for a single enormous elevated building extending west from McCormick Place.[40] None of these proposals advanced far enough to actually threaten the neighborhood, just far enough to alarm its defenders.

The fair promoters' documented sins were at worst those of outlook. To men who drove home each evening past the gleaming towers of the Magnificent Mile and the Gold Coast to the comfortable suburbs of the North Shore, the ragged patchwork of buildings, vacant lots, and disused rail yards of the Near South seemed a terrible waste. And as men who regarded themselves as city fathers, they felt an obligation to do something about it. "Here's a part of our city we should be trying to lift up," Considine put it, "and if we can do it through the fair, it's fine." Architect Graham called Near South redevelopment "completing the city."[41] That there might be people along 18th Street who did not want uplift on these terms, to whom, in fact, being lifted up meant in all likelihood being lifted out, simply never entered into the equations of the fair planners. And when this viewpoint was forced to their attention by the neighborhood activists who mobilized against the fair, they still didn't get it. Publicly, the Fair Authority adopted goals compatible with neighborhood preservation and development and increased social services to the Near South. Privately, Considine told an interviewer he had to bite his tongue when presented with lists of neighborhood demands. He wanted to say, "Well, why don't you get out and get your people organized and get them to clean it up and fix it up and paint it up? That's what they do in other countries." But, he added, "You have to be careful."[42]

In the end, it was social geography—North Shore vs. South Side, Lakefront and Loop vs. "the neighborhoods"—that brought the fair down. This is true whether or not one credits neighborhood activists with the victory or the mayoral administration of Harold Washington. The activists opposed the fair outright and kept up a steady drumbeat of pointed questions and hostile publicity throughout the period 1982–85, when the fair planners should have been consolidating their support rather than continuously having to shore it up. The Washington administration did not have to oppose the fair to kill it; it only had to decline to support it. The questions raised by the activists provided plenty of ammunition to advisors who wanted the mayor simply to sit tight.

In the spring of 1982, anti-fair activists formed the Chicago 1992 Committee, a coalition of opposition groups embracing everything from tenants' rights organizations and neighborhood development groups to the committee of powerboat owners who banded together to oppose a potential threat to their lakefront slips in Burnham Harbor. Eventually the coalition grew to forty-eight groups. Foundation grants supported a paid staff member who forced the Fair Authority committee meetings to be held openly and attended them faithfully. Grants also supported research. The committee commissioned studies of the Fair Authority's financial scenarios and of neighborhood and environmental impacts. Protests they launched led to further independent studies, and data they uncovered helped to focus those studies in ways not helpful to the prospects of the fair. Recounting this history in 1985, the *Tribune*'s economics reporter argued that the fair's demise meant a new politics for Chicago. The Old Guard of Loop businessmen and city hall politicos had fallen before a "New Guard" of community activists and reformers, city bureaucrats, and "a new breed of businessmen" (a reference to the business leaders who had remained aloof from the fair).[43]

Don Petkus and John Kramer believe that the 1992 Committee flattered itself in claiming credit for the fall of the fair, but both concede the importance of the failure of the Harold Washington administration to climb on board.[44] Washington's defeat of his rivals in the Democratic mayoral primary of February 1983 and his subsequent victory in the April general election inaugurated a new era in Chicago politics, an era of ambiguity and conflict in place of the smoothly running accommodations of Boss Daley and his two immediate successors, Michael Bilandic and Jane Byrne. With Byrne, and in negotiating and finding accommodations with their fellow elites in Washington, Paris, or Spain, the fair promoters had validated their reputations for "getting things done," but they failed utterly to adapt to the political style of the new era. They were shocked that their right to speak for Chicago was challenged, and they were uncomfortable with the confrontational style which accompanies bargaining in today's world among conflicting urban leadership cadres. Instead, they engaged in a futile search for accommodation with Washington and their critics which would not require them to relinquish or share control of their project. The search continued right up to the day of Washington's death.

Washington did not oppose the fair at any time, but he did not have to. His election affected the fair's prospects in two ways: it "took the lid off" of Chicago politics, allowing all manner of opposition to flourish that would have been restrained by Democratic Party discipline under Daley Sr. or Byrne. And it placed in the mayor's office a man deeply skeptical of the Loop crowd's intentions and deeply cautious about making the city government commitments which were essential for the Fair Authority's plans to proceed. He gave the fair a verbal endorsement of sorts in June 1983, but he appointed his own advisory committee to look into the matter. Its recommendations set a heavy price on his support: under no circumstances would the city provide money for the fair, and any infrastructure it provided, such as street relocation or beefed-up sanitation and security requirements during the fair's 1992 run, had to be underwritten by the Fair Corporation. This effectively eliminated the very concept of residuals. There were further requirements regarding neighborhood protection, affirmative action, and the like—easy to accede to but hard to effect without a lot of cash—but the rub remained the city's refusal to spend tax money on the fair.[45] Washington's election and the bitter racial antagonisms it had inspired within the Democratic Party had politicized every conceivable issue in Chicago, indeed in all of Illinois. As long as Washington refused to make any commitments to the fair, none of his Democratic or Republican foes were going to make any. And if no one in Cook County would take risks for the fair, certainly no one in Springfield would either. The deadlock seemed unlikely to be broken unless some outside force, not entangled in the underbrush of Chicago and Illinois politics, could be brought to bear on it. This was where the U.S. Jubilee Commission might have played a role.

However, as we saw in the previous chapter, nervousness about the prospects of the fair had led Chicago boosters, with the help of Republican U.S. Senators Charles Percy of Illinois and Strom Thurmond of South Carolina, to impose both financial and legal restrictions on the Jubilee Commission's ability to do anything that might complicate the fair. They would rather have had no commission at all. Many of Philadelphia's world's fair promoters had blamed the federal American Revolution Bicentennial Commission for their city's failure to make good on its plan to host a fair in 1976. If a Quincentenary commission had to be created, it was better from Chicago's standpoint that it be a weak one. Thus, Percy succeeded in attaching an amendment to the commission's enabling legislation that enjoined it from interfering with the Chicago fair or duplicating its programs and also enjoined it to make the fair "a major highlight of the quincentenary celebration." The promoters also placed one of their number on the commission via a presidential appointment. This was James O'Connor, Ayers's successor as CEO of Commonwealth Edison and Petkus's later boss. O'Connor's interest in the commission was strictly defensive; apart from the swearing-in ceremony in September 1985 and a Columbus Day event at the White House in 1988, he attended only one meeting of the commission, in Chicago in September 1986, and he sent Petkus in his place on only a few other occasions. In his absence, another commissioner, Aldo DeAngelis, became the de facto spokesman on the commission for the Chicago World's Fair.

Unlike many Chicago politicians, DeAngelis was a Republican and represented a suburban Cook County district in Springfield, where he was assistant minority leader of the state Senate. Most Chicago observers credited him with a good deal more power than he actually had. Supposedly, he was the link between the Loop's business community and Governor Thompson, but insofar as the commission's concerns provided a test of this matter, he could deliver little support from either. He planned by his own assertion to run for the U.S. Senate in 1990; instead he ran for and lost the post of Cook County Commissioner. "Aldo is a small-fry trying to act like a big fry," another midwestern commissioner explained to those who expressed frustration at DeAngelis's many unkept promises. Be that as it may, he spoke for Chicago at the commission's first business meetings in 1986, arranged for the commission's meeting in the city in September of that year, and set up a closed-door luncheon between the commissioners and the Fair Corporation directors at which the latter's last-ditch strategy to save the fair was discussed.

Behind this strategy was the assumption that Harold Washington would either be defeated in the mayoral election of 1987 or that he would consolidate his hold on city hall and thus be willing to take a less cautious and (from the Fair Corporation's perspective) more statesmanlike view of the fair. On the strength of this theory, the BIE gave Chicago an extension of its site registration in 1985 and, with the Jubilee Commission's endorsement, another extension in 1986. After Washington won a second and decisive victory early the next year, the theory looked like it might work. Petkus, who had continued to seek accommodation with the mayor's advisers, reported that they appeared to be mellowing. Plans were made to invite Washington or one of his aides to the BIE meeting in December 1987, where a final and crucial extension would be sought. Afterwards Petkus and his companion would join the Jubilee Commission at its meeting with Italian Quincentenary planners in Genoa. Everything seemed to be set when Petkus scheduled a round of appointments in Washington for himself and Brenda Gaines, Mayor Washington's chief adviser. They were to visit Illinois congressmen, Commerce Department officials, and the Jubilee Commission office on Wednesday, November 26.[46]

Harold Washington died in his office of a massive heart attack on

Tuesday, November 25, 1987. With him died the last hopes of the Chicago World's Fair. The BIE made it official, pulling its own plug on Chicago on December 4. Don Petkus showed up in Genoa the next day, glum but resigned. The next year found him involved in promoting a sports and culture festival that would be organized around the centennials of Chicago's celebrated arts and educational institutions in 1991–94, but nothing came of that project either.[47] Meanwhile members of the Chicago 1992 Committee had organized to oppose the renewal of Commonwealth Edison's franchise as a public utility. Gentrification had edged a few blocks farther south along State Street, but subway riders still sorted themselves into black and white streams under the Loop.

In the fall of the Chicago World's Fair can be read the eventual fate of the entire Quincentenary enterprise, although this was by no means apparent at the time. The contested meanings in Chicago had as much to do with a new era of local activism as with the failure of patriotic myth, and the Fair Corporation's failure to articulate a unifying theme or vision could be chalked up to the deficiencies of a specific set of individuals or corporate types as well as to the vortex of social problems that made big cities generally, and race-ridden Chicago in particular, seem "ungovernable" during these years. Thus one message of Chicago—that the Quincentenary was over before it even started—was obscured by what seemed at the time to be more pressing concerns.

The Jubilee Commission was left with only one comparable event on which to focus the 1992 observance in the United States. This was AmeriFlora, a horticultural exposition scheduled for Columbus, Ohio, in the spring and summer of 1992. In layman's terms, "horticultural" means flowers. International floral expositions have a long history in Europe, where they serve the commercial flower industry in much the same ways trade shows serve other industries. AmeriFlora would be the first such exposition held in the United States.

Civic and state authorities in Columbus launched AmeriFlora partly to promote Ohio's cut-flower industry, the nation's third largest. But mostly the idea was to promote the city of Columbus, which far more than Chicago suffers from an identity problem. If Chicago smarts from its Hollywood image of being a gangster town, Columbus suffers from having no image at all. This was particularly rankling in view of two developments of the 1970s and 1980s. During these decades Columbus had enjoyed Sunbelt-style growth despite its Frostbelt location, doubling its population and attracting a host of new and expanded service industries. But it had not gained a Sunbelt-style reputation for urban amenities. What was worse, Indianapolis, Columbus's smaller and once-sleepier neighbor and rival, seemed to have solved its no-image problem through a concerted and ultimately successful civic effort to become a center for professional and televised amateur sports. Thus, in further contrast with Chicago, Columbus's 1992 promotion grew less out of fears of economic contraction than from the frustrations of economic success.

The brighter economic picture in Columbus ensured that there was less controversy over public investment in AmeriFlora. The city of Columbus appropriated $500,000 for planning the event; in 1988, the Ohio legislature appropriated $6.8 million of the estimated $50 million total cost. Corporate sponsorships and exhibitors fees were expected to cover the rest. Ohio State University contributed the expertise of its nationally prominent horticulture department and in 1987 designated horticulturalist John C. Peterson to serve as AmeriFlora's director. But by early 1991, while AmeriFlora's success was assured in that there would be a floral exposition of some kind in Columbus in 1992, its scope and educational program, along with some of the residuals the city expected, had been cut back considerably because of insufficient corporate support. Public officials who had backed the event enthusiastically in earlier years were now in retirement (Governor Richard Celeste) or in disgrace (Mayor Dana Rinehart). Peterson himself returned to his teaching post at Ohio State in January 1991, retaining a pro forma connection with AmeriFlora but yielding actual direction of the exposition to a manager brought in from the Disney Corporation. The fair ran as scheduled from April 20 to October 12 and attracted nearly 2 million visitors, beginning with President Bush on opening day. AmeriFlora won high marks from experts and visitors for its beauty and management. But the visitors were far fewer than the 4 million initially projected, and the scaled-back event can scarcely be said to have put Columbus "on the map." Significantly, as the fair closed, a new mayor was talking up the idea of a major sports arena.[48]

The Los Angeles Olympics of 1984 and Statue of Liberty Centennial in 1986 were thought by promoters to have introduced an age of megaevents, public spectacles on a scale commensurate with the audiences that global communications was able to provide. Speaking of the Quincentenary, Lisa Uckman, publisher and cofounder of *Special Events Report*, commented that "there is not a better hook until the year 2000" on which to hang a mega-event.⁴⁹ The program and financial strategy of the U.S. Jubilee Commission were based on this premise. Indeed, during the commission's first year, the autobiographies of Peter Ueberroth and Lee Iacocca were favored reading for several commissioners. But Iacocca's publicists did not advertise the fact, known only to insiders and careful readers of obscure reports, that the organizers of Liberty Weekend (July 3–6, 1986) had actually lost rather than made money for the statue's restoration fund.⁵⁰

More importantly, the examples of Chicago and Columbus suggest instead that the extravaganzas of the mid-1980s marked an end rather than a beginning. A huge audience is necessarily diverse; an event big enough to attract it must therefore touch upon universal themes, and there may be no such theme capable of arousing enough interest that does not also arouse an equivalent amount of controversy. Controversy may be a wholesome sign of the health of a democracy, but it scares away both public and private funders from any event which is neither bland nor modest in scope. Thus, organizers of events focused on the year 2000 moved quickly to dismiss "cynics, pedants and otherwise unclassifiable grumps" who pointed out that this date originates in Christian tradition and that, in any case, December 31, 1999, was nothing more than the last day of the century's and the millennium's penultimate year. The millennial celebration was not about religion or culture but about time, according to the *New York Times*—representing the city that proclaimed itself the center of the global commemoration. "The things that bind us, however arbitrary, are worth noting and making a fuss over."⁵¹ In Britain, official planners secured funds from the National Lottery to build a billion-dollar "Millennium Dome" on the polluted Thames waterfront east of London. The symbolism of a big tent seemed appropriate to the inclusiveness needed for a successful mega-event, while the exhibition theme—Time—seemed certain to achieve the required vapidity. On the other hand, much about the proposed event remained controversial down to the wire. An activist opposition, organized under the ominous name of Time Bomb, denounced the entire program as "a pompous monument to the throw-away consumer society in which we live."⁵²

Sports competitions may be the exceptions that prove the rule. As we noted in the previous chapter, a promoter involved in the 1988 Super Bowl suggested to us that a mega-event such as this should be the model for 1992. The Super Bowl is an event created by and for television, he noted, yet the targeted audience believes that the event is not staged, that it would take place and be meaningful even if the cameras were not in place. The event itself is over in a few hours (although it does carry a build-up of several weeks). Most people participate not by turning out in person as they must for world's fairs, but by virtue of their identification with the competing teams. Professional and commercialized "amateur" sports such as college football and basketball have sustained this illusion of authenticity even in the face of the acknowledged reshaping of most competitions into media events that only superficially resemble the historic contests from which modern games evolved. Yet participatory events such as the Chicago World's Fair seem contrived and vapid when they are conceived on a scale large enough to attract more than local interest. The boom in special events has thus been confined largely to small, localized affairs that provide a tight linkage between targeted audience groups and commercial sponsors, and even here the emphasis is sports and food or music festivals. For example, the first sponsor willing to pay for the use of the Jubilee Commission's Quincentenary logo was the Hispanic marketing wing of the West Coast division of Procter & Gamble, which used it to attract audiences to a Columbus Day festival in San Jose featuring mariachi performers and Mexican food. It was not that the commission did not want something grander or more in keeping with its congressional mandate. This was simply the best it could get.

The experience of Baltimore Quincentenary planners provides another example. "Columbus 500" organized there in 1986 first as a private group of businessmen and journalists, then as the core of Maryland's state Quincentenary commission. As in Chicago, the group hoped to use 1992 as an agenda-setting device, with two major objectives. First, they wanted to keep alive during the transition from white ethnic to African American control of city hall an effective business-government alliance that had earlier succeeded in revitalizing the city's business district and in building a tourist and convention trade focused on a new cultural and entertainment complex, a so-called festival waterfront on the historic Inner Harbor. Another objective was to stimulate international investment and new service industries to replace the city's declining economic bases of heavy industry and its port. Columbus 500 planned a number of public events focused on the city's waterfront to dramatize their objectives and mobilize public support. It also proposed joint public-private financing for a showcase residual: a

"Christopher Columbus Center" that would incorporate university-based marine science and nautical archaeology research institutes, a marine biotechnology research center, a business "incubator," and a public exhibition area, all to be located on the waterfront near the museum, hotel, and shopping facilities that had been built during the 1970s.[53]

As in Columbus, the Baltimore program enjoyed mixed success, and the character of the mix is revealing. The promoters had secured federal funds for their planning phase and a promise of city and state construction funding financed through the sale of bonds. Groundbreaking was scheduled for Columbus Day, 1992. The "hook" both for congressional budget committees and the spokesmen for the black community was not mega-events, but the center's promises of jobs, economic development, and the example of Japanese public investment in emerging biotechnology industries. They sold the center as "Baltimore's computer chip, the key to its economic future."[54] But Columbus 500's schedule of special events remained mostly unrealized. The city's Columbus Day parade, the oldest continuous such parade in the nation, was "upgraded" somewhat but still the centennial 1990 version was much like previous efforts, attracting interest chiefly among Italian-Americans, while efforts to transform and expand the 1992 parade for national television did not succeed. Still, some 75,000 people turned out to welcome the Spanish-financed replicas of Columbus's ships when they visited the Inner Harbor between May 29 and June 7, 1992. About 28,500 persons elected to pay their way on board for the official tour, as did roughly the same number when the caravels docked in nearby Annapolis a few days later. Otherwise, apart from providing the original "hook," "Christopher Columbus's name on the door has not offered a thing to us so far," Columbus 500's president Stanley Heuisler commented in 1991.[55] It was the combination of jobs and science, plus careful tending to communications both with city hall and "the neighborhoods" that accounted for the project's funding. This was enough to get the Columbus Center's doors open in 1995 in a handsome new waterfront building with a roof like billowing sails. But it was not enough to keep them open. Failing to attract significant corporate sponsorship, the Columbus Center closed its doors within a few months. Today, its roof billows above a quiet and weedy spot on the busy Inner Harbor, its public exhibition areas are mostly empty, and its offices and laboratories have been leased out as spillover space to Baltimore's two medical schools.

Meanwhile the governor of Maryland, former mayor William Donald Shaefer, was able to mobilize political support and public revenues to build not one, but two new stadiums in Baltimore's harbor area, brushing aside an opposing coalition ("Marylanders for Sports Sanity") much like Chicago's 1992 Committee. The public financing of the stadiums was a fait accompli in 1991, while bonds for the Christopher Columbus Center were still just a promise (although by the time that the second stadium opened, the Columbus Center had come and gone).[56] This success in funding sports activities echoes the emphasis on sports we saw in Indianapolis as compared to the difficulties in events-oriented efforts in Columbus, Ohio, not to mention Chicago. Still another test of the relative appeal of spectator sports and participatory events was provided by the Seville World's Fair and the Barcelona Olympics in 1992. Even though the Olympics of 1988 in Seoul attracted fewer television viewers than expected, worldwide interest in the Olympics continued to grow. The television rights for the 1992 Barcelona games went to NBC for a then-record price: $401 million when the Spanish authorities auctioned them in December 1988.[57]

The world's fair controversy in Chicago provided a confrontation between the City Father and the Concerned Citizen, two contrasting styles of civic leadership whose dimensions have been mapped by Robert Bellah and his colleagues in *Habits of the Heart*.[58] The former style requires trust between leader and citizen, trust which in most American cities has foundered on the shoals of race and class. That it broke down so completely in Chicago, the former "city that works," is testimony to the depth of the changes that the Bellah study documents. It may be that only professional sports are meaningful—and meaningless—enough to bridge this gap, but whether this bridge is strong enough to sustain the weight of Chicago's ethnic and racial tensions remains to be seen. When the owners of the Chicago White Sox threatened to move the team to Florida, politicians united to find funding for a new stadium next door to the old one, brushing aside the objections of taxpayer and neighborhood groups and nostalgic fans who wanted to keep the old park. But the real test will, as usual, come on the lakefront, as the problem of what to do about the aging football stadium Soldier Field eventually has to be faced. In February 1990, Don Petkus and Frank Considine had become part of an "Illinois Leadership Authority" exploring options for a domed stadium somewhere on the Near South Side. Newspaper reporters voiced suspicions that the stadium builders were none other than "the old 1992 gang."[59] Many of the issues that the fair controversy generated seem destined to come to the fore again in this context, and it will be interesting to see whether sports can provide the inspiration for citizens to direct their gaze from their mutual mistrusts toward an imagined and common future, an inspiration that, at least in our cities, Christopher Columbus is no longer able to provide.

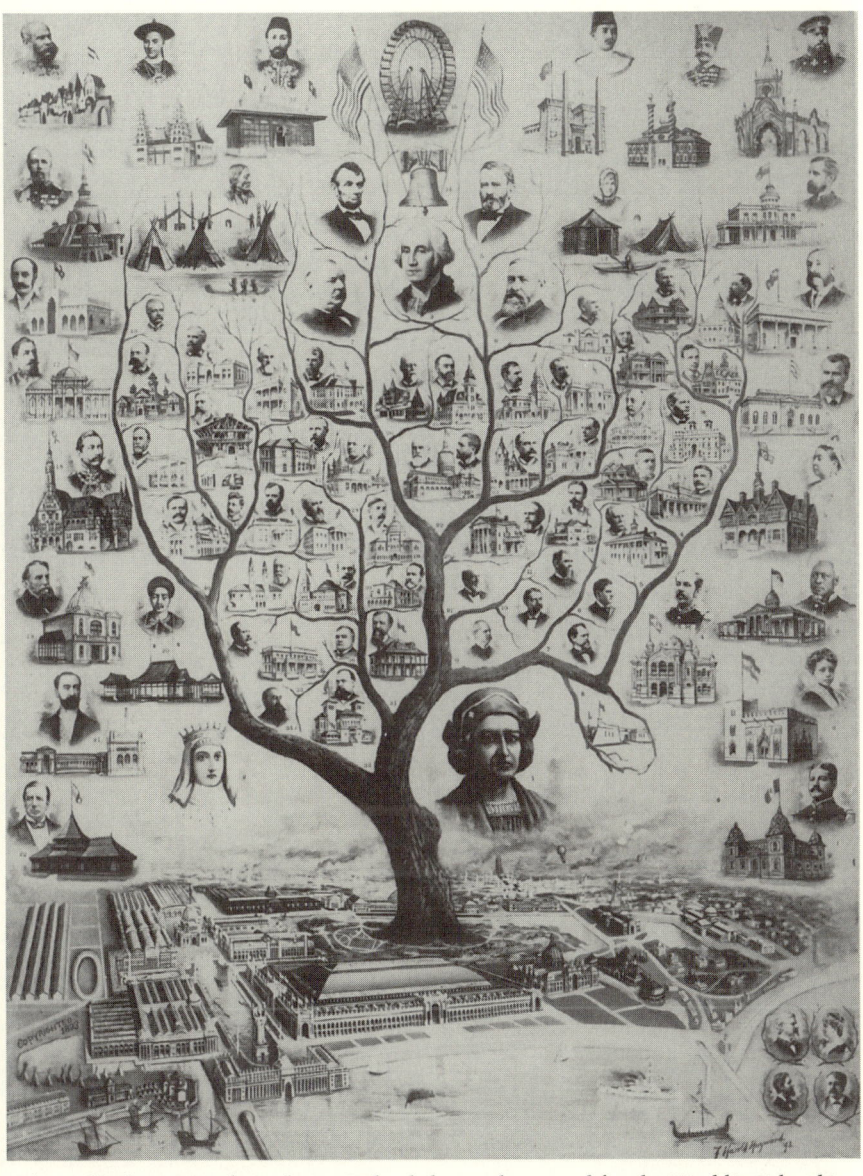

"The Columbus Genealogical Tree." This lithograph, created for the World's Columbian Exposition in Chicago in 1893, shows U.S. leaders as descendants of Queen Isabella and Christopher Columbus, a reference to the latter's status as a quasi-official Founding (Grand)Father. Courtesy The Chicago Historical Society. Photograph; ICHi-30624; The Columbus Genealogical Tree; World's Columbian Exposition, Chicago (Ill.); 1893—F. Harold Hayward, copyrighted & published, 1893, E. S. Farah & Co., Brisbois Photo.

The Landing of Columbus by John Vanderlyn. Commissioned by Congress, this large and influential icon hangs today in the rotunda of the U.S. Capitol. Although Vanderlyn based his representation on historical documents, art historian Barbara Groseclose has pointed out that the painting includes several images not supported by documentary evidence, such as religious figures and symbols and cowering natives (who in the actual event recorded by Columbus and others were friendly, lively, and curious). Courtesy U.S. Capitol Historical Society.

FACING PAGE BOTTOM AND ABOVE: A "re-enactment" of Columbus's landing, based on the iconic Vanderlyn painting, has been staged annually by Italian-Americans in San Francisco since the early twentieth century. In the 1989 event pictured here, Joseph Cervetto Jr. made his debut as Columbus, a role he inherited from his father. The Indians greeting him are Yaquis from Sonora, Mexico, hired for the occasion. American Folklife Center, Library of Congress (photos by Ken Light, IAW-KL-B175-5, 21, 26).

Luis Yáñez Barnuevo, president of the Spanish National Quincentenary Commission, entertains U.S. Jubilee Commission chairman John Goudie (*center*) and commission member Jane Lee García during a tour of Barcelona harbor, 1988. Photo by Manuel Canetti Magrans, Foto Studio Canetti, Barcelona. Used by permission.

Eminent Columbus scholar and inspiration of the Italian 1992 commemoration Paolo Emilio Taviani receives a Doctorate in Humane Letters from President Edward Jennings, Ohio State University, December 1987. Courtesy Ohio State University Photo Archives.

AmeriFlora '92, Franklin Park Conservatory, Columbus, Ohio, showing the centerpiece Navstar sculpture of Stephen Canneto. Photograph courtesy of Gail Summerhill.

Aerial view of the 535-acre Cartuja Island with the full site of Expo '92, Seville, Spain. A p[art] of the city is visible at the bottom, across the Guadalquivir River, with surrounding coun[try] across the canal at the top. Photograph courtesy of the Spanish Cultural Office, Embassy of [Spain,] Washington, D.C.

Aerial view of a portion of Genoa harbor showing one of the most characteristic sights of the Genoa Expo, the decorative booms or masts called *Il Bigo* standing beside Festival Place or Piazza delle Feste on the Embriaco Wharf. Photograph courtesy Tormena Industrie Grafiche, S.R.L., Genoa, Italy.

Side view of the Faro a Colón or Columbus Lighthouse, Santo Domingo, Dominican Republic. Built in the shape of a massive cross (unintentionally, also a sword), the lighthouse was first proposed in the nineteenth century and finally built by President Joaquín Balaguer in time for the Quincentenary. It celebrates not only Christopher Columbus but also the arrival of Christianity in America. Photograph courtesy of Pamela Connell.

American Indian Movement (AIM) activist Russell Means pours symbolic animal blood on the Christ-like statue of Columbus in Denver's Civic Center, October 9, 1989. Photograph courtesy of the *Denver Post*/John Prieto/Steve Nehf.

AIM protestors succeeded in forcing Italian-American organizations to cancel the planned Columbus Day parade in Denver in 1992, but police removed them when they tried to block parade participants from access to a rally at the Colorado state capitol on October 10, 1992. Photograph courtesy of Glenn Asakawa/*Denver Rocky Mountain News*.

Mounted police escort costumed Knights of Columbus to a rally at the state capitol after cancellation of Denver's Columbus Day parade, October 10, 1992. Photograph courtesy of Glenn Asakawa/*Denver Rocky Mountain News*.

Protestors and their slogans at Aquatic Park, San Francisco, October 11, 1992. Demonstrators succeeded in preventing the annual Italian-American mock landing and disrupted the Columbus Day parade. Photos by John Alexander Williams.

Model Lisa Hayward of Houston poses as "Miss Liberty" in the denouement of Antoni Miralda's "Honeymoon Project" in Red Rock Canyon near Las Vegas, February 14, 1992. The image of the Columbus statue in Barcelona was projected on the screen suspended on the canyon wall (*background, right*). Behind the musicians in the middle background are "pelvic sculptures" created by the artist for the occasion. Photo by John Gurzinski/lasvegasphotography.com.

4

Ethnos, History, and Myth

"Come on, let's get out of here," an Italian-American friend whispered as a hush fell over the room and a speaker began clearing his throat. "I know exactly what they're going to say: 'We found this country, we named this country, we made this country what it is today.'" Indeed, this used to be the standard after-dinner toast at an Italian-American banquet, encapsulating 500 years of New World history through the eyes of an ethnic group which has been present in the United States in large numbers only during the last century. The figure of Christopher Columbus was critical to the emergence of an Italian-American identity. At the same time, the linkage of Columbus with Italy was central to the popular American view of the Admiral during the twentieth century. Columbus in his fifth century became an ethnic hero. When the Admiral and his meaning were contested during the Quincentenary, this immediately generated controversies that were symptomatic of the conflicts surrounding the meaning of ethnicity in contemporary American society, and these in turn sprang from the same forces that made ethnopolitical conflict a global problem in the 1990s and beyond.

The Jubilee Commission's early deliberations about its program for 1992 took place in the shadow of the Statue of Liberty Centennial of 1986, an event which brought into the public eye the transformation of ethnicity that has been taking place in the United States over the last quarter century. The logical climax of this event was not the barrage of fireworks that burst over New York harbor on the night of July 4, 1986, but rather the competition between major party presidential candidates two years later over which had the better ethnic credentials. The confrontation of Harvard Law School graduate Michael Dukakis, with his recently reclaimed Greek heritage, and Yale aristocrat George Bush, with his Mexican daughter-in-law and "little brown grandchildren," was ludicrous but revealing. Lee Iacocca and the Statue of Liberty celebrants of 1986 had proclaimed the parity of southern and eastern European ancestry with that of central and northwestern Europe. Ellis Island was now equal to the Mayflower, at least for all practical purposes short of admission into WASP ancestor clubs such as the D.A.R. The brief flare-up of "Greek chic" inspired by the Dukakis campaign confirmed this. And while Dukakis spoke in Spanish and danced in Greek, we heard Jesse Jackson attacking Lee Iacocca while emulating Iacocca's sentimental view of ethnicity and family in his Democratic National Convention speech.[1] We also saw—though we heard little from the candidates in this regard—cities such as Chicago move further toward ethnic and racial polarization while Sunbelt states and cities faced controversies over language policy.

Bush's rather embarrassing references to his Mexican-American grandchildren touched on an issue less easily resolved: what about the descendants of involuntary Americans, those who came over on slave ships or who were incorporated forcefully into the United States by conquest? For them, the so-called melting pot had never been more than a fiction anyway. This tension between two variants of contemporary ethnicity was not resolved in 1986 or 1988 and, indeed, continues to confront us. Much of the ethnic infighting between Hispanic- and Italian-Americans which characterized the congressional establishment of the Jubilee Commission as well as subsequent issues such as the choice of commission chairmanship and programs, was in fact a reflection of unresolved tensions between different types of ethnicity.

These variants of ethnicity need names. Sociologists use the labels "symbolic" or "neo-" ethnicity to describe the phenomenon that Dukakis or Iacocca represent—ethnicity which is a matter of personal style. "I knew Dukakis before he was Greek" was more than a humorous boast in Massachusetts in 1988; it reflected the notion that Dukakis was free to embrace or ignore his ethnic identity as he chose and in fact had done both at different times during his life. The same choice is open to nearly all other Americans of European descent, whether they are the children of immigrants from Greece or Italy, or fourth-generation Scandinavian-Americans, or fifth-generation Germans or Irish or descendants of the earliest British and French settlers of North America. With the exception of a relatively small number of truncated urban ethnic enclaves, there is now no practical way of distinguishing descendants of a particular European nationality from the general run of so-called Anglo-Americans: neither by language nor culture nor place of birth nor residence, income, educational attainment, or choice of mates. Religious preferences are still distinguishable among ethnic groups, political preferences much less so, but these preferences are less significant in today's climate of ecumenism and independent voting than they used to be. Ethnicity for such people thus becomes a symbolic act, divorced from the everyday part of their life. Unless an individual makes his or her living by running an ethnic organization or purveying ethnic foods—or running for office and trying to capitalize on what's left of the advantages that appeals to fellow ethnics used to bring—it makes no difference whether he or she chooses to be ethnic or not.[2]

Scholars differ in the amounts of respect they accord symbolic ethnicity. Those who define ethnic behavior in terms of survivals, such as language and customs, from antecedent cultures overseas tend to look on symbolic behavior as superficial expressions of personal taste rather than of group values. Some scholars argue in fact that symbolic ethnicity among specific European-derived groups masks the more important fact that "a new white ethnic group" of "unhyphenated" people has emerged in the United States, an assertion that probably accounts for the fact that on most college campuses the term "ethnic studies" does not apply to Euro-American groups but refers exclusively to African American, Asian American, Native American, Latino, and Chicano studies.[3]

A more respectful view defines the phenomenon more dynamically. Ethnic behaviors are not merely survivals; they derive from creative interactions between the ethnic group and the dominant culture. Thus the notions of Italian-American identity fostered by the Columbus complex or the red sauce "Italian food" repertory, though both were developed in the United States rather than in Italy, constitute markers of ethnic behavior as valid as cultural survivals from Europe. In the end, symbolic ethnicity permits a group to establish a nonthreatening form of local community that may be a defense against homogenizing forces in American society. In any case, regardless of how its content is validated or its collective strength assessed, there is little disagreement that symbolic ethnicity remains at bottom a matter of personal choice.[4]

But there is another kind of ethnicity, one which reflects—and enforces—a determining influence in people's lives: in where and how well they live, what language they speak, whom they marry, how far they go in school, and so on. This is ethnicity as it is experienced today by Native Americans, African Americans, Mexican-Americans, Cuban-Americans, Puerto Ricans, and most first- and second-generation Asian Americans. Labeling this sort of ethnicity is not easy. Political scientist Ted Robert Gurr distinguishes between the positions of Native Americans, whose circumstances and needs are shared by "Fourth World" or indigenous peoples on every continent, and those of African Americans, whom Gurr identifies as an "ethnoclass . . . [peoples] who have distinct economic roles in societies which are dominated by other ethnic groups." Gurr does not extend this definition to U.S. Latinos, but it would generally seem to fit most of them. The majority of ethnoclass members suffer as a result of their ethnicity, but not all. Cuban-Americans, for example, are generally better off economically than the others, usually vote differently, and achieve higher educational attainments. Still, their demographic parameters—geographic, economic, and cultural—set them apart in ways that do not apply to comparably well off Italian- or German-Americans but which do apply to poorer Mexican-Americans or Puerto Ricans. This type of ethnicity offers affected individuals little choice: they are ethnics whether they want to be or not. This is ethnicity pure and simple, although for purposes of distinguishing it from the symbolic variety we can call it "traditional."

The classic scholarly interpretations of the Italian-American experience make it clear that Italian-Americans were affected by the traditional type of ethnicity through the first half of this century. The works of Shirley Williams, Edward Banfield, and William F. Whyte, for example, delineate problems of social disadvantage and maladjustment similar to those which elicit expressions of academic and official concern in studies of Hispanic- and African Americans today.[5] But today sociologists write about the "twilight" of Italian-American ethnicity. Sociology has traditionally defined ethnicity as a linear process, wherein immigrants and their descendants move past certain demographic checkpoints in a seemingly inexorable process of assimilation.

Measurements taken at these checkpoints today show slight differences, if any, between Italian-Americans and Americans of British descent in terms of residential location, educational attainment, family incomes, or intermarriage with members of other ethnic groups. Marketing experts reach much the same conclusion. Special events producers and advertisers told the Jubilee Commission that there are discernible black and Latino market segments along with well-recognized and effective strategies for reaching them. But despite the prominence of "Italian" food and food purveyors in symbolic Italian-American ethnicity, there are no distribution networks, media outlets, or events categories that can be relied upon to distinguish Italian-American consumers from any others.

How this transition from traditional to symbolic ethnicity worked in practice can be observed in California, one of the first states to create a Columbus Day holiday back in 1909. Schoolchildren there, as elsewhere, recite the Pledge of Allegiance, a ritual first developed as part of the fourth centennial back in 1892. But they establish a more direct link with the Yankee origins of the Columbian tradition when they pose in groups in front of the 1882 monument to Columbus and Queen Isabella in the rotunda of the old state capitol, a ritual that forms an essential part of any student trip to Sacramento. San Francisco's Columbus Day parade is not the country's oldest—New York had one earlier, and Baltimore's has had fewer interruptions. But it is certainly one of the more colorful, and it has spun off an array of companion rituals which collectively make San Francisco's Columbus Day the most colorful and elaborate celebration in the nation. As such, it provided an irresistible target for both planners and protestors as the Quincentenary approached.

By 1992, San Francisco's Columbus Day had expanded over a two-week period, embracing no fewer than eight separate events, each one representing distinct elements and traditions within the Italian-American community and coordinated by a volunteer committee which could trace its organizational genealogy back over a century. A mock landing followed a half-century-old script, with the impersonator of Columbus—a role handed down by Joseph Cervetto Sr. to his son Joseph Jr. in 1989—being greeted by welcoming Indians and a mock Spanish queen, "Queen Isabella," who is actually a beauty queen chosen competitively from among young women required to have at least one Italian-American grandparent. "Queen Isabella" and "Columbus" ride together in the parade, which is held on a different day—usually the Sunday before the federal Columbus Day holiday—and they also appear at the speechmaking in front of the Columbus statue on Telegraph Hill, which is held on the Saturday before the parade. Yet another component is the procession of the devotees of SS. Maria del Lume, who still march in their white capes from the Basilica of St. Peter and St. Paul down Columbus Avenue to the waterfront. A recently added component is a "Festa Italiana," a commercial food and street fair organized by the restaurant owners of the Fisherman's Wharf area, an event which organizers of the traditional Columbus Day activities regard as intrusive.[6] It has to be stated, however, that non-Italian observers have difficulty keeping track of the various events and their meanings and sponsors. The *San Francisco Chronicle,* for example, regularly—when it reports on the contemporary festival at all—emphasizes the unusual rather than the traditional features. These include, for example, the parade participation of Filipino- or Chinese-Americans, or the San Francisco Gay Freedom Day Marching Band and Twirling Corps, or the self-parodying behavior of Italian-American princesses, or special events such as a "Renaissance Football Game" sponsored by the importers of the Italian liqueur Amaretto. One reporter called the 1984 celebration "as traditionally Italian as a guacamole pizza."[7]

Such lighthearted characterizations call to mind the attitude of most sociologists toward symbolic ethnicity. But beneath its heterogeneous and superficial surface, the contemporary form of the Columbus complex in San Francisco engages deeper levels of ethnopolitical conflict: with Latinos, with Native Americans, and with the rapidly expanding Chinese-American population next door to the traditional Italian neighborhood of North Beach. For the twenty years prior to the Quincentenary, Italian-American *prominenti* had succeeded in managing these conflicts. However, the seizure of Alcatraz Island by Indian militants in November 1969 served as a warning to Columbus Day organizers. While the mock landing in nearby Aquatic Park was held in 1970 without disruption, organizers of the pageant were concerned enough to abandon their traditional practice of welcoming Columbus with whites dressed up in Plains Indian garb. Instead of the Redmen and Order of Pocahontas fraternalists with whom "Columbus" smoked peace pipes and paraded during earlier ceremonies, real Native Americans were imported—and paid—to participate, first from northern California and later from Mexico. The Indians who came to Aquatic Park in 1989, 1990, and 1991 were Yaquis from Sonora. They brought impressive-looking costumes of a vaguely Aztec design.

The Italian confrontation with Chinese-Americans concerned territory as well as symbols. North Beach is adjacent to Chinatown, but the population history of the two neighborhoods has diverged sharply over the years. As they have moved into their fourth and fifth generations in California, Italian-Americans live everywhere in the Bay Area, which means that no part of the region can fairly be characterized as an "Italian neighborhood." North Beach remains the ethnic community's symbolic core, with Peter-Paul church, old and famous Italian restaurants, delicatessens and food stores, book stores and travel agencies, the offices of Italian-American organizations, and the North Beach Museum organized to display the historical collection of cultural impresario Alessandro Baccari. Yet the Italian-American proportion of the neighborhood population declined from 21 percent in 1960 to 11 percent in 1970. By the latter date, 55 percent of North Beach's residents were nonwhite, most of them Asian, and Chinese enterprises had become almost as common as Italian shops on Columbus Avenue, the district's main street. To head off "a helter skelter" extension of Chinatown which would deprive both communities of North Beach's considerable tourist appeal, Baccari convened a meeting of Italian-American and Chinese-American business leaders in 1978, who hammered out a private "treaty" governing the neighborhood's further development. In order to preserve the tourist draw, the Italian share of North Beach's business sector was stabilized by Chinese restraint and by a considerable infusion of cash from Italian-American investors—a new generation of Medici, as Baccari characterized them—into the district's venerable restaurants and shops. The Chinese-American share of the neighborhood's resident population continues to grow, without impediment from Italian property owners or politicians. The result was "an Italian boutique" in an Asian neighborhood. Peter-Paul retained its traditional Italian shrines and feast-days, but it added masses in Chinese and Chinese-American personnel. Chinese New Year became an occasion for parish festivities. In 1981, when a Chinese festival fell close to the federal Columbus Day holiday, North Beach residents were treated to back-to-back parades.[8]

As the Quincentenary approached, Mayor Art Agnos created a San Francisco Bay Columbus Committee chaired by a prominent businessman and with an executive director of mixed Hispanic and Native American heritage. It had no fewer than five "ethnic advisory committees" to help it plan "an inclusive, accurate, and balanced commemoration of this critically significant turning point in world history."[9] An official visit by Fred Guardabassi in August 1988 led the Jubilee Commission to designate the city as the host for a second tall ships regatta scheduled for the weekend of October 10–12, 1992. But as with its other projects, the Jubilee Commission offered no funds. Indeed, city officials later charged that Chairman Goudie had demanded as much as $2 million from the city for the honor, which otherwise brought nothing from Washington but a congratulatory letter from President George Bush.[10] Consequently, most of the committee's plans revolved around the traditional Italian-American celebration, whose funding was at least assured. When Agnos lost his bid for reelection later that year, the new mayor replaced his committee with his own appointees, with the organizers of Festa Italiana and the Italian-American Columbus Day celebration as co-chairs.[11]

Italian-Americans in these contexts showed themselves willing to settle for symbolic ethnicity. The same was true of the Italian-American members of the Jubilee Commission. Their outnumbered Latino colleagues such as John Goudie or Jane García were not victims of ethnicity in the same way as are Bob García's former Bronx constituents or the Marielito hotel maids and bus boys who shop at the strip shopping centers built by Goudie's company in the barrios of Miami's south and west sides. Yet the Latino members of the Jubilee Commission came from an ethnoclass, and their Italian-American colleagues did not. This helps to explain the intensity of their feelings about promoting a Quincentenary of *hispanidad,* and it also helps to explain why they and the academic Hispanophiles on the Jubilee Commission prevailed against Italian-American viewpoints in constructing the commission's official mission statement and program. The Italians, though more numerous, cared less. Occasionally they grumbled about the unofficial but pervasive bilingualism of commission meetings and about Goudie and García's eager courtship of Spanish government patronage. In general, however, as long as the figure of Christopher Columbus remained in the forefront, the emotional needs of symbolic Italian-American ethnicity were easily met.

The Columbus Quincentenary took shape during the third of the United States' greatest periods of immigration. As in the two earlier peaks, 1840–60 and 1880–1920, the cultural impact of immigration today leads to political conflict as rival groups seek to shape and control that impact. Concurrently we are living through a period when a sentimental view of ethnicity seems to have solidified the national commitment to cultural pluralism, as when, for example, the Statue of Liberty

Centennial celebration elevated Ellis Island to a position of symbolic parity with Plymouth Rock. How are these two trends related? Is the embrace of symbolic ethnicity a response to—or an evasion of—the challenges posed by the influx of immigrants? The Quincentenary provided a logical framework for addressing these questions. From an ethnic perspective, the commemoration gave us a view of the American future, less through its formal programs than through the processes of ethnic confrontation and negotiation that shaped the ways in which the occasion was observed, controverted, or ignored. Initially, the confrontation between Italian-American and Hispanic ethnicity during the mid-1980s appeared to point toward a new Columbus myth, one that expressed the current entrance of Latinos into the arena of public life in the United States.[12] At the same time, this new myth would acknowledge the dreams and longings of the millions of Spanish-speaking people living in the rest of the New World. Such an idea would be similar to Spain's understanding of the Quincentenary in that it would be less focused on Columbus the mariner than on the societies his enterprise created. And of course, it would reflect the shift in U.S. immigration patterns during the twentieth century from European to Hispanic sources.

The problem, however, is that this new emphasis could never produce a real ethnic, quincentennial myth. For if the Italian-American Columbus complex served a wealthy and fully integrated group pursuing symbolic ethnicity, a Latino version, if one were possible, must have been embraced by a community that lives the conditions of traditional ethnicity, that is, a tendency toward social marginalization into economically disadvantaged groups that retain their language and customs on the fringe of mainstream "Anglo" America. Some Hispanic groups cannot even be called immigrants in the usual sense because they have lived in North America since before even the English arrived, have maintained their cultural patterns for centuries, and seem unlikely to follow the Italian path of eventually becoming so fully integrated that their ethnicity will be mostly symbolic. Perhaps most important of all, it is incorrect to speak about just one Latino community, since the differences among Puerto Ricans, Mexican-Americans, Cuban-Americans, and perhaps even now Dominican-Americans, Nicaraguan-Americans, and still others means that a common heritage takes distinct colorings depending on where you live and work.[13] Then there is the fact that most Latinos in the United States are of Latin American or Caribbean descent and this makes them very different from Spaniards.

Spain is one place, Latin America quite another; and the profoundly problematic history of the relations between the two means that Columbus's "Enterprise of the Indies" has always been understood on this side of the ocean as an extremely ambiguous process that gave Hispanic America a significant element of its being but that also played a major role in the centuries of deprivation and poverty that so many Latin Americans have suffered. Just what dreams or longings could be represented by a commemoration of what in Spanish is straightforwardly called *la conquista de América*, the conquest of America? Although Latin Americans feel great pride in their heritage, is this thanks to Spain or in spite of Spain? Or is it because of some other factor, such as Amerindian or African origins? Or is it a combination of these and still other factors?

Our point here is quite simple. It is to suggest that during the 1980s there was a lot of talk about the Quincentenary as time for a new Hispanic myth, a time to promote the importance of Latinos in the United States, but this talk derived from no more than a counter-image of the Italian-American myth and could have been imagined only by those who know little about the variety of Hispanic cultures. Hispanic ethnicity as a single or common cultural ideal does not exist anywhere in the world today, and Christopher Columbus and his enterprise cannot stand as a Hispanic myth even in Spain because the real history of what happened has always been too well known and inevitably challenges the realm of myth altogether. Thus, the real issue here is a problem alluded to by the *New York Times* when the Jubilee Commission's troubles first came to its attention in 1988: "In the usual opening skirmish, the ethnic mix of the Commission was challenged. It is strong on businessmen and citizens of Italian origin, including Governor Cuomo of New York, and weak on those of Hispanic background.... Beyond that, there were no American Indians among the original appointees."[14] That is, the troubled question of the indigenous peoples on whom the conquest had and continues to have such a profound impact had been overlooked in the original formation of the commission and was still mostly an afterthought in 1988. But by 1992 this issue came to dominate the Quincentenary and rendered the earlier Italian-Latino squabbling moot.

Here, finally, we reach the controversial aspect of the Quincentenary, the one which, it can be said, ultimately became the really significant dimension of 1992: not the epic story of feats beyond compare but the tragic tale of invasion and loss; not a sublimely romantic fable of discovery and creation but a sadly ironic narrative of misunderstanding and error; in short, anti-myth, which was still basically myth, in this case the myth of invasion, contrasting sharply with the earlier one of discovery. This vision had been simmering since at least the 1960s when the colonial system definitively passed from the world. It started to catch the public eye in the early 1980s when many Indian groups announced that they would protest 1992 as a year of mourning for their cultures. It was simply overlooked by the creators of the Jubilee Commission, distracted as they were by the internecine struggles between Italians and Latinos. The commission itself, prodded by its academic members, sought to make up for this somewhat by making Dave Warren, a prominent Native American cultural spokesman, an honorary commissioner, but this feeble gesture had little impact. Warren resigned this appointment in 1990 and was never replaced.

It seems possible to suggest that the invasion myth became dominant in the United States around this time. A survey organized by the "Indigenous Communications Resource Center" at Cornell University reported that 74 percent of the Native American leaders responding saw 1992 as "an opportunity to expose our vision and put our voices together." Public education about Native American issues was the preferred objective among this group, followed by legislation, "networking," and "apologies." "We've finally gotten most people to say it was an encounter, not a discovery," wrote Ladonna Harris of Americans for Indian Opportunity, but most other leaders were willing to go beyond that, with "colonization" being the preferred label for 70 percent of the respondents compared with only 20 percent for "encounter" and 6 percent for "discovery."[15] In April 1990, a traditionalist network known as the Circle of Elders sponsored the creation of an indigenist "1992 Alliance," headed by Suzan Shown Harjo, a former director of the National Congress of American Indians. The alliance's objectives included traditional indigenist goals such as strengthening native values and guaranteeing religious freedom and innovations such as an invitation "to establish a moral partnership between traditional American Indians and environmental organizations." Later that year the projected alliance was cemented: quietly at a meeting attended by traditionalist leaders and white environmentalists at the Onondaga Longhouse in upstate New York;[16] and noisily a few weeks later with the publicity attending the publication of environmentalist Kirkpatrick Sale's *The Conquest of Paradise, Christopher Columbus and the Columbian Legacy*. Meanwhile, such mainstream organizations as the National Council of Churches and the Council on Foundations endorsed some form of indigenist program, with the Council of Churches—founded in Chicago during the World's Columbian Exposition of 1893—formally describing Columbus's voyage as "an invasion" that led to "slavery and genocide of native peoples."[17]

These relatively quiet developments were not what attracted the media to the indigenist point of view, however. Indian militants who had imbibed deeply in what one scholar called "the culture of liberation" first established at Alcatraz in 1970 and repeated at numerous sites of indigenist direct action in subsequent decades dramatized the new perspective in ways that made headlines. One of the first manifestations greeted the startled organizers of *First Encounters*, an ambitious exhibition mounted by the Florida Museum of Natural History and funded by the National Endowment for the Humanities. Showcasing a generation of research by University of Florida and other scholars, especially in historical archaeology, the exhibition texts carefully noted Native American perspectives and justified the research in large part by the contributions it made to understanding native societies at the time of "encounter." Nevertheless, museum exhibitions are inherently low-resolution media. Their enduring impressions are made by objects, not words, and no amount of careful qualification in the exhibition labels or catalog could counteract the overall impression that the exhibition celebrated the Spanish perspective on the Quincentenary, with objects such as European artifacts found at the DeSoto expedition's campsites and a two-thirds-scale reconstruction of Columbus's caravel *Niña* based on the latest archival research in Spain. Accordingly, militant protests by indigenist and student activists greeted the exhibition's opening in Gainesville and threatened to dog it throughout its proposed tour to other museums in Florida, South Carolina, Texas, New York, and the Midwest.[18] From the militant viewpoint, the exhibition was "propaganda, not history." "Maybe if the archeologists dug up the bones of their own ancestors they could learn something about them that would explain to the Indian peoples of North, Central and South America the nature of these violent, greedy and bloodthirsty Europeans who destroyed, not discovered, America."[19]

Pouring symbolic blood over a Columbus statue in Denver in October, Native American activist Russell Means was widely quoted comparing Columbus to Hitler.[20] Kirkpatrick Sale, in interviews launching his new book, was somewhat more measured, but barely. "What kind of a man was Christopher Columbus?" he was asked. "He was unstable, rootless, avaricious and deceptive.... a man without a center." "In the final analysis," he added, "it is not really so important whether Columbus was a good man. What matters is that he brought over a culture centered on its own superiority. The failings of the man were and remain the failings of the culture." Not least among those failings, Sale concluded, were Columbus's and Europe's attitude toward nature "— that man should dominate—and this attitude has subsequently been imposed on the entire globe."[21]

The Conquest of Paradise was the first anti-Columbus book to achieve national attention. As the popular press picked up the issue, the Quincentenary began to project a negative public image and to become "politically incorrect" in progressive circles. Matters only became worse when cultural conservatives, many of whom saw Columbus-bashing as another example of the weakening of traditional Western values, undertook an eleventh-hour rescue attempt. For example, official indigenist stances by the American Historical Association and the National Council on the Social Studies were promptly challenged by dissident minorities within the two organizations, while conservative writer Russell Kirk denounced the handiwork of "whining radicals" who convicted Columbus of crimes not against humanity but against present-day "political correctness."[22] In a highly publicized venture, the National Endowment for the Humanities under its Republican chairman Lynne Cheney waded into the fray by withdrawing funds it had earlier authorized for a television documentary series that it now said went too far in depicting Spanish *conquistadores* as cruel while supposedly overlooking the brutality of the Aztecs. Here finally, the Quincentenary had outdone itself. No longer an innocuous ethnic celebration of Columbus's discovery of America, it had become a battleground for our entire view of Western culture. And since the battle was being waged in the press, which always likes controversy but hardly ever complexity, it turned into a political "hot potato." Funding agencies began to shy away from supporting projects that appeared too Quincentenary-oriented and therefore controversial.

In effect, 1992 was over before it even began. Consider, for example, the fate of a program at Ohio State University that had received start-up funding from the NEH. The objective was the creation of a research center in Seville, Spain, that would help American scholars produce new research on the history of Latin America. Seville, of course, contains the major repository of Spanish colonial documents, the General

Archive of the Indies, and even today much in that building has yet to be studied. But in 1991, while the first two scholars were working in Seville, the NEH backed away from the project, refused further support, and caused the center to die. Though endowment staff would never admit it, it seems probable that the upset surrounding the Quincentenary made the NEH concerned that the project would appear to be controversial, and it shied away before the center could really get started. In terms of its long-term impact, such a center—which was modeled on the academies for classical studies that the United States and other nations maintain in Athens and Rome—could have been a truly significant outcome of the commemoration, especially in contrast to so many ephemeral events envisioned by the Jubilee Commission.

Be that as it may, the anti-Columbus or invasion myth that swiftly took shape challenged traditional viewpoints in provocative ways. First, so it goes, the Admiral of the Ocean Sea was far from a courageous epic hero; on the contrary, he was a dishonest petty man who was not even the first to reach America, for other Europeans had preceded him and in any case native people had been here all along and did not need to be discovered. And when Columbus did arrive, he perpetrated genocide by causing the deaths of thousands, perhaps millions of Taino and Carib Indians in the Caribbean islands.[23] This immediately raises the specter of another major accusation: the arrival of Europeans in America can be called civilizing only if one overlooks the fact that within the first hundred years, close to 90 percent of the native population perished from exploitation and disease, which means probably more than 70 million people. Everywhere one could have looked in that time, native cultures were disrupted or destroyed in the name of civilization. And then when there were no more Indians left to perform the inhumane labor imposed by the colonizers, the equally inhumane institution of African slavery was created. According to James Axtell, 10 million black Africans were brought as slaves to the New World, not counting some 25 percent of these numbers who died under the inhumane conditions of the Middle Passage.[24] And behind all this, it can be said that the conquest of America involved a profoundly biased Eurocentrism that deprived native people, blacks, mestizos, mulattos, and many others of a recognition of their cultural viability by imposing upon them the inferior status of *other* against which the European defined himself as the only meaningful form of humanity. This mechanism of alienation occurred at every level of the process because it was inherent in the very structure of the colonial system, which is what 1492 was really about. Columbus created colonialism and thereby introduced an enduring system of exploitation by which native peoples everywhere throughout the world were subjugated to a presumptuous Eurocentrism that decrees other cultures barbaric, savage, uncivilized, or simply inferior. Only if one were a European immigrant could one escape this demeaning characterization. In this light, most of the programs envisioned by the Jubilee Commission and by other quincentennial planners could be seen not simply as relatively innocuous manifestations of symbolic ethnicity but as an effort to devote yet more public funds and attention to the perpetuation of neocolonialist ends.

It is easy to find a number of exaggerations in the anti-myth and one can therefore appear to be a defender of the older discovery myth. For example, it is simply not accurate to say that Columbus was guilty of genocide or that he can be compared to Adolf Hitler, as Russell Means proposed. Columbus did not decree a mass destruction of the native population and he did not propose to eliminate any race or ethnic group, all of whom he wanted to convert to Christianity. Columbus was certainly no epic hero, but neither was he a demon. In reality, he seems to have been a weird, obsessive man even in the eyes of his contemporaries, a self-educated luminary who saw himself as chosen by God for a great feat, to go east by sailing west. This would permit the Christian world to outflank its greatest threat of the time, Islam, while also making him rich through the easier trade routes he thought he would develop. Always looking for ways to ingratiate himself to the Spanish monarchs by finding gold and other wealth, he quickly realized he could establish colonies on the islands he found but then turned out to be a poor administrator who had to be removed from his command because of his incompetence. He died always resisting the truth that he had landed in a "new world," always insisting that he had found Japan, probably because he possessed a remarkable and ultimately medieval ability not to trust his eyes and to trust only his obsessions. Does this make him a great villain of history? Or merely an ordinary man who accomplished an extraordinary feat without even knowing it? To those who value human complexity above the demands of myth-making, the contradictions and complexities of this real human being are far more interesting than the simplifications about him purveyed by both the discovery and invasion myths. Thus, for example, the indigenist novelists Michael Dorris and Louise Erdrich created in their novel *The Crown of Columbus* a sympathetic portrayal of the Admiral and a plot that did justice to the ambiguities of his deeds. Nevertheless, it was the far more simplistic view of Kirkpatrick Sale that prevailed in the bookstores.

The anti-myth established a fashionable lexicon in opposition to the word "discovery," which was rejected as incorrect and insensitive. Admittedly, the word is excessively Eurocentric, but if we understand it in the archaic sense that "to discover" means "to reveal,"[25] the word is not an inappropriate way of stating what Columbus achieved: making Europe fully and permanently aware of America for the first time in 1493. The Genoese explorer may not have been the first to reach the New World, but as one of us unadvisedly joked to the press, he was the first to return to Europe, hold what amounted to a press conference about his trip, and then get government funding to go back.[26] This was the really novel part of what happened. Because of Columbus's voyages, America became incorporated into the world system for the first time and Europe became able to dominate this system thanks in part to the resources, foodstuffs, and ideas it extracted from its experience in America, not all of which merely expresses cruel exploitation. Many would argue, for example, that the first real theories of human rights were developed precisely in the early colonial period when outraged Spaniards such as Bartolomé de las Casas attacked the barbarity of the colonizers for their cruelty to the natives. A culture capable of incorporating and learning from such self-criticism cannot be entirely evil, and the defense of the Indian no doubt fed into eighteenth-century ideas of emancipation and human rights. Thus, the argument might run, not only can one say that Columbus *did* discover America in the sense of making it a part of the world, but humankind accomplished major advances as a direct result of its American experience, whether parts of this experience were brutal or not.

Because both the discovery and invasion myths obviously distort the history of European settlement in America, whether for good or evil, and leave attention centered on the Europeans, a new word emerged that supposedly corrected them. Neither discovery nor invasion were adequate descriptors; the most fashionable word came to be "encounter"—an "encounter of two worlds." As we discuss in chapter 6, the word seems first to have appeared in Mexico, from where it was developed into the official slogan of the Organization of American States, taken up in modified form by the Smithsonian Institution and, in due course, used by the Spanish government. The appeal of this word—which was plastered all over the quincentennial consciousness in the titles of newsletters, lectures, conferences, and symposia—consists in speaking to our desire to believe that Amerindians and Africans contributed to a multicultural experience in America.

But let us be careful and ask: just what is an encounter? If we think of it as a meeting in which different parties enter a dialogue leading to a new perspective that changes both, one has to admit that extraordinary changes did occur as a result of the European arrival in America, but rarely as a result of any true dialogue. Indeed, Amerindians and Africans *did* contribute major dimensions to the new American experience but the kind of dialogue that really took place can probably best be summarized in an incident reported in a 1588 chronicle that tells us about the arrival of Spaniards in Mexico: "When the Spaniards discovered this land, their leader asked the Indians how it was called; as they did not understand him, they said *uic athan*, which means, what do you say or what do you speak, that we do not understand you. And then the Spaniard ordered it set down that it be called *Yucatan*."[27]

This of course has been the name of the Yucatan peninsula ever since. In other words, the supposed encounter was like a series of monologues among the deaf. The European side did not consistently believe that natives, slaves, or ordinary people had much worth saying; the latter groups certainly had to listen but they always tried to adapt what they heard to their own way of life, difficult as it may have been to do. In this sense, we are inclined to agree with Latin American novelist Augusto Roa Bastos when he says that there really was no encounter and that the word is mostly a euphemism invented by the purveyors of the discovery myth, who took up the idea when they realized some years into their commemorative planning that they were beginning to appear insensitive.[28] Of course, examples of real dialogued encounters can be found in the history of America, and just like the word "discovery," nothing prevents us from continuing to use the term "encounter" in the wide sense of a meeting that changed the participants, whether violent, confrontational, or of some other nature. Still, the word "invasion" remains a more accurate term to describe what really happened.

During the Quincentenary, the invasion myth captured public attention in several dramatic, media-oriented events. The American Indian Movement, building on earlier public relations coups in Washington and Denver, organized a crowd of several thousand demonstrators in San Francisco that kept the Italian-American Columbus from staging the traditional mock landing in Aquatic Park and that also disrupted the ensuing Columbus Day parade. Instead of the grand culminating celebration envisioned by the Jubilee Commission, 1992 Columbus Day in the Bay Area became a "Day of Concern for Indigenous Peoples," the highlight of which was a rock concert featuring Native American, African American, and Latino performers. "'In fourteen hundred and ninety-two, a white male European oppressor sailed the ocean blue,'" grumbled the widely read local-color columnist Herb Caen. "Happy

Columbus Day, Cristóbal, no matter what the revisionists are trying to do to you."[29]

The reputations of Indians and Columbus had, of course, been joined together since 1492, but in contrast to earlier Columbian commemorations that featured Indian images and artifacts but few Indians, the Native Americans of 1992 were neither vanishing nor silent. Nor did they speak with a single voice. While militants were comfortable with boycotts and protests, Indian scholars viewed the observance with mixed feelings. Thus, in 1991, an activist in Columbus, Ohio, said to one of us, "We have no quarrel with Columbus or anything else in history. The past is the past and should be understood as completely as possible. But as Native Americans, we must object to the conditions in which our people live today. The Quincentenary is the only opportunity we have had to call people's attention to our situation, so we have to take advantage of it before it is gone and we return to the silence in which we have always lived. Continue to study history *and* please begin to care about us."[30] "Our celebration will not be like the celebration of the white man," wrote George Horse Capture in 1990. "We must celebrate our survival over the last 500 years. To date we have outlasted the Spaniards, Dutch, Russians, French, and maybe even the Americans. . . . We do better than survive."[31]

Several issues were at the heart of Native American outlooks on the Quincentenary. One was an increasingly unyielding demand to place the cultural representation of Indians in Indian hands. This position manifested itself at one of the earliest scholarly conferences, held under NEH auspices in Santa Fe in November 1983. Then astonished anthropologists heard themselves denounced for imprisoning Indian life and culture in the glass cases and dioramas of natural history museums, classifying indigenous peoples in the same categories as flora, fauna, and minerals, while studying European expressive culture and beliefs under the more dignified rubrics of philosophy, religion, and art.[32]

The second demand, growing out of the first, was for the repatriation of human remains and religious artifacts from museum collections to tribal authorities. As public support grew for this position, Congress enacted it into law in a series of measures adopted in 1989 and 1990. In 1991, the Smithsonian Institution, whose National Museum of Natural History—or at least its most senior anthropologists—had vigorously opposed repatriation, agreed to abide by the legislation, from which Congress had earlier exempted it. A third victory had been won when the Smithsonian, after congressional prodding and a complex negotiation with New York authorities, agreed to acquire the one-million-item

Heye Collection of New York City and to incorporate it into a National Museum of the American Indian. Congress awarded the new museum relatively little money, but it did give it the last remaining building place on the National Mall.[33]

Behind all this was the increasingly successful Indian strategy of seeking redress from the courts for the many broken treaties negotiated in the nineteenth century between the U.S. government and different Indian tribes. Indian groups could hoist the government by its own petard, so to speak, by using the legal system to show the violation of its treaties. The strategy was successful and began to bring in money and rights, not to mention a wider recognition of the indigenist argument against dominant settler discourses.

This growing indigenist movement coincided with the increasing importance of ethnohistorical research into colonial America that first appeared during the 1940s and by 1992 had achieved real maturity for at least a generation or more. This work has provided a far richer understanding of colonial history than existed before because it includes the other side: indigenous people, slaves, and other groups who were always overlooked in earlier periods because they were not thought significant.[34] Indeed, modern scholarship is doing things today that were never attempted in earlier periods: studying Indian society in the 1500s, looking at agriculture, demographics, indigenous social systems, and other aspects of the lives of different groups. At the same time, with the help of critical theory it is re-reading texts that we thought we understood but that we now realize are ambiguous because they carry ulterior motives that often make the authors less trustworthy than we thought.[35] And what emerges from this work is a balanced understanding that does not try to find villains and heroes, does not look only for great epic feats or miserable failure, and yet does not hide the basic fact that beginning in 1492, Europe undertook a huge invasion of America that would effectively undermine the societies already there and change the course of history forever. The picture is neither pretty nor simple. It is a tapestry rich with the complexity of real human beings trying to survive as best they could with the resources at their disposal and within the terms and limitations of their time. Any one of their lives, as ordinary or uneventful as it may have been to the person who lived it, is much more interesting than all the myths purveyed about them.

Colonial historiography did not need the Quincentenary to come into its own, but it undoubtedly received stimulus and encouragement from the attention and money directed its way as 1992 approached.

Moreover, to the degree that it tended to support the indigenist perspective, we can say that the 1992 commemoration was at least partly a consequence of the insights developed by ethnohistorians over the previous two or more generations. In this sense, the forces that opposed the official Quincentenary gained much of their strength from the greater currency of their understanding, even when issues were sometimes exaggerated for media effect. While the various official Quincentenary commissions wallowed in futile debates about Italians versus Latinos, Columbus versus *hispanidad*, the indigenist perspective gathered strength from its relationship to contemporary research and articulated a compelling moral argument for historical justice. This made official plans and programs look precariously out of touch, as if unaware of current research trends and insensitive to ethnic constituencies outside their own narrow interests. The official Quincentenary was thus doomed before it started, though its failure implied a greater success, the victory of an unofficial, *other* Quincentenary that gave voice to the subaltern. In the end, then, 1992 succeeded because it failed. It succeeded because the old-fashioned views of official planners were superseded by a reaction based in contemporary social reality that forced itself into our consciousness and demanded to be heard.

5

The Quincentenary as Excess

The Case of Spain

More than twenty nations established official or quasi-official quincentennial planning bodies, including most Latin American countries, Spain, Italy, Portugal, and even Japan, which was after all the intended destination of Columbus's 1492 voyage. While the scope and character of efforts varied widely from country to country, it is not unfair to say that in terms of time, funds, and energy invested, what went on in the United States was often just a background compared to the foreground played out elsewhere. At the same time, the outcome was generally the same, though for different reasons. Whether the investment was large or small, the Quincentenary was usually a big disappointment. From the shores of other nations, Columbus often sailed in a luxury liner, but his boat usually sank anyway, sometimes from carrying too much cargo. Let's begin by looking at the fanciest vessel of all, the one that set the terms against which all the others were defined, Spain.

Among the nations that chose to commemorate 1992, none was more ambitious than Spain. The socialist government of Felipe González set loftier goals, undertook more programs, and spent more money on the Quincentenary than probably all other nations combined. Spain also took more risks with the Quincentenary, not only in the enormous costs associated with its 1992 programming but especially in the potential loss of national prestige if things went awry. None of this is surprising, of course, for the Quincentenary touched Spain in ways more meaningful than ever could have been the case for Italy, Portugal, Latin America, or the United States. Italy had the birthplace of Columbus; Portugal had the early lead in maritime exploration; Latin America had the societies that 1492 produced; and the United States had a long history of Columbus myths associated with manifest destiny. Spain, on the other hand, had the overall undertaking that connected these into a whole. It had the voyages of Columbus and other explorers that launched modern New World history, and above all it had the huge colonizing enterprise that produced the cultural encounter on which the Quincentenary was based. Whatever else one might have thought about the 1992 commemoration—whether one believed it glorious or infamous—one had to admit that it was an essentially Spanish affair.

Official Spanish publications always stressed that the primary goal of the Quincentenary was to strengthen cultural ties with Latin America. Writing in 1992, the president of the Spanish National Commission, Luis Yáñez Barnuevo said: "El Gobierno, la sociedad española, el Estado en su conjunto, decidieron hace diez años, poner en marcha un proyecto de conmemoración que era necesario compartir con la totalidad del mundo iberoamericano, a todos los niveles sociales, ya que tan protagonista como España de esa fecha lo es toda Iberoamérica, y tanto como los Gobiernos, los pueblos" [Ten years ago, the Spanish government, society, and state jointly decided to undertake a commemoration that it was necessary to share with Latin America at all social levels because both the people and the governments of Ibero-America are protagonists of 1492 as much as Spain].[1]

Given the nature of the Quincentenary, this Latin American emphasis was inevitable and always remained a strong feature of Spanish planning efforts. In Spain, Latin America can never be just another part of the globe, like Asia or Africa. Beginning in 1492, Spain created Latin America in the sense of colonizing the continent and making it part of the world system. Though relations between the two have often been problematical, the linguistic and cultural ties that bind them together can never be ignored. With the Quincentenary, Spain sought to enhance these ties through a program of cultural politics focused on a common history and a shared recognition of the need for Latin America to achieve economic and political integration into the contemporary world. The government was also seeking to show Latin Americans that the "mother country" is no longer burdened with colonial ideas and that it wants to deal with the New World as partner and equal. Of course, as a relatively small world power, Spain could not do much in a practical sense to improve conditions in Latin America, whether through technical assistance or other programs, and skeptics can legitimately say that nothing has changed there just because of the Quincentenary. Still, the goal was sincere and led to several programs we will mention further on.

With its Latin American emphasis, Spain became one of the early leaders in the shift of the Quincentenary away from the figure of Christopher Columbus. The Genoese mariner was given a place in the commemoration, but the real goal was to celebrate Hispanic culture as a whole. The developed nations had too long ignored Spain and Latin America, and the time had come to redress the balance by insisting on the importance of their contributions to Western culture. Such an argument had limited appeal outside the Hispanic world and seemed mostly intended to make people feel good about themselves. It also drew on a traditionalist view of Hispanic culture that is largely meaningless in today's world because the Hispanic peoples are too diverse to be covered by a single ideal. For Spain to promote *hispanidad* made her appear neocolonial even when she argued otherwise. Moreover, the growing indigenist perspective, itself partly a product of Latin America, was perceived as either irrelevant or a threat to the Hispanic emphasis and was therefore ignored until the end. Spain may have looked fashionably up to date when it downplayed Columbus, but its promotion of *hispanidad* and its resistance—or indifference—to indigenist ideas made its concept of the Quincentenary deeply anachronistic.[2]

At the same time, Spain had a different and much more important goal in 1992, to celebrate the nation's historic "return to Europe" as shown by its recent consolidation of liberal democracy and membership in the European Union. This goal was rarely mentioned in publications, probably because it was more than obvious to most Spaniards and the government did not want to appear to diminish the Latin American connection. Still, it was the most significant aspect of 1992 because it touched on one of the most troubled issues of modern Spanish history, the nation's long and difficult struggle to achieve democracy.

In this context, it might be helpful to recall that over the last two centuries many different groups of Spanish liberals had pursued modernization and democracy but had always been defeated by a powerful conservative oligarchy drawing from the Catholic Church, the military, and the upper classes. This oligarchy believed that modernity was a form of decadence contrary to the spiritual values of "eternal" Spain, and its goal was to preserve traditional Spanish culture by preventing change and progress. Such an attitude resulted in a recurring pattern of civil wars between progressives and conservatives of which the worst and last, from 1936 to 1939, produced the military dictatorship of Francisco Franco. As a particularly harsh incarnation of the traditional Spanish oligarchy, the Franco regime sought to keep Spain isolated from the rest of the world and to preserve the values of the privileged few. And because Franco lasted from 1939 until 1975, it came to appear that freedom and democracy would always remain the impossible dream of Spanish history.

And yet when the Franco regime was followed by a peaceful transition to democracy during the years 1975 to 1982, it was as if a never-ending nightmare had suddenly disappeared. Probably in spite of himself, Franco had begun much of the modernization process that made Spaniards dissatisfied with anything but consumer society and democracy. Moreover, fearful of returning to the polarized environment that had led to the 1936 Civil War, politicians and public officials worked hard to achieve consensus and compromise. A key figure in the transition was King Juan Carlos I, the monarch picked by the old dictator to continue his regime but who used the Franquist legal system to dismantle it from within and create a democratic constitution.

The king also saved democracy on a famous night in February 1981, when a last-gasp effort by a few disgruntled members of the Civil Guard sought a return to military rule. Facing them down alone, he demanded that the democratic process be allowed to continue. When he prevailed, King Juan Carlos went down in Spanish history as the savior of the new order. With the election of the Socialist Party of Felipe González in 1982, the transition was complete and Spain could now, after centuries of seemingly endless, failed struggle, begin to fulfill its European destiny as a modern—or even postmodern—liberal democracy. The socialist policy of entering NATO and the European Union, no matter what the cost, drove the message home. Spain had come back to Europe and the demons of its past had been buried forever.[3]

No wonder, then, that the Quincentenary was to be a celebration of democratic Spain. Under the leadership of King Juan Carlos, whose prestige was now immense, the government poured what seemed like unlimited resources into a huge public relations campaign focused on past and future, Latin America and Europe. The goal was to mobilize civil society with a view to making Spaniards feel proud about their modern, democratic society while at the same time recognizing the important role they had played in world history.

Linked to this was the idea of modernizing the image of Spain in the rest of the world. Spaniards believe that their country is often stereotyped as either a nation of religious fanatics and military dictators, or a land of bullfighters and flamenco dancers. Such old-fashioned images obviously fail to correspond to today's Spain, and they tend to make the society appear incompatible with the contemporary world, as if Spaniards preferred to strum guitars rather than become computer technicians or successful business leaders. One goal of the Quincentenary was to change the image of Spain in the world by showing a different, more contemporary face.

The year 1992 was an especially fortunate one because, in addition to serving as the five hundredth anniversary of the first voyage of Columbus, it was the year originally targeted by the European Union for full economic integration. In response to this opportunity, the government set about formulating an ambitious program of activities that would showcase both the heritage of the past and the vibrant, new Spain that was busily building its future. Since Spain has long been one of the main European tourist destinations, with now more than 55 million visitors a year—some 15 million more than the nation's population—a major thrust would be to enhance tourist attractions while also developing transportation and communications infrastructure, areas still in need of serious improvement. If all these tasks could be accomplished, and if, in addition, scholars could provide the cultural veneer that would give prestige and meaning to the historic commemoration, it was assumed that the Quincentenary would be a success.

Of course, this multiple thrust of focusing on both Latin America and Europe, of attracting tourists and building infrastructure, and of involving both scholars and the media produced a variety of tensions and misunderstandings that were difficult to reconcile. For example, to emphasize Europe could be seen as appearing to turn away from Latin America, while to renew Latin American ties could be interpreted as undermining the push toward Europe.[4] To spend a lot simply for the purpose of attracting tourists could be seen as crass commercialism while to build infrastructure could lead to overspending and corruption.

Official organizations were inevitably committed to promoting the Spanish experience in America as a glorious historical achievement and therefore resisted acknowledging the less positive aspects. Above all, to launch programs in so many directions at once could and did lead organizers to spread themselves too thin, with the result that they were always at risk of failing to accomplish much of what they proposed.

Still, one sign of Spain's self-assurance in the years leading up to 1992 was its conviction that no problems were insurmountable and that the Quincentenary could be everything the nation wanted it to be. Latin America was not only Spain's past but also its future, part of a common struggle to achieve the economic and democratic modernization that Spain itself was now accomplishing. Europe was not only the future of Spain, it was also a potential market for Latin American goods that might be funneled through Spain. More tourists meant more money for everybody, and better highways or train stations were to all people's benefit. In short, Spain thought it could be all things to all people. Though ingenuous to the extreme, its attitude expressed the energized environment of the 1980s when prosperity followed on the heels of democracy. Spain had entered a new era and was determined not to overlook its once-in-a-lifetime opportunity for a moment of glory on the world stage.

The three high-profile events of 1992 were the Games of the XXV Olympiad in Barcelona, the Universal Exposition of Seville, and the celebration of Madrid as Cultural Capital of Europe. In reality, the first of these, the Olympic Games, was not an official quincentennial event at all and was rarely mentioned in official publications, although the Games were obviously awarded to Barcelona in recognition of the importance to Spain of 1992. Barcelona, we know, is in Catalonia, and Catalans sometimes say that the Spanish experience in America had nothing to do with them, as if they were one country and Spain quite another. Such sentiments have more than a little truth to them but they are also often exaggerated. Catalans were excluded from trading with the New World until the eighteenth century, but of course King Ferdinand was lord of Catalonia and different levels of activity took place anyway. In the end, however, Catalonia *is* different from the rest of Spain, and to the degree that the Olympic Games were not part of the Quincentenary but could be seen as essential to the overall "Year of Spain," they provided exactly the right balance to maintain the "separate-but-together" mentality so important to Catalonia. Catalans could receive much attention and money from Madrid, but they could also organize an event less directed toward the Spanish past and more in tune with Catalonia's traditionally greater sensitivity to the outside world.

The Barcelona Olympics were used both to showcase Catalan culture, which had been repressed under Franco, and to undertake a much-needed modernization of Barcelona, whose overall appearance had declined. Indeed, the real purpose of the Olympics was to serve as a pretext to transform the city, pursuing the same logic of "residuals" we saw earlier with Chicago, Baltimore, and other cities. The transformation started with the port, which had been cut off from the urban environment by rail lines, factories, docks, and customhouses. It was completely renewed and is now a hub for luxury liners. The city also got a remodeled airport, new outer circulation highways, widened avenues, parks, restored buildings, and many other projects—not to mention the Olympic sites themselves. Barcelona and Catalonia generally gave themselves a face-lift fitting their self-image as Spain's commercial and cultural center. In addition, the Olympic Games were well organized, well attended, and highly successful. Whereas an economic boom did not immediately follow the Games, 1992 is now considered a major turning point for the city because the last few years have witnessed a veritable take-off of tourist and economic growth. Barcelona has become one of the liveliest, most prosperous, and most attractive cities in Europe.[5]

The World's Fair or Universal Exposition of Seville, popularly called Expo '92, was Spain's major quincentennial event and dwarfed all others by comparison. Like the Barcelona Olympics, Expo '92 had its own planning structure separate from the main Quincentenary organizations. In many ways, the whole venture was one of those throwbacks to an earlier era that only a somewhat naive country—in the best sense of the word—could have attempted. Of course, unlimited funding helped. As we saw with the case of Chicago, many nations can no longer afford the prohibitive costs of mounting mega-events like world's fairs, and much of what used to be so engaging about them—seeing exotic places or experiencing the latest technology—is now available every day on television. As Penelope Harvey has noted, however, it was important for Spain to show that it was capable of carrying out a project of this magnitude in order to corroborate that it belonged as one of the world's "advanced" nations.[6] The idea was to make Expo '92 so attractive that 15 million people would flock to it. Of these, organizers believed that about a third would come from foreign countries, mostly European. When the Chicago effort collapsed in 1987, the nation had the stage to itself.

Although skeptics said that Seville was chosen as the site of Expo '92 because the president of the government, Felipe González, and many of his key advisors were from there, it is also true that the city is the capital of one of the most historically rich but economically underdeveloped regions of Spain, Andalusia. By locating the exposition there, the government was creating a pretext to fund residuals that would hopefully jump-start the local economy when the fair was over. As a result, plans to convert the exposition site into a high-tech research and development park for after the fair were front and center from the beginning. A basic assumption was that Andalusia had what it takes to become an "amenities zone," comparable to the U.S. Sunbelt or the Riviera in France, attracting high-technology industries whose negligible transportation costs would allow for location in places where the living, rather than the shipping, was easy.

At first, this later effort, called "Cartuja 93," had difficulty getting off the ground. Although 60 percent of the pavilions and other buildings were quickly designated for private-sector investment, they ran at barely more than a 25 percent occupancy rate for several years. This was better than Baltimore's Columbus Center but still disappointing in terms of original goals. More recently, occupancy has risen to 66 percent and includes about 140 companies and government offices. Along with biotechnology, computer, and telecommunication enterprises, an engineering school has located on the site and additional educational institutions are planned. At the same time, another area has been developed as a "Park of the Discoveries" that includes several of the original Expo pavilions, a cinema, planetarium, concert venues, discotheques, and an amusement park called "Magic Island." Whereas crowds can be large on summer evenings, tour guides describe this part of the island as "overpriced and uninspiring."[7]

As for the exposition itself, Expo '92 involved a massive ultramodern installation on Seville's Cartuja Island, a 535-acre site in the Guadalquivir River close to the central city. The island contains an old Carthusian monastery—whence the Cartuja name—where the remains of Christopher Columbus had once been buried before his bones were transported to America. Until the 1960s, the monastery had been transformed into a ceramics plant for a unique English-style chinaware carrying the Cartuja name that is highly regarded in Seville. To construct

Expo, the monastery, buildings, and surrounding waterways were completely restored or rebuilt, and the famous inverted cones of the ceramic kilns were retained as a motif from the past. During construction, several potentially important archaeological finds were made around the monastery, some of them dating from Roman times. Though scholars suggested that work should be halted until assessments of the finds could be made, planners were concerned about delays and disregarded pleas to slow down. As we will see in chapter 6, the same thing happened in Genoa, Italy.

The huge effort in planning, development, and construction generated many tensions between officials in Madrid, who were paying most of the costs and expected their views to prevail, and a local citizenry who had to endure years of upset throughout their city and often resented the intrusions from outside.[8] Launched with the theme "The Age of Discoveries," Expo '92 sought to combine public education about the past, present, and future with an intense entertainment program that fit Seville's fun-loving reputation. As it turned out, the entertainment became the great star of the fair, with hundreds of performances of popular and classical musicians, theater, opera, dance, movies, and many other attractions lasting every day until 4:00 A.M. As for the exhibits, reports were what one might expect, ambiguous at best. Pomp and gimmickry usually outdo substance in high-tech events such as this and Expo '92 was no exception. Harvey and Richard Maddox both comment on the widespread use of technology, electronic media, and film to communicate the usual sense of progress and enlightenment so typical of world's fairs.[9] Spain's main newspaper, *El País*, summed up the exhibits this way: "Pese a que la mayoría de los 110 países participantes anunciaron unos contenidos espectaculares, lo cierto es que ha habido un abuso de las técnicas audiovisuales, exposiciones de tono menor, pocas piezas originales y mucho cartón piedra que dejaba poco lugar para el asombro" [Although the majority of the 110 participating nations announced spectacular events, the truth is that there was an abuse of audiovisual techniques, an excess of very ordinary exhibits, few original displays, and a lot of *papier-mâché* that left little to get enthused about].[10]

On the other hand, attendance can surely be taken as an indicator of overall success, and in this light, Expo '92 was indeed a triumph. An average of 232,000 persons a day visited the 98 pavilions for the six-month run of the fair, and on peak days, the number reached as many as 500,000. Overall, a total of about 15.5 million people came to Expo '92.

Counting those who attended more than once, officials suggest that the fair received nearly 42 million visits, which is about 5 million more than originally targeted. Several pavilions, such as the one dedicated to navigation, or those of France and Japan, were widely praised as imaginative and interesting. Others with high-tech film shows, such as Spain, Canada, and Fujitsu, were extremely popular, and lines could be up to seven hours long. Then too, the fair offered many tasteful exhibits of original works of art from the Renaissance to the present.

Beyond this, the sweltering heat of Seville was moderated by a water-mist cooling system that was praised by some though criticized by others. Besides the entertainment, the achievements lauded by the press included the strict health controls on the food—*sevillanos* were amazed that no cases of food poisoning were reported—and the fact that, among the 2 million cars and buses negotiating the 40,000 parking spaces, there was only one recorded accident. Anyone who has experienced driving in Spain will be astounded by this detail alone. Besides being a break from routine and a lot of fun, Expo '92 must have been a great *calmante* to the hectic pace of modern Spanish life.

Shortly after Expo ended, official government estimates announced that Expo '92 cost $630 million but that not only had it paid for all costs, it also made a profit of $120 million. The government also acknowledged several billion additional dollars for bridges, highways, train and bus stations, a revitalized airport, and other residuals in Seville and the surrounding region. This figure includes an $850 million high-speed train to Madrid, the AVE, which has reduced what used to be a seven- or eight-hour trip to just over two. Of course, like the archaeologists who wanted to slow down the restoration of the Carthusian monastery in Seville, Spain's growing ecological movement was quashed when it expressed concern about potential environmental damage caused by construction of the train line. The AVE was completed in time for Expo and it is still popular today, with new lines now being planned to connect Madrid with other cities. Although the AVE has put the Madrid–Seville air route almost out of business, it is still receiving a hefty subsidy from the central government.

One problem with the final cost figures was that they were submitted by the same socialist government that created Expo '92. It was not in its interest to admit to cost overruns or major financial problems because it had bragged for many years about how socialism had overcome the corruption of the Franco regime and introduced accountability into public life. However, as the 1990s developed, scores of high-profile politicians, including President González himself, found themselves or members of their families implicated in cases of influence peddling, stock market manipulations, and corrupt land deals. How could anyone think that corruption would not also have infected Expo '92? No one could know until the cloud of corruption finally caught up with the socialists and they lost the 1996 election to the conservative Partido Popular. Spain had a new government for the first time in fourteen years.

At this point, investigations into the real costs of Expo '92 began. By late 1997, government auditors were estimating that the famous profit of $120 million was really a deficit of $250 million. Outraged conservative politicians demanded that the socialists reimburse the public treasury every *peseta* they were alleged to have plundered, while former Expo officials rushed to declare that the extra funds were not stolen but simply spent as part of the cost of getting the job done. Everyone vehemently denied that they had taken any funds for themselves or paid them illegally to any entity associated with Expo. An especially touchy item was the $43 million paid to the promotional firm Telemundi; no one could figure out why the services had been so expensive and everyone suspected kickbacks.[11] Subsequently, Baltasar Garzón, the same magistrate who later sought the extradition of former Chilean dictator Augusto Pinochet from Great Britain, required eight of the most well known Expo officials to testify in a special investigation into corruption and fraud in Expo '92. *Sevillanos* always expressed special resentment toward one of these eight, Jacinto Pellón, an engineer from the north of Spain who was brought in around 1988 to head up site construction because the local administration under the gentlemanly Manuel Olivencia was far behind schedule. With a direct, imperious manner that irritated many, Pellón was extremely effective and got the job done. When called to appear, he denied any wrongdoing; in the end, neither he nor the others were charged with crimes. Socialist politicians insisted that the investigation was mostly a show trial intended to humiliate those who ran the country for years. Still, the issue of cost overruns remains substantial and suspicions of corruption may never be stilled.

Spain's third major quincentennial event, the celebration of Madrid as Cultural Capital of Europe, was less oriented to popular activities. For this reason, though it may have been as impressive in its way as the Olympics and Expo '92, reports tended to be less enthusiastic. Madrid had only four years to prepare for the occasion, so infrastructure was mostly disregarded and money was spent on events, most of which differed little from the normal range of cultural activities available in a metropolitan city. About $60 million went into the occasion. The funds were provided from the national lottery, city hall, and, to a lesser degree, the autonomous region of Madrid, the central government, and private donors. The number of official events was staggering and most were considered of high quality. According to *El País*, 1,800 different groups or companies performed in the city during the year in six different categories: music, art exhibits, dance, theater, public lectures, and film. Although young people complained that none of the music was for them (programs included not one rock concert), there is no doubt that during 1992, Madrid was host to some of the world's great orchestras, artists, and dance and theater companies. And though many complained that a lack of advertising made it difficult to know what was going on, a total of 1,270,000 spectators viewed the different performances.[12]

Planning for the rest of the Spanish commemoration started a year before the 1982 election of the first González government. Signaling his personal commitment to the effort, King Juan Carlos signed a royal decree creating a Comisión Quinto Centenario del Descubrimiento de América [Commission for the Quincentenary of the Discovery of America] on April 10, 1981. Thus, like other national commissions that were named before controversy appeared, the old-fashioned idea of discovery was built in from the beginning, although, as we noted earlier, this did not mean giving emphasis to the figure of Christopher Columbus. The president of the commission was the secretary of state for Ibero-American relations, a position of relatively high rank in the Ministry of Foreign Affairs. This showed the importance being given to Latin America. The commission itself was housed in the offices of one of the most prestigious cultural organizations in Spain, the Institute of Ibero-American Cooperation (ICI), in Madrid. It had a forty-member board of directors chaired by the king that included the president of the government, a variety of cabinet ministers, and representatives from all major institutions, including the legislature, labor unions, the Church, the military, the private sector, and others.

The national commission performed the usual duties of coordinating and overseeing official events, often with the participation of the Spanish royal family. Following the 1982 elections, the government of Felipe González began funding allocations that were eventually conceded at more than ten billion dollars but probably went well beyond that. González named a close political ally from Seville, Luis Yáñez Barnuevo, to be president of the commission. Yáñez tended to be aloof or distant, lacking the affability one might have hoped to find in the person holding his position. In 1991, he ran on the socialist ticket for mayor of Seville but lost convincingly, partly as a result of the reputation he had developed as a political hack, and also because of fallout from what was perceived as intrusion from Madrid.[13]

In 1985, the national commission created a second entity, the Sociedad Estatal para la Ejecución de Programas y Actuaciones Conmemorativas del Quinto Centenario del Descrubrimiento de América, S.A., that is, the State Society for the Execution of Quincentenary Programs, a semi-public corporation whose primary function was to raise funds and implement programs. It functioned as a private business, without the usual reporting constraints of governmental agencies. Rarely paying full price for projects, it encouraged other entities by nudging, cajoling, and negotiating funding agreements that usually carried a cost-sharing component either with government ministries, private donors, or both. To help the effort, in 1988 parliament passed a historic Law of Fiscal Benefits that offered tax write-offs for those donating to official quincentennial programs. Because this kind of law was unknown in Spain, it is difficult to know just how much impact it had on corporate funding of projects. Throughout most of its life, the State Society was run by an economist, Angel Serrano, whose intense but open and communicative manner quickly turned him into the most effective leader of the Spanish Quincentenary effort.

From the beginning, Spain put a lot of effort into creating and maintaining a forum of national commissions, the Ibero-American Conference of Commissions for the Commemoration of the Quincentenary of the Discovery of America—Encounter of Two Worlds. The idea was to use the Quincentenary as a vehicle to encourage cooperation with Latin American governments. Meeting every year in a different place, representatives of each of the Latin American national commissions as well as those of Spain and Portugal would debate issues and propose goals. We noted earlier how in 1988, the chairman of the Jubilee Commission, John Goudie, had sought membership for the United States in the Ibero-American Conference. Spain successfully opposed the effort because it did not want to lose importance in the group. It was also trying to keep the group untainted by the troubled history of American foreign policy in Latin America. Excluded from the main body, the United States remained with a number of other nations as an observer state, and the emphasis remained strictly Hispanic, just as Spain wanted.[14]

The presence of the king at several of these meetings guaranteed a certain prestige and attendance. The culmination took place in 1991 and 1992 with two *cumbres* or summit meetings of heads of state, first in Mexico and then in Madrid, with a decision to make the conference permanent.

The Ibero-American Conference continues to meet every year but is largely ceremonial and has produced little more than idealistic rhetoric. Some might argue that it has been useful in communicating the sincerity of Spain's wish to support democracy in Latin America. The 1980s did in fact witness a reappearance of democratic tendencies in parts of Latin America—Argentina, Chile, Brazil, Mexico, and Nicaragua, for example—and Spain continues to go out of its way to make sure that these trends receive encouragement.

Following its admission into the European Union in 1986, Spain also made the Ibero-American Conference one of a number of forums from which to stake out a position as a bridge between Latin America and Europe. From this perspective, the nation has been seeking—with limited success—to soften the EU's protectionist stance against products and immigration from Latin America while at the same time advocating technical assistance for the region by the EU. By the late 1980s, Quincentenary officials were making similar gestures toward the Inter-American Development Bank (IDB) in Washington, which agreed to manage a $500 million program of low-interest technical assistance loans for Latin America in the areas of education, agriculture and rural development, public health, communications, and urban development. Though not large by international standards, such programs at least back up the rhetoric with action.

It would be tedious to list even a small percentage of Spanish quincentennial projects. Official publications promoted the trite symbolism of "Five Hundred Years: Five Hundred Programs." However, besides the national commission and the State Society, each of the seventeen autonomous regions had its own set of Quincentenary activities, plus also the fifty provinces, dozens of town councils, city halls, universities, museums, and other educational and cultural institutions spread throughout the country. Programs and events must certainly have reached into the thousands. In one way or another, *everyone* in Spain was touched by 1992, so much so that many complained that the commemoration was excessive and that other kinds of activities were being postponed or passed over. No wonder there was a sense of relief when

1992 finally ended. On the other hand, the extraordinarily high rate of participation by all kinds of institutions suggests a degree of consensus that is rare in public programming anywhere. Either the State Society was successful in encouraging organizations to support its cause or the availability of money led everyone to line up for their share.

Projects fell into three overlapping categories: education, science and technology, and culture. Participation by the State Society provided a veneer of official sanction and a partial subsidy, while interested individuals or groups carried out the bulk of the task. Thus, there were projects to modernize the teaching of Spanish through interactive technology. A program of more than 700 fellowships brought U.S. high school Spanish teachers to study in Toledo. A "floating university" took more than 2,000 youngsters sailing between Spain and Latin America each summer. There were several enrichment programs on Latin American history and culture for more than 150,000 students in some 3,000 Spanish schools. Archaeological restoration projects embraced 29 Latin American sites and another 30 in Spain, ranging from the Temple of the Great Jaguar in Tikal, Guatemala, to the Columbian Library in the Cathedral of Seville. A start was made toward computerized access to the great General Archive of the Indies in Seville, where IBM began a pilot program of transferring the 40,000 most frequently used documents to a computer format that would permit scholars to consult them more easily. This project has proven enormously successful because, besides being much more accessible, documents no longer deteriorate through constant handling.

In the scientific arena, the Quincentenary was involved in launching Hispasat, two multipurpose, telecommunications satellites intended to provide up-to-date telephone, television, and other communications capabilities between Spain and the New World, including the United States. The first satellite was launched in September 1992 and the second in July 1993. Spain eventually hopes to establish commercial and educational programming from New York to Cape Horn.

In the cultural area, a consortium of 55 Spanish publishers brought forth the Biblioteca Quinto Centenario or Quincentenary Library, consisting of more than 1,300 books. It included new editions of hard-to-find older works, new scholarly work on the colonial period, and even a long list of popular and children's literature on Latin American themes. Another major project was the restoration of the Museum of America in Madrid. This is a major collection of pre-Columbian artifacts brought to Spain over the centuries. The building had been closed for many years but was finally reopened following restoration in July 1992.

Then there was the effort to create a series of cultural centers to permit local communities to program activities. More than a thousand such venues were developed, sometimes as large projects costing lots of money, such as the new opera house of Seville, and other times as specialized activities with more narrow goals, such as the *casa-museo* or museum dedicated to poet Rafael Alberti in Cádiz. Overall, nearly 150 museums, 120 libraries and archives, and 31 art galleries were set up in this program in addition to the thousand other centers mentioned above.

The State Society also funded countless exhibits and learned conferences on topics such as pre-Columbian cultures, early scientific expeditions, Spanish and Latin American art, Sephardic Jewish culture in Spain, and many others. It sponsored musical concerts, theater productions and festivals, several productions of Spanish light opera (*zarzuela*), and a long list of dance festivals. It supported several compact disks of classical Spanish music, and it subsidized fourteen feature films, eighteen documentaries, twelve television series, and an opera. As commercial and critical ventures, the films failed badly, as did the opera. Even the great director Carlos Saura was not immune. *El dorado* premiered with great panoply and royal patronage in Madrid in 1988, but it turned out to be a mediocre version of the same story that German director Werner Herzog had already made into a fine film, *Wrath of God*. *El dorado* quickly disappeared from view. Equally disappointing was the film version of one of the great stories of the early encounter, Cabeza de Vaca's *Naufragios* or *Shipwrecks*,[15] which though faithful to the text was unfortunately quite tedious. Though Carlos Fuentes's *The Buried Mirror* was probably the closest the State Society came to achieving a moderate success in its film ventures, the series presented a traditional approach to Spain's achievement in America, and in any case arrived too late to make an impact.[16] The society's reputation as a producer of contemporary entertainment ended up becoming a sad joke in Spain.

This brief compilation of Spanish Quincentenary activities is far from complete but is probably enough to help us see that the effort was major. Moreover, unlike in the United States and other countries, much of what planners set out to do was actually accomplished, probably because of the large amounts of money available to them. One assumes then that in spite of a failed performance here or a bad film there, the Spanish Quincentenary must be considered a solid success. Interestingly, most Spaniards have long believed just the opposite. During the years leading up to 1992, the Quincentenary was so heavily promoted by the government and it so dominated the funding of research and entertainment that it soon made everyone weary of it all and most just wanted to get it over with. Many had such negative reactions that by 1993 they were angry and did not want to talk about the Quincentenary any more. It was as if they had had to put up with so much empty rhetoric for ten long years that once it was over, they didn't want to hear another word about it. In an informal survey of about fifty Spanish friends from different walks of life, all but one roundly condemned the whole 1992 effort. The one who favored it had been heavily involved in it.

Much of the anger was reserved for what people considered the excessive amount of money spent on ephemeral events that disappeared not long after they had begun. Expo '92 took much of the criticism, but the many short-lived conferences, exhibits, and performances that came and went in 1992 were not exempted. Many believed that the government had squandered an opportunity to bring a more enlightened understanding of Latin American history into the public arena. To be sure, some of this discontent can be attributed to what was called the Quincentenary *resaca* or hangover, the inevitable let-down following a major event when bills must be paid and reality sets in once again. But there was no denying that billions of dollars had been spent on activities that had come and gone without lasting effects of any kind. The Quincentenary, one heard so often, was just a frivolous, one-shot deal that made a few people rich but did not change a thing.

Such sentiments may be understandable in context. Many Spaniards are cynical about public institutions and presume that a *pícaro* or thief lurks behind most governmental activities. If one has power, it is not to help others but to become rich. If Expo '92 cost billions, one just *knows* that somebody skimmed millions off the top. It did not help that in the early 1990s, newspapers were full of the Filesa scandal in which nearly $8.5 million were illegally funneled to the Socialist Party. If the scandals had stopped there, perhaps the Quincentenary might not have provoked such animosity, but as we've seen, issues of overspending and corruption became worse and still lurk around the fringes of public consciousness.

Then too, the long period of socialist rule in Spain produced a growing disillusionment about the gains of the 1980s, including the goal of European integration, which many came to say the government of Felipe González defended mindlessly, without considering if some aspects should be reconsidered or slowed down. Spaniards still strongly favor European integration, but during the build-up to 1992 they began to question the high cost of unity, the periods of weak investment, and the high unemployment rates that never seemed to drop below 20 percent of the workforce. This led to a new "Euroskepticism" about the future of the nation that coincided with the Quincentenary year. If 1992 was meant to be a celebration of Spain's "return to Europe," most think it should have been less extravagant and more thoughtful, with a more practical recognition of the country's limited resources.

Indeed, the Quincentenary necessarily lost on all counts because few ever believed the Latin Americanist rhetoric either. How, they ask, could a small nation such as Spain ever expect to make serious inroads toward solving the huge economic and political problems of Latin America? How could relatively small projects—these included, for example, the building of a train line and construction of an electric plant—really change the massive problems of the continent? Spain has enough difficulty just keeping its own house in order, these people say, and to the degree that the Quincentenary thought it could straighten up someone else's house, one that, moreover, represents 500 years of frustration, it was a sad tale of misused resources.

All of this came to a head in the recession that was finally admitted by the government toward the end of 1992 and that in the following two years reached the highest levels in a quarter century, that is, since the Franco era. In such a context, the Quincentenary appeared as a waste of increasingly scarce public resources. Begun during the boom of the mid-1980s when foreign investment was strong and public coffers were full, the Quincentenary did not take place until the balloon had burst and Spain was in trouble. How should we expect Spaniards to react any way other than to say it was a waste of money? Subsequently, the recession has passed and the economy is booming again, but the Quincentenary has not recovered a good image. Rather, it has simply disappeared from view.

It has been impossible to determine the final cost of the commemoration, but the many billions of dollars far exceed what a small country like Spain could reasonably afford and must surely have contributed to a worsening of the already serious national deficit. Moreover, one has to agree that Expo '92, the Olympics, and much of the rest were excessively focused on a single, short period of time and thereby gave too much of an impression that lasting effects were unimportant. Spaniards often say that their culture lives only for the moment and that few in Spain ever worry about the future. To the degree that many Quincentenary activities seemed to do the same, they perpetuated a traditional vice and deserve to be criticized. Quite simply, too much of the Quincentenary was the superficial one-shot deal so many in Spain predicted.

There were other problems too. Although public commemorations provide great opportunities for encouraging thoughtful debate about important national issues, Quincentenary officials rarely looked for interesting or challenging ideas and ultimately failed to articulate a meaningful relationship between the programs they were developing and larger issues of national and historical life. For example, if the Quincentenary was intended to focus on a democratic, European Spain, one looks in vain for serious debate about democracy and the national relationship with Europe within the context of 1992 programs. One has to conclude that officials were more interested in celebrating than in encouraging a thoughtful citizenry. This was even truer with respect to the whole Latin American side. For most of the period up to 1992, Spanish officials were oblivious to the debates about discovery, invasion, or encounter. Gradually, under pressure from the growing indigenist movement outside Spain, they began to use the word "encounter" in many of their presentations although, as the Latin American novelist whom we cited earlier, Augusto Roa Bastos, pointed out, they never really changed their meaning and were simply trying to appear more fashionable.[17] Thus, when they issued statements in defense of Indian rights during 1992, they had taken on the sad air of people who were ready to say anything just to appear current and please the other side. Clearly, they had missed the boat and many of the deeper issues of the Quincentenary had been disregarded.

This failure to encourage a national discussion concerning either the past or the present was probably the major lost opportunity of the Quincentenary. Programs were not intended to make people think but to encourage them to spend money. Officials were seeking to attract visitors who would come to Spain, open their wallets, and see that the society was no longer old-fashioned. This means that much of the Quincentenary came down to tourism, a point to which we shall return momentarily.

It must also be said that Spain largely wasted its Quincentenary effort in the United States. Officials assumed that, because of the strong

Italian-American lobby, the U.S. commemoration would emphasize Christopher Columbus and the old-fashioned myth of discovery. Though they hoped to avoid this by promoting Hispanic culture, they failed to offer solid programs and ended up concentrating their efforts on a project that perpetuated the Columbus myth. This was the tour of replica caravels from Texas to New York in 1992. Though the tour did attract solid crowds, it was not the kind of major activity focused on *hispanidad* that Spain would have wanted. In addition, officials were chronically unable to detect the multiplicity and pluralism of U.S. culture and therefore failed to see the groundswell of revisionism that eventually recast the meaning of 1492 in the United States. As a result, Spanish Quincentenary officials in the United States spent their time in hopelessly anachronistic public relations that had little or no effect on improving Spain's image in this country.

Part of the blame for this must surely go to the famous—or infamous—Spain '92 Foundation in Washington. Created by the State Society, the foundation admittedly was hurt early on when it was unable to secure financing it originally thought would be available from the McDonnell Douglas Corporation, then a major purveyor of military hardware to the Spanish armed forces. However, the foundation also developed a poor working relationship with the Spanish diplomatic corps operating in the United States and wasted many opportunities to develop cooperative programs with it, not to mention taking advantage of the considerable knowledge of U.S. culture possessed by these individuals. Then too, the foundation did what many organizations in Spain did—spread itself too thin. Never wanting to say no to anyone, but lacking the resources and personnel really to pursue projects, it agreed to all kinds of activities and then had no choice but expect the other party to do all the work. Anyone dealing with the foundation came to learn quickly that it would agree to whatever was proposed and never be heard from again.

After all these harsh words, can we find anything good about the Quincentenary in Spain? Apart from the films, most cultural productions and performances were of high quality, while achievements such as the restoration of libraries and the publication of the Quincentenary Library in particular deserve special mention because they carry some permanence. When compared to such events as Expo '92, these activities were certainly not as spectacular, but neither were they nearly as expensive, and in many ways they were just as worthwhile. They were also long overdue from a nation that has not distinguished itself by its attention to the arts. Efforts to showcase the rich cultural tradition of Spain were a useful accomplishment of the Quincentenary for which officials can be proud. At the least, they made more people better informed about the nation, just as one also thinks that, thanks to the Quincentenary, a few more Spaniards are better informed about Latin America.

On the other hand, indications do not suggest that the Quincentenary contributed to major changes in the way Spanish scholars understand the past such as happened, for example, in the United States. American scholarship has always been more open to new ideas, and controversy about the meaning of 1992 encouraged some interesting, albeit uneven, new work. Spanish universities, on the other hand, did not experience a similar phenomenon. Scholars were active of course, and lots of research was published, but most of it was of a very traditional nature, though of course this does not disqualify it. Educational institutions in Spain, especially the universities, still have a long way to go before opening up to new methods and ideas, and it is natural for interest in issues of Native Americans to be less immediate or compelling in that environment.

Another area of accomplishment touches tourism. Long one of the nation's most important economic sectors, tourism in Spain goes back to the early 1960s and depends on sun and beaches. During the 1980s, the sector came on hard times because resort locations had grown old and needed refurbishment. Spanish beaches also acquired a reputation for being dangerous. One of the goals of the Quincentenary was to reinvigorate the tourist sector by building highways, new hotels, and other facilities in inland areas that had not yet attracted the large numbers of foreign visitors that annually made it to the beaches. It was hoped that, with new roads and facilities throughout the country, hotel owners in the beach areas would also be encouraged to improve their locations. The ultimate goal was not only to bring back the tourists who had stopped coming to Spain but to begin to attract the so-called inland or monumental tourists, the ones interested in visiting artistic locations—of which Spain has plenty—and who are thought to be less careless and more sensitive than the beach crowd. Like all tourists, they of course want good highways, tasteful but inexpensive hotels and restaurants, and safe conditions in which to travel.

The results of this effort seem positive. After serious declines in the late 1980s, the tourism sector increased by 6.6 percent during 1992 and has followed with continuing strong increases of about 7 percent per year throughout the 1990s.[18] Statistics do not distinguish among kinds of tourists, but the prominence of alternative destinations such as the pilgrimage to Santiago de Compostela in Galicia, and the popularity of inland cities such as Salamanca, Burgos, and Segovia suggests that not everyone comes to Spain for sun and sand. Though it is not clear that the Olympics or Expo '92 did much to change the international image of Spain, we can almost certainly say that by helping to generate great improvements in highways and hotels, the Quincentenary did make Spain more attractive to foreign visitors and led to solid payoffs throughout the tourist sector.

Related to this is the expansion of Seville and Barcelona. Although some have complained that Expo '92 was not the kind of investment needed for the long-range development of Seville,[19] the considerable investment in infrastructure around these two cities has positioned both for a much stronger economic future. To the degree that capital projects such as roads, airports, and trains support both business and tourism, the residuals of 1992 seem to have been worth the effort. We have already mentioned the improvements in Barcelona, and those of Seville are no less impressive. The city has been given a face-lift one would not have thought possible, and yet its traditional character of being both carefree and mysterious to outsiders seems not to have changed a bit. Perhaps as a way of trying to find more uses for the facilities it now enjoys, Seville submitted a bid for the 2004 Olympics. Though unsuccessful, the city obviously wants to play on a larger stage. Though it remains vulnerable to economic problems, at least steps have been taken toward improving prospects for the future.

When the Quincentenary ended, unfinished educational and cultural projects were to be completed by the Cervantes Institute. This is a Spanish version of the British Council, Alliance Française, or Goethe Institute, that is, a network of cultural centers located in major foreign cities that foster the teaching of the Spanish language and promote Spanish culture. It was not established until after the Quincentenary, operates several centers worldwide, and has begun a solid development. However, whatever projects it inherited from 1992 received little public attention and appear to have been abandoned. This, indeed, has been the fate of the entire Quincentenary effort in Spain, which has simply evaporated. Spaniards seem indifferent and the nation cannot be said to have changed significantly because of its year on the world stage.

The balance, then, is ambiguous at best. The Quincentenary was a gargantuan expenditure of money for programs that have now largely disappeared. A few good things were done, especially in the cultural and tourist sectors, but opportunities to raise significant issues were mostly ignored as programs stayed within the safely conservative world of celebrating *hispanidad*. Most of all, far too much money was spent, especially on superficial activities that ended up appearing vacuous and lacking in substance. In many ways, it was a problem of excess, of having the luxury of doing almost anything imaginable, but for that reason, pursuing much that lacked real interest. To the degree that the Spanish Quincentenary did what it set out to do, it appeared to be a huge success. But considering how ephemeral and unimportant so much of it was, we have to conclude that it was also a major disappointment.

6

The Same and the Other

Italy and Latin America

The three countries we want to look at now—Italy, the Dominican Republic, and Mexico—followed their own paths but could not avoid the tensions and political issues that bedeviled Quincentenary planners everywhere. Each of course had its own way of dealing with them and each tells us something different about the problems of managing public programs in the contemporary world. Let's begin with the land where Christopher Columbus was born, Italy.

The shift of the Quincentenary away from the figure of Christopher Columbus was a problem for Italy. Ultimately, the Genoese navigator was the only real connection Italy had to 1992, and without him, the nation lacked a meaningful reason even to hold a commemoration. Whether one liked it or not, the Italian version of 1992 had no choice but to focus on Columbus. This is not to say that Italy wanted to avoid its famous native son or that it would have preferred to dedicate the Quincentenary to a different topic. Obviously, Christopher Columbus will always be an important figure in Italian history, and he was the logical point of reference for any national commemoration. But whereas other nations were moving away from Columbus, Italy had little option but to pursue the time-honored tradition of celebrating "the discoverer of America." Where other nations were facing controversial questions that made the Quincentenary difficult to manage but also interesting and important, Italy was obliged to stay within a traditional course whose parameters had been defined a hundred years earlier. Even when controversies arose about Columbus—one thinks of the landfall debate, for example, or the issue of his exploitation of Native Americans—they were outside the scope of Italy's focus, which seemed stuck with less interesting questions such as the navigator's childhood and upbringing. Christopher Columbus was on the defensive everywhere but in Italy, where planners tried to tell us that he was alive and well, as always.

Perhaps it was as a consequence of this situation that Italy ended up with a relatively modest commemoration that was limited in scope. Where Spain went in all directions at once and was able to declare almost anything Quincentenary-related, Italy concentrated almost exclusively on the era and places associated with the youthful Christopher Columbus, that is, the city of Genoa and its surrounding region of Liguria. This emphasis on the navigator and his time inevitably created a tendency to appear old-fashioned. Often it was difficult for officials to resist the temptation to refer to Columbus in terms such as "one of mankind's greatest heroes," or "a genius of vision whose daring shaped subsequent history." Such inflated rhetoric owed much to the influence of eminent Columbus scholar Paolo Emilio Taviani, who was a key organizing figure in the Italian commemoration. Taviani provided most of what passed for the intellectual framework within which the Italian 1992 commemoration was carried out, and though one cannot deny the importance of his scholarship and eloquence as a defender of Columbus's significance to Western culture, he represents an earlier period of historical understanding that felt a need to argue the grandeur of national heroes as a way of affirming the greatness of the nation itself. Taviani's leadership had many positive aspects, but he also brought to the Italian commemoration an air of anachronism that shielded it from controversies that could have helped it become more thought-provoking or appealing.[1]

Related to this were the complaints one frequently heard about the excessive localism of many events and their tendency to be focused almost exclusively in and around Genoa. Several surveys leading up to

1992 suggested that those living outside Liguria were mostly unaware of or indifferent to the Quincentenary. This was echoed by the frequent complaints of Ligurian officials against the indifference of Rome (that is, the central government) to their ongoing plans and needs. Perhaps communities everywhere are unconcerned about events affecting other cities, but the fact that Italians perceived the Quincentenary as almost exclusively Genoese shows how narrowly it was defined and how poorly those responsible for it reached the country as a whole—another point of sharp contrast with Spain, where Spaniards in every corner of their nation were inundated with Quincentenary talk to the point of complaining that they were not being allowed to think about anything else.

Before looking at the details of the commemoration, some additional issues should be mentioned. It is important to recognize that, notwithstanding official protestations to the contrary, decisions about programs were often influenced by political rivalries among the different parties. Where Spanish organizers were almost always members of the Spanish Socialist Party and therefore quite united in their vision, planning in Genoa and Liguria, for example, depended on a coalition of various political affiliations that rarely saw eye to eye. There was the further complication of rivalry between Genoese officials who were predominantly Social Democrats or Socialists, and a national commission dominated by the Christian Democrat Taviani. More often than not, relations between Rome and Genoa were cool, with each tending to go its own way. Taviani controlled the national commission and, though himself from Genoa, was disdainful toward certain Genoese leaders such as the Socialist president of Liguria, Rinaldo Magnani, a strong-willed politician who, as a former port worker and union organizer, had less formal education and was somewhat unpolished. Of course, relations were cordial in an official sense, and it was often stated with some pride that projects would never be hurt by political shifts as a result of elections. But this could not obscure an obvious antagonism between Genoa and Rome and among political parties that marked all Quincentenary planning. To be sure, such struggles are common in many places and must be considered standard in public programs, but they were especially evident in Italy even when they were not always obvious to outsiders.

Beyond issues of local politics, it should also be pointed out that no one anticipated the tumultuous political scandals that began to tear Italy apart after 1990 and eventually brought government after government to its knees in a crisis of public trust that is even yet not fully resolved. Italy revealed itself to be a nation where bribery and kickbacks had become an ordinary part of government life. *Tangentopoli*—"bribe city"—became the catchword of the time and inevitably infected the Quincentenary as much as it did every other aspect of Italian public events. But though Genoa too would be hit by scandal and though several officials would be put on trial, it was as if these were just further sordid details in a national paroxysm where every new day brought a still worse scandal, suicide, or politician fleeing into exile. *Tangentopoli* touched every city, whether Genoa, Rome, or many others, and it infected every political party, whether Christian Democrat on the right, Social Democrat in the center, or Socialist and others on the left. Through it all, the Quincentenary became tainted by scandal and yet also appears much like everything else: just another occasion for governmental dishonesty and a violation of public trust. Indeed, in certain instances such as the building of highways in parts of the country not linked to Genoa or the Quincentenary, the commemoration sometimes ended up as an unfairly blamed scapegoat because it served as a convenient funnel for kickbacks that might otherwise have taken a different route. In this sense, bribery was part of 1992, but it is not clear if it was worse for the Quincentenary than for other kinds of government contracts, or if it influenced the success or failure of what was attempted. *Tangentopoli* was a way of life, and as such was present nearly everywhere. On the other hand, precisely because many legal issues surrounding *tangentopoli* remain open, details are still unclear, not everything is known, and many issues may never be clarified. In the end, we need to be aware of it but we cannot know for certain exactly how much impact it had on the Quincentenary.[2]

Finally, during the 1980s one often read that different groups hoped to use 1992 in order to promote the latest Italian business interests, especially tourism. There was even some talk about trying to update the international image of the nation from the stereotype of a society emphasizing art and high fashion to a more businesslike world that is heavily committed to scientific research and advanced technology. Rather than fashion models and fancy racing cars, Italy hoped to spotlight its computer industry or advanced medical research. However, apart from a few efforts to promote Genoese tourism, this more contemporary approach never took hold. For example, when the Italian Trade Commission organized a commercial display called *Piazza Italia* that toured various American cities in 1992, it emphasized exactly the kinds of products that were supposed to be avoided: ladies' fashions, perfumes, and the latest in Italian design.[3] As usual, commercial interests promoted what they thought would sell, and attempts to refashion the national image were left for another day.

Italy formed its Comitato Nazionale per le celebrazzioni del V Centenario della Scoperta dell'America—National Commission for the Celebration of the Quincentenary of the Discovery of America—through presidential decree exactly ten years before the commemorative day itself, on October 12, 1982. The seventy commission members came from political, business, and academic backgrounds throughout the nation, and they were presided over by the president of the republic, who was usually represented by the minister of culture. In those early days, it was not yet politically incorrect to speak about celebrating the discovery of America, so this became the main charge of the commission. The decree also says that the commission "promotes and carries out cultural events and initiatives designed to provide knowledge about Christopher Columbus's achievements, and the cultural ambience which helped to conceive this enterprise, as well as the characteristics of the civilization which evolved from the discovery of America."[4] Three years later in 1985, parliament followed up with an act of law that fully authorized the commemoration while also allocating funds to carry out activities. By 1987, the commission had distributed $28.5 million for Quincentenary programs, and it would distribute another $75 million in the next three years. Assuming that spending continued roughly at this rate or that it increased somewhat through 1992, the commission may have disbursed a total of about $200 million. Unfortunately, there is no way to be certain because, for reasons no doubt linked to the delicate matter of *tangentopoli*, neither the commission nor the government has ever publicized its full ledger of expenditures.

Of the committees established within the commission, the thirteen-member "scientific" or scholarly committee quickly emerged as the most prestigious and effective. The key was Senator Taviani, who served as chair of the committee and therefore as de facto spokesperson for everything that would be undertaken. Taviani is a man of principle who was not seeking economic gain from the Quincentenary and who defended programs out of personal conviction, especially his long-standing idea that Christopher Columbus represented the best of the Italian Renaissance spirit. He would never be touched by the scandals that toppled other public figures, and he maintained his full prestige throughout the Quincentenary years. He also possessed a great deal of energy in spite of his advanced age. Whatever he said carried enormous weight and usually became policy, especially because he was vigorous enough to make sure that his wishes were carried out.

Governed by Taviani's vision and with the goal of celebrating Columbus and the Italian past, the national Quincentenary program sought to avoid commercialism by emphasizing scholarly activities such as publications, research, exhibitions, conferences, and archaeological restoration. Smaller amounts of money were reserved for student contests, scholarships, commemorative coins, and other activities associated with public education. The two major exceptions to this scholarly face were the committee's responsibility for developing the Italian exhibit at the Seville World's Fair and its overseeing of the *Gran Regata Colombo 92*. Concerning the former, *Palazzo Italia* was an exhibit of some 60,000 square feet focused on the theme of Italy and the sea from antiquity to the present. Costing several million dollars, it ran parallel to the theme of the Genoa Expo.

The *Gran Regata* was a widely publicized Quincentenary event that began in Italy and ended in New York. Fourteen tall ships and some eighty smaller sailing boats from all over the world gathered in Genoa in April 1992 prior to setting sail for the New World. During the week or more when these boats were present in Genoa harbor, several thousand local boats came to see what was going on, while thousands of spectators lined the shore. Once the main fleet departed for the high seas, it made brief stops in Cádiz, Lisbon, the Canary Islands, and then San Juan, Puerto Rico, where additional ships joined in until a flotilla of some 450 boats eventually made its way to New York on July 4, 1992. By this time, it was accompanied by the three Spanish-built reproductions of Columbus's Niña, Pinta, and Santa María, which of course attracted much of the attention. Still, Italy had been the point of departure for the effort, and government officials were present for the New York arrival.

The national commission's main project was a favorite idea of Taviani that will undoubtedly remain as one of the major Italian contributions to the 1992 commemoration, the publication of the *Nuova Raccolta Colombiana* or New Columbian Collection. Italy's celebration of the fourth centenary in 1892 had included publication of the first *Raccolta Colombiana*, produced in sixteen volumes from 1894 to 1896. These works long stood as important contributions to Columbian scholarship and are still sometimes cited in research. The 1992 national commission wanted to replicate that success by producing another, more up-to-date series that would take advantage of contemporary scholarship. Perhaps motivated by a desire to avoid confusing the names of the two collections, planners in 1985 were calling the contemporary project the *Nuovo Corpus Colombiano*. It would contain twenty-four volumes, eight more than the series of a century earlier. By 1988, the time-honored name had crept back in and people were speaking of the *Nuova Raccolta Colombiana*, which was now projected at twenty-seven volumes. The first three works were presented at a 1988 ceremony, and, as might be imagined, the initial volume was by Taviani: a new edition of Columbus's log that was coedited with the major Spanish Columbian scholar Consuelo Varela. As the Quincentenary came and went, the projected number of volumes was scaled back to the original twenty-four works of which more than twenty eventually became available. In 1991, the Italian commission reached agreement with Ohio State University in Columbus, Ohio, to translate twelve of the volumes into English. The commission also shared with the Spanish State Society and the American NEH the cost of publishing *The Repertorium Columbianum*, a series of eleven important texts from the early discovery period edited by prominent scholars under the auspices of the University of California at Los Angeles.[5]

Because the emphasis of the national commission was so strongly oriented to scholarly activities, the number of conferences and exhibitions it supported in the years leading up to 1992 ran into the hundreds, nearly all of them focused on demonstrating the importance of Columbus and Italian culture in early modern history. The commission also concentrated on architectural restoration, notably of important buildings located in the historic center of Genoa, with a few in other locations. In Genoa, the commission made certain that the house of Columbus was restored by 1985, making it among the earliest Quincentenary projects. This was soon followed by work on San Giovanni di Pré, an important medieval building that had once served as a lodge for an order of knights, then as a hospital, and now functions as a public exhibition site. Additional restorations were conducted at other important historic buildings such as the cloister of San Lorenzo, the facade of the Palazzo Tursi, and the Porta Sant' Andrea. All are associated with the time of Columbus and their restoration was part of a general face-lift given Genoa throughout the 1980s. Also given much publicity was the restoration of three highly prized, eighteenth-century silver bowls with depictions of Christopher Columbus. They are located in the Palazzo Spinola of Genoa. A notable effort outside Genoa was the restoration of the cathedral in Santo Domingo, a collaborative effort funded by Italy, Spain, the Dominicans, and various international organizations.

Finally, we can mention that because of concern among Italian-Americans in the United States that the Quincentenary was being dominated by Hispanics, the Washington-based National Italian-American Foundation (NIAF) signed a 1988 agreement with the Italian national commission to cooperate in lobbying for Italian interests among the American government and public. NIAF publications of the period suggest that this came down to promoting American tourism to Italy.[6] Later, in October 1991, NIAF sponsored a reception on Capitol Hill in honor of Senator Taviani, who formally presented his new book, *Columbus, The Great Adventure*.

With the possible exception of the *Nuova Raccolta Colombiana*, projects of the national commission tended to be less important, or at least less spectacular, than those mounted directly by Genoa and Liguria. The local-regional coalition in Genoa had about $830 million to spend on 1992, which was four times as much as the national commission. Since much of the latter's funds were spent there too, Italian Quincentenary efforts centered on a single location more than in any other nation. Following the familiar pattern of linking desirable "residuals" to mega-events—and consciously imitating redevelopment planners in Baltimore and other waterfront cities—Genoese officialdom used the Quincentenary to launch an ambitious program of urban and economic renewal to overcome years of decline and neglect. In this sense, not only were Genoese efforts more ambitious than elsewhere in Italy, but they also had a lot more at stake and faced many more challenges.

Genoa is often called the "secret city" of Italy, a once powerful hub of banking, shipping, and industrial activity that has recently come upon difficult economic times. Long one of the most bustling Mediterranean seaports, the city was once an essential stop on the Grand Tour of eighteenth-century European aristocrats and later served as a major stopover for both luxury liners and freighters carrying goods for all of northern Italy. Nowadays, middle-class tourists flock to the Riviera beaches that extend east and west of the city, but they bypass Genoa's medieval and Renaissance monuments for those of Venice, Florence, and Rome. Passenger liners have largely disappeared and freighters move goods in containers requiring large mechanized docks. These have had to be built over the last thirty years toward the outer limits of the city. This has left the older docks and port in the center of the city run-down, unused, or in a state of abandonment.

In addition, strong working-class organizations that originated in Genoa's vigorous industrial and shipping development of the late nineteenth and early twentieth centuries have tended to prevent the modernization of older factories and industrial plants. As a result, many have fallen into disrepair, and businesses based on more recent technology have preferred to become established elsewhere. It was said that more than 20,000 jobs were lost over the twenty years preceding the Quincentenary as the city struggled unsuccessfully to adapt to changing conditions. Prosperity remains of course, but it is much less widespread than in the past and has become tempered by an uneasy sense that Genoa is a site of decayed grandeur. Indeed, until well into the 1980s several buildings damaged during World War II sat untouched and needing repair. In spite of its illustrious past and many possibilities for the future, it was often suggested in recent years that the city was unable to stop a seemingly inevitable slide into decay. To the extent that Quincentenary planners during the 1980s amounted to a league of distressed cities—and this label applied with some justice though for different reasons to places as diverse as Barcelona, Seville, Santo Domingo, Columbus, Chicago, and Baltimore—Genoa was one of the most distressed. At the same time, it was also one that had the great potential for residuals that would endure long after the excitement of 1992's megaevents had faded from view.

Because Genoa's former glories stretch directly into the Middle Ages, the city possesses an important and well-preserved medieval neighborhood, the so-called *centro storico* or historic center, sitting adjacent to the largely dilapidated older part of the waterfront. This historic center is truly an architectural and archaeological treasure containing many important monuments, not least what is left of the house where Christopher Columbus is said to have been born. On the other hand, as hard times overtook the city during the last few decades, the historic center fell into disrepair and was gradually taken over by less desirable elements such as drug dealers, prostitutes, and displaced or impoverished immigrants from northern Africa. By the 1970s and 1980s, the medieval core of Genoa had come to be perceived as an unsafe haven for crime. This in combination with the city's somewhat isolated location in Italy made Genoa less attractive to tourists, and it was excluded from the usual itineraries of visitors to Italy. Even the hotels were insufficient because the local leadership had never sought large numbers of visitors and indeed had managed to channel Riviera tourists across the city without stopping by means of a raised highway—*La Sopraelevata*—built along the waterfront and separating the historic center from the old port. Thus when planners turned to the task of restoring Genoa to tourist maps, they faced the problem of historic zones that were not only crumbling but that were effectively cut off from—although within sight of—each other.

This was the context that made local planners turn to the 1992 Quincentenary as a way of transforming the local economy by shifting emphasis away from the traditional manufacturing and shipping base toward a new tourist industry. Genoa would move toward postmodern capitalist enterprise even as its traditional charms were enhanced. Planners believed that the key to accomplishing this was a revitalization of the historic center by cleaning out the undesirable elements and making the place safe for citizens and tourists. No less importantly, buildings would need to be restored and the old port area would have to be recreated into something resembling Baltimore's made-over waterfront. In effect, 1992 would become a pretext for the revitalization of the ancient city core.

In 1984, a group of prominent local citizens led by Carlo Perrone, publisher of the local newspaper (revealingly titled *Il Sècolo XIX*), called for a program of urban renewal focused around the upcoming 1992 celebration. Perrone's goal was to establish a private corporation of local businessmen who would take responsibility for the commemoration. This quickly ran afoul of local authorities, who did not want their thunder stolen by businessmen. The city and regional governments quickly organized a special local commission called Ente Colombo '92, representing the Chamber of Commerce, Port Authority, and city, provincial, and regional governments. Perrone was left with no choice but to let them have their way. Subsequently, whenever his newspaper criticized mistakes in the commission's planning or program implementation, it was suggested that Perrone was showing his resentment at having been shunted aside.

The 1992 event on which redevelopment activities hinged was Colombo '92, usually called the Genoa Expo, a specialized international exposition that was officially authorized by the Bureau of International Expositions in 1986. Focused on the theme of "Christopher Columbus: Ships and the Sea," the Genoa Expo was open for only three months, from May 15 through August 15, 1992. This brief period of time was said to be a result of pressure from Spain, which agreed to participate in the Genoa fair only on condition that competition with the Seville

World's Fair be kept to a minimum. Thus, the fair ended in mid-August, long before the commemorative day of October 12 and at the height of the vacation period when the largest crowds could have been expected to attend. There is little question that this time limitation blunted the final attendance figures, which were disappointingly low. Planners hoped to attract 4 million visitors or approximately 43,000 per day (tickets cost the equivalent of twenty dollars), but though final figures were never officially announced, attendance appears not to have come even close to that, perhaps standing at about 43,000 a day.

In addition to the limitation on the number of days the fair was open, funding delays from Rome became serious obstacles to early progress in construction and advertising. Over and over again, officials complained about not receiving promised funds and about delays in authorizing construction. Eventually, Rome sent all the promised money, but Expo would never be able to overcome images of ineptitude and bad planning. Indeed, as late as 1991, the city was rife with rumors that the fair would not open on time. There were also problems in finding a target audience. Promotional efforts were first focused on North America and later, after 1990, on Europe. In the end, however, Colombo '92 remained a mostly local and national event seen by relatively few international visitors.

True to the purpose of local planners, the fair itself was located on the waterfront, in the very heart of the old medieval port adjoining the *centro storico*. Inspired by Baltimore's Inner Harbor redevelopment, the idea was to transform an area of some twelve acres or five hectares into a modern and lively cultural center. By installing clean and safe facilities for educational, cultural, and recreational activities as well as for business conventions, new uses were sought for buildings that had been sitting unused or in disrepair. The designer was the well-known Genoese architect Renzo Piano, who said he was seeking permanent change on the waterfront while hoping to avoid the superficiality and mindlessness that often characterize public fairs. In this sense, a substantial portion of activities prior to and during 1992 was dedicated to conferences and lectures on historical themes. These did not attract much public attention but they did give to the whole an air of scholarly seriousness.

The Expo site extended from the Molo Vecchio or Old Wharf and moved west over two piers (called the Ponte Embriaco and the Ponte Spinola) to a third one, the Darsena, several hundred meters beyond. On the Old Wharf was a group of large, nondescript buildings from the nineteenth century, called the Cotton Warehouse (Magazzini del Cotone), which was transformed into a somewhat small but modern convention center with a 1,500-seat theater or viewing area. Here is where many of the scholarly and other conferences were held. The center is operational today but is underutilized.

The pier closest to the old dock area, the Ponte Embriaco, became the location of a decorative construction called Il Grande Bigo. This was a modern assemblage of booms reaching into the sky as if forming a cluster of ships' masts for sails. One of the booms had a carriage that carried spectators into the air for viewing the port. The next pier, Ponte Spinola, was the location of the Italian Pavilion. It was constructed in two parts, one a large aquarium built into the sea, which was announced as the largest in Europe, and the other a boat set up as a floating exhibit on Italy's maritime past. The aquarium was not finished by the opening of the Expo, though it did open later and, similar to its counterpart in Baltimore, became quite popular.

Several buildings along the adjacent waterfront were renovated to accommodate the different national pavilions and exhibitions. Subsequently, the spaces have been used by local businesses and for other activities, including a gym, a day care center, the local tourist office, several restaurants, and so forth. Close by these buildings, architect Piano created a Plaza of Festivities with a reflecting pool and a thousand-seat open-air theater. This became a center for performances at the fair.[7]

One of the more difficult problems faced by fair planners was encouraging other nations to participate. By 1988, only five nations had signed on: Argentina, Colombia, Ecuador, Uruguay, and Spain. Local newspapers complained bitterly that delays in naming a general commissioner for the fair were making the city look foolish and unorganized. Finally, in 1990 a seventy-six-year-old local academic, Alberto Bemporad, was appointed commissioner. Clearly, he was a compromise candidate who would not offend anyone and whose age made it unlikely he would use his position to seek important office after the fair was over. As a result of Bemporad's efforts, many additional nations were quickly signed on. Less wealthy countries were subsidized to the tune of some $12 million, and eventually, a total of thirty-seven nations and five international organizations participated. These included the United States, most European nations, a large number of Latin American countries, Japan, China, Korea, and others.

As if the many construction delays and uncertainties about the commissioner were not enough, the most controversial part of the Genoa Expo was undoubtedly Piazza Caricamento. This is a large square adjacent to the Expo site under which planners sought to construct an underpass so that traffic would be diverted out of the square and the open space would remain for pedestrians. Unfortunately, the project was plagued with problems from the start. Soon after beginning construction, workers found remains of early dock construction that suggested they had come across the original port from before the time of Columbus. This led several local groups to advocate stopping all construction until the site could be assessed for its archaeological importance. Planners became worried, however, that delays would prevent completion of the underpass by 1992, so just as at La Cartuja in Seville, they overrode all objections and pushed forward, much to the chagrin of local scholars.[8] Then, when the underpass was finished, it was discovered that an error in design made it useless for larger vehicles such as buses and trucks, which therefore had to proceed through Piazza Caricamento. The chain of misfortunes reached its peak in September 1992, when heavy rains flooded the underpass and it had to be closed. There ensued a great hue and cry over the incompetence that had led to so many problems, but no one had easy solutions. Piazza Caricamento had to be reconstructed following the Genoa Expo, and it reopened only in September 1996.

Though given many highly positive reviews for the tastefulness of its presentation and the laudable attempt to become a permanent source of renewal for the older part of the city, the truth is that from the beginning, Colombo '92 was rowing upstream against the Spanish surge of 1992 and never was able to attract enough interest to offset the attention being directed toward Seville. Moreover, Colombo '92 alone could never have been enough to solve the problem of safety and cleanliness in the historic center or to shift the local economy toward tourism. The key to this objective was the *centro storico*. If tourists were to be welcomed to the city, the *centro storico* needed to be cleaned up and made safe for sightseers. Buildings throughout the neighborhood would have to be restored, and residences would have to be renewed so that local citizens would consider living there. It was even speculated that the attractiveness of living in a restored historic core might foster the growth of high-income professional services in Genoa, serving not only that city but also the booming economy of inland Milan, whose dreary winter climate is one of the many causes of satisfaction the Genoese feel about living where they do. But whereas some incentives for the reconstruction of apartment buildings were in fact developed, relatively few buildings were completed, and gentrification of the area was not fully successful.

One of the important promotional ideas for the historic center was that of a "Columbus Walk." Tourists would start at the Columbus House and stroll through the many winding streets on an itinerary that would let them see the main architectural monuments. Gradually, they would make their way to the waterfront where they could enter the Expo site. If this was to be successful, streets needed to become safe and several dilapidated buildings would have to be restored. The elevated highway would also need to be dealt with, something that did not happen. Restoration efforts concentrated instead on two especially important historic buildings—both of great symbolic importance to the Genoese but neither located so as to have a transforming effect on the crumbling *centro storico*. These were the Opera Carlo Felice, a nineteenth-century opera house that had stood in semi-ruinous condition since being bombed in World War II, and the Palazzo Ducale or Doge's Palace, which was one of the city's great Renaissance architectural monuments. Actually, restoration had begun on the Doge's Palace in the 1970s, long before the Quincentenary effort, but 1992 provided the incentive and money to complete the goal of turning the building into a museum and cultural center. The palace was reopened on May 17, 1992, in time to hold several major exhibits during the quincentennial year. As for the Opera Carlo Felice, work on it was completed earlier, in 1989, and today it functions as a somewhat underutilized but highly regarded opera house.

Among several other restorations that were undertaken in the period, that of Saint Ignatius is worth mentioning. This is an old church in the historic center that was targeted for restoration and conversion into the home of the state archives. The idea was to make it the main location for historical documents of Genoa and Liguria so that it would become an important research area for those studying Christopher Columbus. Though more than $1.5 million was spent on the project up through 1992 and though many papers were transported there, problems with the restoration made the building unusable. As a result, the papers had to be removed for safe storage and further work undertaken. Local wags thought that the situation deserved investigation for questions about the quality of work and possible links with *tangentopoli*. The full story about St. Ignatius has yet to be told.

In the end the Quincentenary did not have the full effect of transforming Genoa. To be sure, the historic center is today far more attractive than it was, but many streets are still unsafe, and the area has not been fully reclaimed for the modern city. Discussions have taken place about converting parts of the Expo site to a research park, but as in the case of Seville, this has not happened, and much of what is there remains underutilized. Nor is the city yet a main tourist attraction. Overall, 1992 was a good but not entirely successful beginning to a renewal project that will take more time, money, and effort.

So then, what do we make of the Italian Quincentenary commemoration? On the one hand, we can say that by seeking to focus mostly on traditional topics and activities without overwhelming publicity, efforts in Italy remained modest but also dignified, not the kind of hyped-up media events one often saw in Spain or even in the United States. On the other hand, this uncontroversial emphasis made the Italian Quincentenary commemoration appear old-fashioned and tired, as if lacking in spirit or verve. This probably explains why the public largely overlooked it. Whereas one applauds the fact that Italian planners avoided generating the resentment and anger found in Spain, it is equally true that, as elsewhere, most of what happened was received without enthusiasm, ended up being ephemeral, and has largely been forgotten. Columbus may still be alive in Italy, but it is clear that very few people care.

Would spending more money have generated the excitement planners wanted? Was the problem that Italy spent only the paltry sum of a billion dollars on its commemoration? In fact, the issue is less one of money than the oft-noted decline of the mega-event. Other than on television, public programs struggle to reach large audiences even if trivial or promoted with the most crass commercialism. In this light, maybe Italy took the smarter route through the Quincentenary by not trying to do too much and therefore not suffering the extremes of disappointment seen elsewhere.

In Latin America, most quincentennial projects dealt with architectural restoration, archaeological and historical research, educational programs, and artistic exhibitions of various kinds, few of which directly engendered debates about the anniversary's meaning as a whole. This means that a survey of every Latin American nation would quickly become little more than a laundry list of similar activities. Moreover, what is not done during a commemoration may be just as important as what is done, so that we need to go deeper than merely providing lists of projects. Rather than saying a little about a lot of countries, we have thought it would be better to concentrate on a few significant cases that can be looked at more closely. Several are possible, including Colombia, Costa Rica, and perhaps Peru, all of which had active national commissions. Two nations, however, seem especially interesting because they were so different from one another and thereby offer a glimpse into the range of ideas and attitudes that governed the Quincentenary in Latin America. These countries are the Dominican Republic and Mexico. Both Mexico and the Dominican Republic could claim major roles in 1992 if they chose. The Dominican Republic was discovered and colonized by Christopher Columbus and therefore stands as the first European society in the New World. Mexico developed from the mingling of Spanish and indigenous cultures and is therefore a preeminent example of the idea of "encounter" that came to be so central to the 1992 commemoration. Indeed, it was Mexico that originally proposed the term "encounter" as an antidote to "discovery," so that the nation obviously had a good grasp of the tenor and directions of the Quincentenary from long before it started.

And yet, two nations could hardly have been more different in their approach to 1992. In spite of—or perhaps because of—being a relatively small country with limited resources, the Dominican Republic sought to attract attention by throwing itself into the commemoration with energy and commitment, quickly becoming the major Quincentenary player in Latin America. Mexico, in contrast, possessed many more resources and possibilities but paradoxically avoided high-profile activities and gradually closed down its participation as 1992 drew nearer. To explore and understand this difference shows the range of issues provoked by the Quincentenary in the Latin American context.

Let us begin by noting that the historical and cultural context of Latin America inevitably implied a more negative, or at least a more ambiguous, understanding of the 1992 commemoration than in Europe or North America. Where people in the United States experienced the Quincentenary as a basic exposure to issues whose complexity they had rarely even thought about, Latin Americans have always lived with debates about the meaning of the New World and are therefore well aware of the ambiguities associated with 1492. Latin America, after all, *is* a product of the Spanish conquest of America. Controversies about discovery, invasion, and encounter, not to mention several other theories about the arrival of Europeans in the New World, are well known throughout the continent and really originate there.[9] This means that differences of opinion quickly become identified with political tendencies and movements. For example, it would not be an exaggeration to say that most Latin American intellectuals, especially those of leftist persuasion (which is by far the vast majority), viewed the Quincentenary either as a trivial event unworthy of serious consideration, a public relations venture of the Spanish government, the fraudulent attempt of conservative groups to celebrate their dominance of Latin American history, or all three of these at once. For many, the Quincentenary implied the specter of neocolonialism. That is, the Spanish dominance of the event suggested that Europe was seeking to renew its competition with the United States for economic and cultural influence in Latin America. In such a context, the continent was destined to be but the pawn in a contest between two giants who would inevitably perpetuate its subaltern position because neither was prepared to acknowledge the difference or *otherness* of Latin American society.[10] Obviously, many Latin Americans wanted nothing to do with the commemoration.

Then too, the years leading up to the Quincentenary, which is to say the decade of the 1980s, were among the most difficult in Latin America from an economic point of view, and this made any kind of celebration problematic, to say the least. Called "the lost decade" by agencies such as the Inter-American Development Bank,[11] the period saw a slow recovery of democracy after a generation of repressive dictatorships, but it was also a time of major recession that worsened Latin America's massive foreign debt while provoking increased economic hardship and a sharp rise in poverty. In May 1985, the foreign debt of Latin America stood at $360 billion with no relief in sight.[12] Not only were many nations hardly able to meet interest payments, but most could not realistically foresee ever paying off their debt. Then, toward the end of the decade, after years of tension provoked by such situations as the trials of Argentine generals, Colombian drug trafficking, a civil war in El Salvador, and a U.S. trade embargo against the Sandinista government of Nicaragua, the collapse of European communism in 1989 led to widespread fears that the rich nations of the world would now concentrate on saving Russia and Eastern Europe while turning their backs on the seemingly intractable problems of Latin America—though, of course, the rich nations had never done much for Latin America anyway. In his introduction to *The Buried Mirror*, Carlos Fuentes tried to express the uneasiness this situation produced for the Quincentenary:

> Five hundred years after Columbus, we are being asked to celebrate the quincentennial of his voyage—undoubtedly one of the great events of human history, a turn in events that heralded the arrival of the modern age. But many of us in the Spanish-speaking parts of the Americas wonder whether there is anything to celebrate.
>
> A glance at the Latin American republics would lead us to reply in the negative. Whether in Caracas or in Mexico City, in Lima or

in Buenos Aires, the fifth centennial of the "discovery of America" finds us in a state of deep, deep crisis.[13]

The Dominican Republic is a small Caribbean nation of about 7 million people located on *Isla Española* or simply *La Española*, "Spanish Island," traditionally anglicized as Hispaniola. After landing there in 1492, Columbus returned the following year on his second voyage with seventeen ships in order to establish the first European colony. Finding no one alive at La Navidad, which was the small settlement in present-day Haiti where he had left the crew of the Santa María the previous year, he moved east to a site he named Isabela, after the queen of Spain. A small colony was established with houses, storage area, church, and cultivated lands. Garrisons were set up at several locations in the interior, and the conquest of the island was begun. Within a few years, however, Isabela was abandoned and everything was moved to the south coast of the island at the site of present-day Santo Domingo. For nearly half a century, the new location became an important Spanish base from which the invasion of the rest of the New World was launched. Then, by about 1540, all the natives had died, the small deposits of gold found on the island had been exhausted, and the discovery of greater wealth in Mexico had led the Spanish government to shift its emphasis toward the mainland. Gradually, Santo Domingo became a forgotten backwater of empire that would suffer periodic foreign invasions and a perpetual suspicion that it was unimportant. Still today, the nation struggles for recognition and a sense of its identity beside the traditionally more prosperous and prestigious environments of Cuba and Puerto Rico.

And yet, as a result of that early Spanish settlement, the Dominican Republic can legitimately lay claim to many kinds of New World "firsts": the first European settlement (at Isabela), the first Catholic mass (also at Isabela), the first city (the Colonial Zone of Santo Domingo), the first cathedral (that of Santo Domingo), the first university, and several others. Of course, certain other "firsts" less compatible with glorifying the past were also part of the early colonial experience: the first massacres of Indians, the first cases of syphilis, the first epidemics of smallpox and influenza, the first black African slaves, and the first destruction of New World flora and fauna. While they don't talk about these very much, Dominicans do take pride in the fact that the first denunciations of the harsh treatment of the natives were issued on the island. In addition, Dominicans maintain a strong though disputed claim that the remains of Christopher Columbus are buried there. This, along with the respectable "firsts," has always been a source of great pride for a very conservative, traditionalist nation that thinks of itself as what is variously called the Source (*Solar*), Cradle (*Cuna*), or Threshold (*Umbral*) of America. Thus, it was logical for the country to approach 1992 as a way of showing respect for its colonial past while taking advantage of opportunities to enhance historic sites and monuments.

A national commission for the Quincentenary was first named in 1979 during the presidency of Antonio Guzmán (1978–82); it functioned in several early events under Guzmán and his successor, Salvador Jorge Blanco (1982–86). These included, for example, the development of Plan Carimos, an OAS-sponsored project in architectural restoration that was announced in 1982 and remained important throughout the period leading up to the Quincentenary. Other early activities included participating in the annual meetings of the Ibero-American Conference of National Quincentenary Commissions convened by Spain every year for the purpose of setting the 1992 agenda. The second of these meetings was held in Santo Domingo in July 1984. On October 12 of the same year, Pope John Paul II visited the city with much fanfare to launch the official Quincentenary period.

Shortly after Joaquín Balaguer, the newly elected conservative president, took office in 1986, the Dominican commission was reorganized.[14] If there had been any uncertainty about the commission's orientation up to this point, it disappeared under the strongly traditionalist direction Balaguer now gave it. Ensuring a dominant role for the Roman Catholic Church, he appointed the archbishop of Santo Domingo president of the commission and drew several of the remaining eleven members from the clergy and the ranks of prominent Catholic laymen. The commission also carried a significant, new title that proudly displayed its Catholic connections: Comisión Dominicana Permanente para la Celebración del Quinto Centenario del Descubrimiento y Evangelización de América (Permanent Dominican commission for the celebration of the Quincentenary of the discovery and evangelization of America). That is, not only did the Dominican commission accept the notions of "celebration" and "discovery" emanating from Spain but questioned elsewhere in Quincentenary circles, but it was the only national group to include the word "evangelization" in its title. The longstanding Catholic idea that the conversion of native peoples to Christianity was one of the great achievements of the conquest was now integral to planning and reflected the close alliance between Church and state in the commemoration.

The idea of evangelization provoked significant disagreements with Mexico in a variety of settings, notably at the above-mentioned 1984 Santo Domingo meeting of the Ibero-American Conference of National Quincentenary Commissions. Representatives of Mexico—including, presumably, the first general coordinator of the Mexican national commission, the eminent indigenist scholar Miguel León-Portilla—argued that the missionary work of the Church contributed to the disruption of native cultures and should not be given such prominence during the Quincentenary. León-Portilla instead favored a word that would soon enjoy great fortune, "encounter," which he believed conveyed greater respect toward Native Americans. At this still early date, the eventual impact of the word was not yet visible but it did begin to have an effect. The Dominicans responded by continuing to defend evangelization, but they made it clear that they felt uncomfortable with the reactionary role into which they feared they were being cast. They wanted it understood that they too respected native Americans, for the Church had been the first to raise its voice in defense of the Indian.[15]

The misgivings associated with these incidents no doubt help explain why one of the first public conferences developed by the Dominican national commission was "First Encounter of Caribbean Indians," a conference held in Santo Domingo in September 1988 and cosponsored with the InterAmerican Indian Institute of Mexico City. Obviously, the commission did not want to appear out of touch with the indigenist turn taken by the Quincentenary, which by this time was becoming much more clear. Interestingly, this sensitivity did not reflect an effort to stay in touch with local constituencies, for there are no Native Americans in the Dominican Republic and no need to pacify indigenist groups.[16] Rather, it was the Catholic elite's desire to appear open to other tendencies. Ultimately, the conservatism of the Dominican approach was more obviously Roman Catholic than most other Hispanic countries would have preferred, but it was consistent with a local tradition of tolerance toward difference and was no more reactionary than many other aspects of this conservative society. At the same time, Mexico was obviously more in touch with our era's concern to open the Quincentenary to the non-European peoples who were often its victims.

Balaguer himself, like other Quincentenary planners in Spain and the United States, appears to have given less thought to meanings than to residuals. Throughout a long political career in the Dominican Republic, he had always emphasized construction projects as a way of creating jobs and encouraging public confidence that the state is committed to progress and development. Cynics had long complained that most of the construction he proposed was unnecessary and too expensive, especially for a small, third world nation. On taking office in 1986, he launched his usual building program and he also made it clear that he wanted to increase tourism as a means of supplying much needed foreign exchange. This would mean not only building hotels and infrastructure but also using the Quincentenary as an excuse to enhance historic sites, create new attractions, and lure to the island those tourists who want to combine time on the beach with visits to museums and monuments. Though popular with Europeans, the Dominican Republic is not a favorite vacation spot for American tourists, who may be avoiding the less modern amenities of many Dominican sites. Balaguer's goal was to change this situation by using the commemoration as a means of making the nation more attractive.

The first, largest, and undoubtedly most controversial quincentennial project was consistent with Balaguer's way of thinking, the Faro a Colón or Columbus Lighthouse. Initially proposed in the mid-nineteenth century and designed during an international contest in 1923, the Columbus Lighthouse had been put off many times before because it was considered too costly and, in truth, not very attractive. Ultimately, it is a good example of the kind of exaggerated or oversized monument once constructed by totalitarian governments as a sign of their power. For Balaguer, it seems to have been an obsession of many years' duration while appearing as a way to carry out what he believed would be the most spectacular quincentennial project in the world. When he returned to power in 1986, he announced plans to complete the lighthouse by 1992.

And complete it he did. Costing $40 million, the Columbus Lighthouse is a huge, recumbent cross (or sword, an unintentional second symbol attaching to it that fits the conquest) stretching several city blocks and containing a bright light or beacon in the shape of a cross intended to proclaim that here, in Santo Domingo, began the great Christianizing and civilizing enterprise of the Indies. The interior contains museum space and a shrine for the remains of Christopher Columbus, whose mausoleum was transferred from the cathedral. Evidently, then, the Columbus Lighthouse invokes the symbols of discovery and Christianity that belong to an earlier era, and it reinforces the sense that the Dominican commemoration was profoundly anachronistic. This, along with its exorbitant cost and the fact that 50,000 people had to be removed from their homes in order to build it, explains why the lighthouse ended up being extremely controversial. How could a poor nation with debts reaching into the billions of dollars invest an additional $40 million into such an unattractive, out-of-date structure? Indeed, if one realizes that Balaguer is blind and that the Dominican Republic has to endure several hours a day without electricity because the government has failed to build enough electric generating stations, the real symbolism of the lighthouse becomes apparent. While it was still under construction several years ago, Alastair Reid reported that Dominican peasants—the same ones who have been enduring unjust governments for centuries—would joke sarcastically that as soon as the lighthouse would be turned on, it would use up all the electricity on the island, and the rest of the lights would go out.[17] Actually, the pope turned it on in October 1992, but the ceremony had to be moved up a few days before the target day of October 12 in order to avoid protests. Balaguer got his lighthouse, but the nation continued to be victimized by a president who failed to see what his citizens really needed.

The remaining Quincentenary projects in the Dominican Republic were far less controversial and in general involved archaeological and historic restoration. Three major projects were undertaken, all of them carrying a certain prestige in Dominican circles: restoration of the Colonial Zone of Santo Domingo, restoration of the cathedral (which is in the Colonial Zone and is therefore part of the same effort), and reconstruction of the Isabela settlement on the north coast. Smaller restorations were initiated at the garrisons or settlements of Vega Vieja, Pueblo Viejo de Azua, and New Isabela.

To our knowledge, the budget for these and other activities was never made public. On the other hand, with all the money that was going to the Columbus Lighthouse, funds were sufficiently scarce that assistance was sought from foreign sources. Spain contributed to the restoration of the cathedral, and Italy, which also helped with the cathedral, promised to build a road from Puerto Plata to Isabela. The Organization of American States provided funds for the Isabela restoration under the framework of Plan Carimos, the OAS project mentioned earlier. Work at Isabela proceeded slowly, partly because questions were continually raised about whether the location was correct, and partly because, just prior to a site visit many years earlier by the dictator Trujillo, a bulldozer that was trying to clean up the place caused major damage that made it difficult to restore. In contrast to this, the restoration of the Colonial Zone and cathedral had made enough progress by 1988 that the Dominican commission sought to include the area on the World Heritage List of UNESCO. This was subsequently approved in 1991. The beauty of the Colonial Zone is indeed impressive, and Santo Domingo has become a more attractive environment. In this domain, then, the Quincentenary seems to have been relatively successful. At the same time, it is not clear that the tourist sector significantly improved. Santo Domingo is not on the same coast as many of the most popular resorts, and American tourists still tend to prefer other Caribbean islands.[18]

In addition to the usual display of educational projects such as essay contests and exhibits, the Dominicans also hosted "a staggering array of international conferences, seminars, and public events."[19] Some of the gatherings were linked to quincentennial issues, but most functioned simply as annual meetings of various associations and so contributed to the goal of using 1992 to make Santo Domingo more important as a convention and tourist center.

Overall, then, the balance is somewhat ambiguous. On the one hand, restoration and similar projects were certainly legitimate and performed a useful function. On the other, little was done to educate the public in a new or changing vision of the world because those in control of the commemoration followed old-fashioned myths of discovery and evangelization that expressed, sustained, and perpetuated their values. One doubts that the Columbus Lighthouse has given the Dominican people a greater sense of national identity, but it has most assuredly succeeded in worsening the national debt. Its only virtue may have been to help make Dominicans more aware of the failures of Balaguer's policies, and to this degree it may have hastened his exit from public life after the 1994 elections. In the end, it will probably stand as a monument to the bad taste of the president's obsessions.

Mexico's circumstances were very different from those of the Dominican Republic. Where the latter is a small, relatively poor country that has always struggled to achieve a sense of identity, Mexico is a large nation of 80–85 million people with a strong national identity based on the idea of *mestizaje,* that is, the mixing of Spanish and Indian races. In Mexico, the concept of Indianness is central to national life, and pre-Columbian cultures are exalted as crucial to what it means to be Mexican. Much of this is pure myth, of course, because the link between the government and the original indigenous cultures is tenuous at best, and many present-day Indians are excluded from the life of the nation. Still, indigenist nationalism has had a substantial role in Mexican history, having developed as part of the break from Spanish colonial rule during the independence period in the early nineteenth century. Subsequently, it was canonized by peasant uprisings during the Revolution of 1910 and is now thoroughly entrenched as an essential element of Mexican society.[20]

Given this strongly pro-Indian tradition, Mexico had a natural opportunity to become a major player in the 1992 Quincentenary. If the peculiar trend of the commemoration was to give voice to Indians, no nation was better positioned to do so than the one most closely associated with indigenous perspectives. Moreover, we already saw that besides disputing the Dominican Republic's emphasis on evangelization, Mexico was the first to argue the idea of "encounter" as a governing concept for the Quincentenary. Indeed, by 1985, Mexico had convinced the Organization of American States to include the phrase *Encuentro de Dos Mundos*—Encounter of Two Worlds—in the title of its Quincentenary programming. Subsequently, this same phrase began to find its way into Spanish publications, no doubt because Spain was responding to Mexican pressures and did not want to appear old-fashioned or out of touch. From the earliest moment, then, Mexico was an eloquent defender of what would later become one of the most characteristic trends of the Quincentenary, the "vision of the vanquished" or perspective of Native Americans.

There is little doubt that this early Mexican position was deeply influenced by Miguel León-Portilla, one of the world's preeminent scholars on pre- and post-conquest Nahuatl or Aztec texts, and the first general coordinator of the Comisión Nacional de México Conmemorativa del Quinto Centenario del Encuentro de Dos Mundos, or National Commemorative Commission of Mexico for the Quincentenary of the Encounter of Two Worlds. The commission was officially established on April 30, 1985, by the government of Miguel de la Madrid, which also appointed nine other members. León-Portilla's illustrious career as a student and advocate of those whose cultures were devastated by the conquest made him both a logical spokesperson and a leader of considerable prestige. Note that not only did the commission's title emphasize "encounter" rather than "discovery," but it also spoke of a "commemoration" rather than a "celebration."

During these early years, several projects were announced that pointed to an enlightened understanding of the indigenist approach to New World history. For example, one of the first was undertaken in cooperation with the National Autonomous University of Mexico (UNAM) and involved analyzing history textbooks throughout Latin America. The goal was to improve the teaching of history in elementary and secondary schools by moving beyond Eurocentric interpretations and including better information on indigenous cultures. Another project was to encourage the publication of early indigenous texts, either in facsimile editions or in Spanish translations. In this context, one can also mention that in 1990, Pope John Paul II acknowledged the importance of the Quincentenary in Mexico by returning the *Badiano* manuscript to the nation. This is an important text on early medicine which had been held in the Vatican.

Archaeological restoration was often mentioned in Mexican Quincentenary programming, but it did not receive extraordinary attention. The problem is that though a huge number of pre-Columbian and colonial monuments still need attention, the nation already puts a great deal of emphasis on archaeological restoration, and the Quincentenary could not really have added much that was new or special. Archaeological research is really a permanent activity in Mexico, and 1992 was no more crucially important for it than any other year. Perhaps one reason for the subsequent fate of the Quincentenary in Mexico is that officials did not target one or more specific sites as a major 1992 project. Thus, unlike in all other Quincentenary environments, the commemoration could produce neither residuals nor the excitement associated with pursuing them.

A major goal mentioned early on by the national commission was to make Mexico a prominent international player in the 1992 commemoration. One way to do this was to make early and firm commitments to both Expo '92 in Seville and the Genoa Expo in Italy. The commission also took forceful early roles in the Ibero-American Conference of Latin American Commissions. Later, Mexico hosted the next to last meeting of the conference in Guadalajara in 1991, when for the first time the conference became a summit meeting of Latin American heads of state. However, the most successful international project was probably the spectacular art exhibit which opened in New York to lavish public attention in 1990–91. Called "From Toltec to Tamayo: Twenty Centuries of Mexican Art," the exhibit offered a window into the richness of Mexico's ancient and modern traditions and was the nation's most visible activity during the Quincentenary period.

Notwithstanding these accomplishments, the federal commission soon acquired a privately funded rival. This was FUNDICE (Fundación

Pro-Difusión del Medio Milenio en América), a private foundation in Mexico City that opposed what it believed was the nation's exclusive emphasis on indigenous or "pagan" issues. FUNDICE advocated a more Christian orientation and held several conferences over the years that sought to create consciousness about the importance of evangelization and the role of Christianity in saving native peoples. It also argued that the conquest was not as violent or destructive as some people, including León-Portilla, usually said. In the end, then, FUNDICE was a conservative group pursuing ideas not dissimilar from those of the Dominican Republic. Its ultimate impact is difficult to determine but may be obliquely present in the subsequent direction of the commission.

In the spring of 1988, Miguel León-Portilla resigned as general coordinator of the Mexican commission. This was prior to the election of President Carlos Salinas de Gortari and therefore was not a political change associated with a new government. Indeed, the new general coordinator, Leopoldo Zea, later said that the previous president had asked him to run the commission as early as November 1987, during a visit to Mexico of Spain's King Juan Carlos.[21] It is not far fetched to suspect that Spanish officials complained during their visit that León-Portilla's indigenism was excessive. There is no proof of this, but the subsequent direction of the commission supports such a contention.

Zea was a prominent philosopher and essayist on New World thought. It was certainly more than coincidental that, when he became general coordinator, the scholarly journal *Cuadernos Americanos* published several articles by him and others that gently marked their distance from León-Portilla for having taken too extremist a position in defending the idea of "encounter."[22] In these pieces, Zea insisted that "encounter" remained valid and that no one deserved greater respect than León-Portilla. But a certain polemical ambience had surrounded the commission up to that point, he added, and a new, more cordial approach was needed. There should be room for all, he argued. Spain had been able to accommodate the term "encounter" in addition to "discovery," so why should Mexico not accept "discovery" in addition to "encounter"? Indeed, Christopher Columbus did accomplish many important discoveries and his voyages did lead to an encounter between Europeans and Indians. Additionally, the arrival of Europeans in the New World had created other effects also, starting with Zea's pet theory of an *encubrimiento*. That is, because America was so totally new, Europeans tended to fit their experiences into preexisting categories, thereby *covering over* the New World they were finding. The historical issue of America was to become "uncovered," so to speak, to be experienced as it really is, rather than through a European lens. This is an ongoing venture that has never been fully accomplished, and the Quincentenary could be an opportunity to help advance it.[23]

Zea and his collaborators did not say that they wanted to change the projects of the commission, and it is clear that they preferred not to interfere with ongoing activities. Their goal was simply to project a more conciliatory image, as if they believed that León-Portilla had hurt Mexico's reputation by a perhaps too-strenuous argument in favor of Indians. At the same time, this inevitably led to an impression that efforts now became less vigorous, as if this calmer approach was gradually turning into a withdrawal. Ironically, as the rest of the world began to pick up on Mexico's idea of "encounter," the nation itself moved in the opposite direction toward more traditional ideas such as "discovery." At the same time, it lost much of its will for a commemoration. Spain was making its voice heard in Mexican circles, but the price was a growing detachment or indifference by Mexico.

This trend was carried further in 1990 when Zea himself was replaced as general coordinator of the national commission by the prominent historian Enrique Florescano, who began to argue a decidedly non-Indian perspective for the Quincentenary. In a 1991 interview published in his own journal, *Nexos,* Florescano offered that Mexico's pro-Indian tradition had "amputated the colonial period from our history" while creating an idealized vision of the Indian that was both historically inaccurate and the origin of a national identity crisis.[24] He was alluding here to the fact that, because Mexico's *mestizo* tradition was born in the independence or anticolonial period, it had resulted in a certain historic aloofness from Spain that contrasted sharply with the strong ties one found between Spain and the Dominican Republic. He believed that such a situation had tended to make Mexico's colonial history less well studied than either the pre-Columbian or the postindependence periods, while at the same time contributing to the stereotyping of both Spaniards and Indians. Some of the anti-Spanish feeling had declined in the contemporary period, Florescano believed, especially because the many exiles who came to Mexico from the Spanish Civil War in 1939 had created a more appropriate understanding of the former colonial motherland. With this decline of stereotypes about Spain, the Quincentenary was coming at a propitious moment to reevaluate the colonial period, question national myths, and reach a less contradictory idea of national identity.

León-Portilla, Zea, and Florescano all have legitimate points that can be defended in context, but the important point here is that the evolution from one to the other in the Mexican national commission clearly reflects the degree to which Spain came to dominate Quincentenary thinking in Latin America by the late 1980s. The commemoration came to be focused not on the pre-Columbian experience of Native American cultures but on the early colonial period under Spanish administration. Of course, this is the one in which an "encounter" between Indians and Europeans—assuming we accept the idea—would have taken place; but León-Portilla emphasized the devastation suffered by non-European societies, whereas now the attempt was to attend to the creation of a Hispanic world. And of course, this was also the approach of Carlos Fuentes in *The Buried Mirror*, with his insistence on Spanish influence in America. Adopting a posture of strong Hispanic traditionalism, Fuentes argued that, rather than emphasizing economic and political problems, one should seize the opportunity of the Quincentenary to celebrate the importance of Hispanic culture. This was the conservative, pro-Quincentenary position that acknowledged the seriousness of the continent's social problems, but that ultimately gave more importance to history and the arts and, inevitably, the fiction called *hispanidad*. This side did not want to miss the chance to celebrate the Hispanic past, whose achievements it hoped other cultures would become more aware of. Its receptivity to Spain can be seen in the subtitle of Fuentes's book: *Reflections on Spain in the New World*. Of course, it helped that the Spanish State Society for the Quincentenary was heavily involved in financing the project.

But the real issue here is that, unlike in the Dominican Republic, this emphasis on Spain ultimately led to the decline, even the death, of the Quincentenary in Mexico. During 1992, Florescano left the commission, apparently without being replaced. Just like in the United States, official activities ground to a halt, and the commemoration disappeared from view precisely at the moment when it was supposed to take off. We see this, moreover, on a variety of fronts. One of the most useful records of quincentennial activities in Latin America is the bilingual OAS newsletter published from 1985 through 1993, *Quinto Centenario del Descubrimiento de América: Encuentro de dos mundos; Quincentennial of the Discovery of America: Encounter of Two Worlds*. During the first five years of the newsletter, Mexico was one of the most frequently mentioned Latin American nations for quincentennial activities, but from 1990 through 1992 allusions to Mexican activities could hardly be found. A review of several well-known journals either published in Mexico or that cover events there turned up almost no mention of the Quincentenary prior to 1992.[25] Perhaps most telling of all, not long after the Quincentenary was over, we asked the Mexican Embassy in Washington for help in locating reports or information about the national commission and its activities. Officials expressed great willingness to help but were puzzled and uncertain. They had no idea where to turn and recommended contacting the U.S. Library of Congress. This is not a criticism of embassy staff but a sign that the national commission either did not write a final report or, if it did, had little to discuss and received almost no public attention.

So, the Mexican case reiterates the general pattern of disappointment, but it also follows a truly unique path of showing a strange weakening of the idea of "encounter." An early indigenist perspective that eventually came to dominate other nations and undermine Quincentenary commemorations everywhere was gradually forsaken as officials became more receptive to traditional New World theories such as "discovery." In this way, the Quincentenary became dissociated from the *mestizo* values by which so much public life is conducted in Mexico, and the event naturally appeared less important or interesting to Mexicans themselves. To the extent that Spain came to be perceived as the real impetus for the commemoration, Mexico's voice and role were lost and the nation gradually abandoned its commitment. At the same time, there is more than a little irony to the fact that the most widely circulated presentation of the Quincentenary, *The Buried Mirror*, was a Spanish vision written by a Mexican, Carlos Fuentes. It is even more ironic but also very sad that Mexico had such difficulty defending in its own home what will always be its principal contribution to the Quincentenary, the idea of "encounter."

The final result, then, is that the Quincentenary in Mexico was more subdued than in many other countries, with few high-profile programs and very little publicity. Like in the United States, the national commission went into a late eclipse and the commemoration passed largely unnoticed. One did not even hear the polemics about Indians that appear everywhere else, probably because they were no longer new or surprising in that environment. To be sure, projects such as revising textbooks or publishing Nahuatl codices will certainly remain as valuable contributions, and the rest of us can continue to debate the theory of encounter which Mexico both launched and abandoned. In the end, however, the Mexican version of 1992 is a melancholic spectacle of loss.

7

Conclusion

Weeds of Change

Oh tierra de la muerte, ¿dónde está tu victoria?

Luis Cernuda

Las Vegas, someone has said, is where "you have all these classic symbols of Western civilization that have come here to die."[1] Christopher Columbus was thus in appropriate company when Antoni Miralda brought his much-scaled-down "Honeymoon Project" to town on Valentine's Day 1992, hoping to stage his "wedding of worlds" amid the Roman, Egyptian, medieval, and Wild West icons that line the Las Vegas Strip. Miss Liberty's gargantuan garments were strewn in museums and galleries all over town, but Columbus himself ended up once again in exile when Caesar's Palace pulled out of a plan to stage the extravaganza as an evening event at its casino-hotel. Instead, Miralda was forced to move the show to the afternoon and relocate it to Red Rock Canyon, a desert park fifteen miles from the city. Here images of Columbus and Miss Liberty were projected against the walls of an old quarry while the wedding guests sipped champagne and picnicked from the trunks of rented cars. "Liberty always loves to be in nature," the artist explained to a reporter; besides, "when you do an art work, you never use words like disappointment."[2]

So it went with most of the special events that were planned for the quincentennial year. Even when the various commissions carried out their charge, as in Spain or the Dominican Republic, the Quincentenary was perceived as a failure and largely disappeared from view. In the United States, the first PBS documentary series, WGBH-Boston's *Columbus and the Age of Discovery*, began broadcasting in October 1991 but was neither surprising nor very interesting. It was shortly followed by two Washington museum "blockbusters," the National Gallery's *Circa 1492* and the Smithsonian's *Seeds of Change*, and then Martha Graham's uncompleted last work, "The Eyes of the Goddess," which was commissioned by the Spain '92 Foundation.[3] Through this same foundation, the Spanish government managed the American tour of the Columbus caravels, which cost $7 million and drew large crowds in Miami as well as respectable ones in Tampa, Charleston, Norfolk, New York, and other Gulf and East Coast cities during 1992.[4] In New York, the replicas sailed—or more accurately, churned, since only the Pinta turned out to be sailworthy, and all depended on diesel power as they entered ports—at the head of the Grand Columbus Regatta on July 4. A faint imprint of the Jubilee Commission's earlier involvement could be discerned in the tall ships parade. This time the ship captains, who had been ignored during the Statue of Liberty celebration, were feted with a Gracie Mansion reception, and the cadets were treated to a ticker tape parade. Much more than in 1986, the ships were the centerpiece, along with the caravels, of the New York celebration. This was in accordance with the Jubilee Commission's early promises and planning, but it also signaled the almost complete lack of imagination governing the final act. The Jubilee Commission itself was nowhere in evidence on July 4 except in official ceremonies that took place out of public view on Governor's Island. The weather—heavy rains on July 3 and fog on the morning of the 4th—reduced crowds to a fraction of original expectations. Cars could easily find parking places in lots along the Hudson River that had had spectators lined up ten deep on July 4, 1986.[5]

The thin crowds and maritime focus made for a more relaxed celebration, but with the single exception of Expo '92 in Seville, the megaevents of 1992 were a flop. The AmeriFlora fair in Columbus, Ohio, suffered cost overruns and disappointing crowds; in the end local sponsors had to dig into their own pockets to make up the difference (estimated to be as large as $30 million) between what the fair cost and what it earned.[6] Genoa was seen by relatively few people, and even Expo '92 was more recognized for its after-hours entertainment than for its connection to Columbus. The Spanish caravel tour also went bust, and January 1993 found the replicas back in New York, temporarily stranded without means to pay their return to Spain.[7] Eventually, the ships were sold to a museum in Corpus Christi, Texas, where they now form the main attraction in a waterfront park. The proposed West Coast tour of the replicas never came off and Columbus Day in San Francisco, which was supposed to be the grand finale of the U.S. Quincentenary, was dominated by protests at the waterfront and the disruption of the annual Columbus Day parade. Couple all this with the protests accompanying the lighting of the Columbus Lighthouse in Santo Domingo as well as the disappearance of the Mexican commemoration, and the Quincentenary provides us a very dull picture.

Indeed, even ideas that seemed positive from one point of view carried problems from another and were ignored or abandoned. The Columbus Scholars program was to have been a multicultural and bilingual corrective to the colonialist Rhodes Scholarships but needed proceeds from sales of commemorative coins that in turn depended on legislation by Congress and public interest stimulated by special events. Neither of these requirements ever materialized. Congress did not pass coin legislation until the spring of 1992, when it was too late. Competition with the nearly 200 other commemorative coins available from the U.S. Mint meant that the Columbus coins brought in only about $7 million. This serves as an endowment to support a "Columbus Fellowships Foundation" dominated by Italian-American patronage appointees.[8]

The reasons for the failure of the Quincentenary are clear. As a commemoration organized by official commissions and governments, from the beginning it struggled unsuccessfully to escape being an anachronism. In this country, Columbus was wounded by Indians and discovery was subverted by invasion. A Quincentenary *of the other* displaced the official event and gave voice to those who were victimized by the Columbian legacy. This was equally true in Latin America, where the plight of indigenous peoples is even more serious than it is in the United States. If Indians found themselves obligated to play the less pleasant role of spoiler, this was required by the situation and had the advantage of giving them the moral high ground. This meant that as an official event, the Quincentenary was doomed before it began because it overlooked or avoided its own darker side while defending positions that were out of touch with the contemporary world. Indeed, even in

Spain and the Dominican Republic, where the Quincentenary might be described as successful because it carried out its major goals and programs, we still have to conclude that it was a failure. By offering little more than self-congratulatory celebrations, both nations condemned themselves to superficial, expensive events that left many indifferent or even angry. If ordinary Spaniards felt antagonistic toward 1992, it was because of the vacuity of it all. They watched as huge sums of money were spent on activities of little moment while opportunities for raising important questions about Spain and the world were disregarded.

The paradox of the Quincentenary is that its failure was its success. As the official commemoration played out its hackneyed homage to the past, the other Quincentenary shifted the debate to the issues we have seen throughout this study: popular versus elite culture, diversity and tolerance versus uniformity and blindness, local versus central government, myth versus history, and many more.[9] In the end, the other Quincentenary overcame the triviality of official commissions by challenging the nation to achieve the democracy and well-being that had too often been the privilege of the few.

To be sure, the complex and sometimes somber messages of Columbian revisionism often failed to connect with mass audiences. The exception that perhaps proves the rule were the millions who viewed the Tournament of Roses Parade in Pasadena on January 1, 1992. The selection of a Columbus descendant as the parade's grand marshal "set off an uproar," which then led to the appointment of a Native American co-grand marshal, Representative (later Senator) Ben Nighthorse Campbell of Colorado, who paraded in full Cheyenne regalia in front of a carriage conveying the latest Cristóbal Colón. "Voyages of Discovery" provided the parade's general theme, but apart from the Spanish float and another sponsored by the Knights of Columbus, no units of the parade referred directly to the Quincentenary. "As you know, there has been some controversy," ABC Television commentator Joe Garagiola mused as the parade got under way. That was it as far as revisionism on a grand scale was concerned. ABC did remind viewers, however, that Columbus had not landed in the United States "as many believe" but came ashore instead "on one of the Bahama Islands."[10]

Official programs could never have accommodated, much less reconciled, the numerous discordant voices offering authoritative interpretations of 1492 and its anniversary. In fact, the programs that flourished best in the United States were those that did not attempt a unified vision but presented the alternatives, however discordantly, side by side. This meant giving space to the indigenist perspective not only as one among many but as a vision that had been too long overlooked. Trying to be open to all, the National Endowment for the Humanities pumped its millions into more than 400 scholarly productions, exhibits, films, and symposia related to the Quincentenary, yet the list of funded projects presents no unifying theme. Columbus's name was associated in some way with only 25 of the projects, funded at a total cost of just over $2 million. "Hispanic" themes account for 130 grants ($9 million) and projects dealing in some way with Native Americans for 136 grants and nearly $10 million. Another 24 grants ($2.5 million) may fairly be termed multicultural.[11] Similarly, the historian James Axtell, who examined some 250 books published on relevant topics during the Quincentenary years, divided these into eleven categories, only one of which had to do with Columbus himself.[12]

The most successful museum blockbusters, *Seeds of Change* and *Circa 1492*, did not present narratives of either European triumphs or pre-Columbian innocence but rather displayed the artifacts and innovations of the two cultures, along with contributions from Africa and Asia, in uneasy but instructive juxtapositions. At the National Gallery, the organizers of *Circa 1492* chose 1492 as "a symbolic date of birth for the modern world." Most of the objects exhibited originated during Christopher Columbus's lifetime or thereabouts; otherwise Columbus did not figure into it. Displaying an influence that few other art museums can match, the NGA accumulated more than 600 art works from more than 200 lenders in thirty-four countries and confidently placed paintings, prints, drawings, and sculptures next to ornamental carvings, maps, scientific instruments, and works of decorative art, the latter category including everything from ceremonial armor and leather-bound books to swords and tapestries. Europe was represented in the exhibition by paintings by Lucas Cranach the Elder, Albrecht Dürer, and Leonardo da Vinci, but also by the Catalan Atlas of 1375, Venetian globes and astrolabes, and King Ferdinand's armored helmet. Africa was represented by wood carvings from Benin and ornamental gold and ivory from the cultures encountered by Portugal; Islam by a wide array of objects from the Mamluk and Ottoman empires; Asia by Japanese, Chinese, and Korean paintings, scrolls, screens, ceramics, armor, and lacquerware. From the Americas came objects never before exhibited in the United States, such as a calendar stone from Tenochtitlán, along with a profusion of Aztec codices and sculptures, Inca and Chimu textiles, gold objects from Central and South America, and delicately sculpted effigy pottery from the Mississippian cultures of the southern United States. *Circa 1492* made "no claims to completeness," the chief curator noted. "We have specifically tried to present each civilization on its own terms," declares the exhibition catalog. "Homogeneity was not a feature of the world of 1492, and under no circumstances could a single theme have done justice to the amazing variety that characterized the cultures that are represented in the show."[13] A similar message was sought in the Museum of America in Madrid when it reopened in the summer of 1992 with displays from North and South America from pre-Columbian and colonial times, and in addition special exhibitions of contemporary artists. The contrast here with the Chicago World's Fair organizers' futile search for a unifying theme is especially instructive.

The organizers of *Seeds of Change* adopted a similar strategy. Rather than trying to show the full implications of the Columbian exchange of peoples, plants, animals, and microbes that the 1492 voyage inaugurated, the exhibition focused in depth on five topics: sugar, maize, the potato, disease, and the horse. Curator Herman Viola explained: "Sugar led directly to the enslavement of Africans and the transformation of New World ecosystems; maize fed the Africans that provided the manpower for American plantations; the potato, like maize, was developed by American Indians and has become a basic food of people around the globe; disease, especially smallpox, measles, even the common cold, wrought havoc with New World peoples.... The horse, the fifth seed of change, was one gift from the Old World that Indians came to embrace and cherish."[14]

No mock-ups of Spanish caravels greeted *Seeds of Change* visitors. Rather they could inspect a reconstructed slave ship, review the archaeology of sugar plantations, witness the astonishing profusion of potato varieties from the Andes, see a recreation of the great Aztec market at Tlatelolco, and examine the elaborate material culture spawned by the North American Plains Indian adaptation of the horse. The overall impression was a careful balance of celebration and reflection. For example, on the one hand, *Seeds of Change* celebrated the achievements of Indian agronomy; yet visitors who scrutinized the displays and accompanying catalog learned that the same crops developed by Native Americans also made possible the demographic explosions in Africa and Europe that supplied the Americas' replacement populations. This focus gave the exhibition organizers the formula for which so many other quincentennial programmers searched in vain—an inclusive, multicultural, and "balanced" means of celebrating the fact that the Columbian voyages had indeed created a new world.[15] As a result, other programmers flocked to it. The NEH funded poster versions of the exhibit for circulation to smaller venues around the country. The American Library Association and the National Council on the Social Studies mounted educational programs on the exhibition's themes, and a junior version of the show was set up in Columbus, Ohio, as part of the AmeriFlora horticultural fair. *Seeds of Change* became the Smithsonian's—and possibly the nation's—most successful quincentennial program. Its success was a personal triumph for Viola, whose assignment to the project had been intended by museum brass as a punishment for siding with the Indians during the repatriation controversy.

When other museum exhibitions were less successful, we can usually understand why. The National Museum of American History mounted an exhibit richly documenting multicultural encounters among the Indian, Hispano, and Anglo population of northern New Mexico, but reviewers were puzzled by the tight focus on a locale distant in time and place from the Columbian voyages. As well they might have been—museum authorities did not disclose to the public two basic reasons for this choice of themes: a subsidy from the New Mexico legislature that made up in part for federal penury; and long-term loans from the Museum of New Mexico that compensated for the fact that the Smithsonian historical collections contain relatively few colonial objects from anywhere but the English settlements of the Atlantic seaboard.

In another Smithsonian offering, the National Museum of American Art's *The West as America: Reinterpreting Images of the Frontier* was an exhibition of paintings and drawings whose original purpose had been to interpret to urban audiences the march of nineteenth-century American civilization across the western half of the continent. Curators hooked this Eurocentric material to the Quincentenary by making the Columbus saga the first chapter in a triumphalist narrative of conquest. Then, in order to "demystify" the art works, they plastered the walls with lengthy and intrusive labels that tutored viewers on the racist and imperialist implications of the pictures they were viewing. The result was a firestorm of protest.[16] A revision of some labels quieted the storm somewhat, but when a friendly critic, historian Alan Trachtenburg, suggested that an appreciation of the multicultural West might have been more effectively presented had the curator used a greater variety of materials—documents, letters, old photographs, folk art, and objects—that could attest without elaborate exegesis to the fact that the *real* West was not the one portrayed in the fine art of the period, curator William H. Truettner shrank from this idea: "I shudder to think of the mix of images, text, and graphics that would have confronted viewers."[17] Such an exhibition, he implied, would confuse visitors, notwithstanding the fact that museum goers could soon encounter a comparable mix of genres at the National Gallery's *Circa 1492* just down the street. The NMAA curators' career investment in painting and sculpture and in the boundaries that kept these objects in higher regard among collectors and patrons than folk art or other "minor" genres undercut their interpretive strategy. To the informed visitor, *The West as America* said more about the politics and finances of the art world than it did about Columbian revision, especially as the exhibition's signature painting—Emanuel Leutze's *Columbus on the Deck of the Santa María*—had recently changed hands and was the object of a determined public relations campaign by new owners hoping to increase the painting's value.[18]

A similar contrast between traditional and experimental narratives could be seen in the differing fates of print and film products of the Quincentenary. In addition to the popularity of Kirkpatrick Sales's *The Conquest of Paradise*, a trio of Columbian novels exposed readers to new perspectives in the years running up to 1992. Two of these novels were promoted through public library reading groups sponsored by the American Library Association and funded by the NEH. One was Argentine novelist Abel Posse's *The Dogs of Paradise*, which framed the Columbus story within Latin American magical realism.[19] Posse's Columbus is a mystical Christian of Jewish birth, a sexual athlete with a secret—webbed feet—that he does not reveal to anyone until that astonishing October morning in 1492. He is also a visionary whose gifts permit him to peer into the future to see the millions who will follow in his wake. His story is that of a man who seeks paradise—and finds it! The novel takes literally Columbus's explanation of the unexpected continent (South America) that he encountered in his third voyage of 1498. In his reports to Spain, Columbus speculated that the coast of Venezuela was near the actual setting of the biblical Garden of Eden. Posse gives us an imaginative account of what it might have been like if this had been true. Alas, the story turns out pretty much like it did in the original garden. Columbus is happy there, but his companions find

Paradise lacking. Satiety is boring. The Iberians prefer excess. But excess requires rules, prohibitions, force. There is a military coup, followed by the emergence of capitalism, slavery, and environmental destruction. Free love is replaced by rape, native homage by tribute. New World history has begun.

Columbus's power to fascinate is at the center of indigenist writers Michael Dorris and Louise Erdrich's novel *The Crown of Columbus*.[20] This book's leading characters are Vivian Twostar and Roger Williams, respectively a Native American anthropologist and a WASP poet. Each is involved in a Columbus project in anticipation of the approaching Quincentenary. They are also involved with each other, and the tension that drives the novel derives in part from our curiosity about how their increasingly competitive projects will affect their complicated relationship. As is often the case in real life, these fictional characters start out by using Columbus as a symbol, a name all but divorced from historical reality but which stands for things that the characters like or dislike about contemporary society. For Vivian, her ambiguous feelings about Columbus reflect the ambiguous position of indigenous peoples in modern societies. For Roger, Columbus is a stand-in for the poet's alter ego: a great individualist whose dream became deed, the man who as another New England poet, Ralph Waldo Emerson, wrote in his essay "Self-Reliance" "sailed the ocean in an undecked boat." Yet notwithstanding their academic tendency to deal with life and history at the level of abstraction, both characters are drawn into engagement with the *real* Columbus and the actual event. Vivian and Roger both modify their views of Columbus and, in the process, modify their views of themselves and of each other. Encounter *and* discovery operate at both the personal and historical levels in this story, and in the end the distinction between them blurs.

Apart from Posse's novel, the Quincentenary inspired almost no fiction of note in the Hispanic world except perhaps Carlos Fuentes's *Christopher Unborn*. The work is a comic tour de force that is not among the author's best but did receive respectful attention when it appeared in Spanish in 1987 and in English in 1989. Fuentes narrates from the perspective of a fetus destined to be the first child born in the Western Hemisphere on October 12, 1992. This provides a small but penetrating window into the near future of Mexican society and in particular its problematic relationship with the Anglophone people to the north. In one passage, a character muses on what Fuentes considers the fascinating result of the cultural and demographic mixing unleashed in the New World since 1492. This is the new nation of "Mexamerica": "independent of Mexico and the United States, in-bond factories, smuggling, contraband, Spanglish, refuge for political fugitives, and free entry for those without papers from the Pacific Coast to the Gulf Coast, 100 kilometers to the north and 100 to the south of the old frontier, from Sandy Ego and Auntyjane to Coffeeville and Killmoors: independent without the need of any declaration, the fact is that no one pays the slightest attention to the government in Mexico City or Washington."[21]

After adventures that allow him to observe from the safety of his mother's womb the assorted dramas of Mexico's disintegration, the unborn Christopher returns to Acapulco, where he was conceived and where he is born on the beach in the first moments of October 12. Just before birth consigns to oblivion his memory of all that has gone before, Christopher muses that "We are all Columbuses, those of us who bet on the truth of our imagination and win; we are all Quijotes who believe in what we imagine; but ultimately, we are all Don Juans who desire as soon as we imagine and who quickly find out that there is no innocent desire."[22] As so often in Fuentes's fiction, Hispanic myths prevail.

As noted earlier, Fuentes's leaden narration in the Spanish- and Smithsonian-sponsored documentary series *The Buried Mirror* befits the anachronism of the project's concept. On the screen, large or small, the Columbus story perpetuated a long record established in some seventy operas and plays over the centuries of never having inspired a critical or popular hit. On film, nothing worked for the Quincentenary: neither a great writer such as Fuentes, nor acclaimed directors such as Carlos Saura (*El dorado*) or Ridley Scott (*1492: Conquest of Paradise*), nor an accomplished producer such as Zvi Dor-Ner (*Columbus and the Age of Discovery*), nor a celebrated actor such as Gérard Départdieu (playing Columbus in Scott's film). Today, classroom audiences are still being put to sleep with Fuentes's relentless tedium and Dor-Ner's endless shots of wooden hulls plowing blue water, but the feature-length Columbus films quickly and mercifully sank from view, notwithstanding a couple of star turns by Tom Selleck as Ferdinand and Faye Dunaway as Isabella that were instantly recognized as camp classics.[23] It also seems unlikely that audiences will see the new Columbus operas again, as Antonio Gala's Columbus opera in Spain and Philip Glass's *The Voyage* in New York added to the list of flops.

The successful quincentennial exhibitions and books had in common a feature that might be called "narrative indeterminacy." That is, they allowed viewers or readers freedom to proceed in a nonlinear fashion, to compare discordant objects and ideas and their sources without inherent bias, and to invent or revise Columbian interpretations of their own. The films, on the other hand, clamped a vise on the viewer's gaze, directing him or her to a narrative that focused on the individual and personal. Their tired plots preempted the larger possibilities of the narrative and really directed the audience toward the classic Hollywood stratagem: that despite the gorgeous costumes, Selleck was not Ferdinand but a Hawaiian detective on television; that Isabella was Bonnie on the prowl for Clyde or Evelyn Mulwray consorting with *Chinatown*'s Jake Gittes; and that Dépardieu was really Cyrano trying to get his green card.

In any event, epics require heroes, and from the revisionist standpoint, the arrival of Columbus in the New World could not constitute epic because Columbus himself was an antihero. At the same time, there was no Taino hero on which to fasten the cape of protagonist against Columbus. Cortés had Cuauhtémoc, Pizarro had Atahualpa; perhaps that will be sufficient when their quincentenaries turn up in 2021 and 2033. But Columbus's enemies were anonymous victims who will forever be lost in the mists of time. Perhaps for this reason, the most successful Columbus work in the performing arts remains Darius Milhaud's opera composed in 1922 which divides the Admiral into two characters, with Columbus as an old man singing counterpoint commentary about the deeds and confusions of Columbus in his prime. This device accommodates the ambiguities of classic Columbian biography, but it could not accommodate the demands of revisionism since the great divide today is not within the hero but within the audience, the guilty beneficiaries of the Columbian exchange.

One could also make the argument that because we live in an anti-Columbus time, successful quincentennial films had to be those that argued the other side, that of Native Americans. A film like Kevin Costner's *Dances with Wolves* (1990) might qualify in this regard. Though it did not address explicit Quincentenary themes, its defense of Native Americans and the ecological concerns that are so important to them struck a popular chord that might be said to have fostered resistance to the official 1992 commemoration. Moreover, the epic grandeur with which the film sought to convey the land and nature transferred the heroic element onto the native inhabitants, the victims of European settlers and the U.S. government. This was myth, of course, and three long hours of it with Costner's plodding style don't make for great cinema. But myth is consistent with the values of the indigenous peoples the film was seeking to vindicate and the overall invasion argument of anti-Quincentenary sentiment.

Appropriately, the greatest and probably most enduring triumph of the Quincentenary in the United States came with the opening of the New York branch of the Museum of the American Indian in October 1994. Here in the neoclassical Custom House, an architectural monument to the primacy of European ideas in the American mind (replete with a stained-glass Columbus in the vestibule), curators displaced the "vanishing Indian" subtext of the 1892–93 celebration with a cry of contemporary indigenist triumph: "We are still here!" While exposing only a fraction of the fabulous Heye Collection, the new museum presented artifacts from past and present, labeled them with the mixed messages of natives, anthropologists, and historians, and celebrated contemporary Indian artworks alongside "masterworks" that in an earlier era would have been arranged in the encased tableaux of natural history dioramas. *All Roads Are Good* proclaimed the title of the museum's first big exhibition. This displaced the concept of "discovery" embedded in Delacroix's representation of Columbus as he returned to Barcelona in 1493 with his Indians and his loot. Now the message pointed to the global society that had evolved over the past 500 years.

In a grumpy sermon delivered in San Francisco's Grace Cathedral on Sunday, October 11, 1992, the critic Robert Hughes denounced the protestors who were at that moment assembling at Aquatic Park and with them the "politically correct polemic[s]" that attributed to Columbus and his voyages so many of the defects of the modern world. Hughes found Columbus bashing to be one of many symptoms of a national "culture of complaint." The United States in 1992 was "a society obsessed with therapies and filled with distrust of formal politics, skeptical of authority and prey to superstition, its political language corroded by fake pity and euphemism." The nation's inability to rally to an inclusive Columbian commemoration was, he argued, symptomatic of an eroding sense of "collectivity and mutual respect." Don't let the rejection of nineteenth-century imperial myths obscure the Admiral's importance, Hughes implored, just for the sake of comfortably "projecting our own morality into the past." "History, like it or not," Hughes concluded, "is pretty much the record of original sin."

But Hughes's defense of Columbus resembled many of the very Columbus bashers he deplored because all still placed human agency at the center of their narrative concern.[24] One of the more significant long-term consequences of 1992 may be that it moved authority definitively away from the linear, personalistic history of the age of print toward something closer to the "di-s," "polys," and "multis" of our time: diversity, dialogical, polysemic, polyethnic, multicultural, multimedia, and so forth. To appreciate this achievement we would like to contemplate for a moment an idea known as "the theory of catastrophic sexual transmutation."

Now the theory of catastrophic sexual transmutation is not an idea imported from France nor was it ever funded by the National Endowment for the Arts. Rather it is a hypothesis about the evolution of corn or maize, that marvelous gift of the Americas to the world, which today is the earth's second largest cereal crop, as important in the diets of Africans, Asians, and Europeans as it is in our own. The catastrophic sexual transmutation theory (CSTT) challenges older theories holding that maize evolved in gradual but thus far unidentified steps from its most logical wild ancestor, a Mexican annual plant called teosinte. Instead, the CSTT holds that maize shifted suddenly when a form of environmental stress, possibly an unseasonable flood, caused a localized wild population of teosinte to mutate. A normally elongated lateral branch of the plant shortened drastically, bringing its flower (tassel) into the female hormonal zone of the main stem, altering the tassel from masculine to feminine, enlarging its central spike into the familiar maize ear, and multiplying the number of kernels. The kernels became sheathed in a husk derived from the vestigial leaves of the ancestral lateral branch, a situation which left the plant inefficiently constructed for self-propagation. In the words of Hugh H. Iltis, the University of Wisconsin scientist who advanced the theory in 1983, "All basic traits distinguishing maize [from teosinte] developed simultaneously with tassel feminization."[25] This explains the absence of intermediate hybrids linking maize and teosinte in either the natural or archaeological record and also explains the genetic similarity of the two plants.

Two things link the theory of catastrophic sexual transmutation to the intellectual climate in which we observed the Columbus Quincentenary. One is the role that Indians played in the propagation of maize, for had not the mutant teosinte come to the attention of local farmers, it would almost certainly have died out within a few plant generations, its greatly enhanced nutritional value lost forever. But the farmers did notice the transformation, according to Iltis's theory, and began propagating and developing the new plant through human selection.

This and other achievements of Native American agronomy formed a main theme of the Smithsonian's *Seeds of Change* program, and they were also a focus of several NEH-funded projects. The question remains: given the twinned reputations of Indians and Columbus, when the Indians' stock rises, does Columbus's stock have to fall? The answer has to do with an aspect of the CSTT that challenges traditional forms of historical explanation. As Iltis puts it, "A commonly accepted aspect of Darwinian evolution by natural selection is the gradual change of species over time. This has been challenged recently by the view that basic structural change occurs during a rapid macroevolutionary phase followed by long periods of relatively little change." The CSTT is only one of a number of scientific theories that have emphasized the importance of "macroevolutionary events," usually catastrophic in nature, in evolutionary history. Think of the recent news about asteroid collisions and dinosaur extinction, of plate tectonics and continental drift, of the Big Bang itself. The comfortable analogy between evolution and human events that equated gradual and incremental change with the story of human progress based on individual accomplishment was central to American intellectual life at the time of the fourth Columbian centenary. Now that analogy is all but impossible to sustain.

Historians and scholars in many fields have come up with modes of inquiry that relegate individual deeds and words to the background of explanation. Demographic history, environmental history, and world history are all relatively new fields, and all take what might be termed an orbital view of humankind, like the NASA "big blue marble" photographs that show the earth whole, its fundamental singularity clarified, but its pattern of wonderful and endless variation obscured. The newest forms of historiography have something of the same impact. They focus on processes in which human intention plays only a partial role and one that can be discerned only in the aggregate effect, not through the more accessible record of individual deeds and specific events. Similar patterns can be found in archaeology, with its interest in all aspects of human experience including those found in garbage dumps, not just what has been monumentalized in written records and works of art. Indeed, the shift in today's cultural commentary away from elite classes and creative individuals toward the more anonymous processes of popular culture is part of the same tendency and is integral to our postmodern concern for the daily life of ordinary people.[26] Such trends are not orbital in the sense of global, but localistic in the sense of attending to what is immediate and ordinary. The two tendencies, orbital and localistic, coexist today along with a host of uneasy pairings. The Quincentenary did not invent these polarities, but by absorbing and expressing so many of them, it captured the tensions of an era that is moving from one way of looking at things to another way. Here might be the real significance of the Quincentenary: not only that it was the first official commemoration to give voice to the other, but also that it expressed our postmodern shift from personality to process. In truth, 1992 exceeded even the most imaginative planner's fondest dreams and worst nightmares.

William H. McNeill, the Jubilee Commission's vice chairman and one of the founders of the field of world history, placed 1492 in the new "macroevolutionary" context when he spoke of it as "the end of one ecological era and the onset of another.... The disturbances introduced by [Columbus] were more abrupt and more catastrophic than anything I know of," he added, but they were not unique events in human history. "Human displacement, migration, and the shifting of cultural boundaries" are recurrent events in world history, often accompanied by the catastrophic spread of disease. If Columbus had not brought the Americas and Europe into permanent contact, someone else surely would have, possibly as soon as 1500, when the Portuguese navigator Cabral bumped into Brazil while sailing to India.[27]

From the orbital perspective, human population history compares to the biological process of florescence. Old populations introduced into hospitable new environments (such as European farmers into the rich soils of Pennsylvania or Illinois, horses and cattle into the American grasslands, or smallpox virus into the bodies of Native Americans) multiply rapidly but eventually run up against natural limits. The present resurgence of Indian peoples, the stagnation of white population growth in both Europe and North America, and the appearance in both regions of millions of legal and illegal migrants of non-European origin are signs that the natural limits of European expansion have been reached. The year 1992 fell during a time of human displacement and shifting cultural boundaries, one that was (and still is) as significant as though perhaps less abrupt than the shifts that Columbus initiated. It is hard to wax poetically or indignantly about the impact of his voyages if we frame such changes in the same dispassionate language that scientists use to explain macroevolutionary events. Indeed, as the boundaries of daily life continue to shift under the pressures of migration, the local worlds of so many peoples formerly destined to otherness gradually move into clearer focus and the Columbian voyages become all the more remote. We are not assuming that old values have been replaced by new ones, but that the stage being occupied by many more kinds of voices therefore presents a much more complex and interesting spectacle.

In this way, we live with many ways of understanding history, but for some, the old habit of searching for moral purpose, of assigning credit and blame, dies hard. Global-localistic perspectives may be fascinating and their explanatory power strong, but like a Chinese dinner they can leave us craving something more. We can accord a sort of generic respect to the men or (more probably) women who had the bright idea of propagating the mutant teosinte plant, but we can't carve their faces into Mount Rushmore or give them a name. Processual history is a history without heroes—or villains.

Except for Columbus. The morning of October 12, 1492, is one of the rare occasions when moment and epoch merged. The chain of events that ensued was, as McNeill says, in the processual sense inevitable. Yet this is also one case where we can also put a human form and name on the face of catastrophe. From the standpoint of linear history, it seems important to know who was first across the Atlantic, where he first landed, how the journey was financed, and all the other myriad details over which dedicated Columbus buffs like to argue. Others want to know how Columbus exploited Taino Indians, misgoverned his new colony, and unleashed the destructive forces of greed that continue to provoke the animosity of Columbus bashers everywhere.

But if history is process and its unfolding a lurching ride between sudden, random, and often catastrophic events, then these details seem far less important. From this perspective, Columbus praising or bashing is a bit like the husk on an ear of corn: vestigial. It is left over from the days of seeing history as the record of human purposes, as a kind of societal balance sheet for toting up credit and blame. Like so many other archaic rituals that were staged in 1992, this attitude is a link not with the future but with the past.

Notes

INTRODUCTION

1. "Sjöfaren Christopher Columbus," produced by Sjöhistoriske Museet, Stockholm, Christen Levedahl, curator. Notes and a poster from the exhibition in the author's collection, box 31, hereafter referred to as Williams Collection. This collection has been transferred to the Quincentenary Archives in Zimmerman Library of the University of New Mexico and may be rehoused, in which case a key linking the old location with a new one will be provided by the library.

2. Damon D. Hickey, "Undoing Columbus," *Friends Journal: Quaker Thought and Life Today* (October 1992): 12–13 (Williams Collection, box 31). We are grateful to Tom Rodd of Morgantown, West Virginia, who with his wife, Judy, wrote the pageant, for bringing it to our attention.

3. "Remarks by First Lady Hillary Rodham Clinton at the White House Millennium Event," as quoted in the "Announcement" section of the Millennium web page (http://www.whitehouse.gov./Initiatives/Millennium). See also *New York Times*, January 1, 1999, A18, and Nick Hanna, *The Millennium: A Rough Guide to the Year 2000* (London: Rough Guides, 1999).

1. CHRISTOPHER COLUMBUS, THE CHICKEN, AND THE EGG

1. Lee Johnson, *The Paintings of Eugene Delacroix: A Critical Catalogue*, 4 vols. (Oxford: Oxford Clarendon, 1981–86), 3: 84–87, 4: pl. 82 and 83; Frank A.

Trapp, *The Attainment of Delacroix* (Baltimore: Johns Hopkins University Press, 1970), 193–96.

2. The interpretation that follows here is based primarily on material gathered for use in speeches and various publications in the course of Williams's official quincentennial career. See especially *The True Cross and the Pseudo-Event: Some Reflections and Readings on the Columbus Quincentenary* (Washington: Federation of State Humanities Councils, pub. no. 5–89, 1989). As 1992 approached, other scholarly assessments of Columbus's symbolic roles became available. See especially Claudia L. Bushman, *America Discovers Columbus: How an Italian Explorer Became an American Hero* (Hanover, N.H.: University Press of New England, 1992); Thomas J. Schlereth, "Columbia, Columbus, and Columbianism," *Journal of American History* 79, 3 (1992): 937–68; Lilian Handlin, "Discovering Columbus," *American Scholar* 62, 1 (1993): 81–95; and Barbara Groseclose, "American Genesis: The Landing of Christopher Columbus," in *American Icons: Transatlantic Perspectives on Eighteenth- and Nineteenth-Century American Art*, ed. Thomas W. Gaehgens and Heinz Ickstadt (Santa Monica, Calif.: Getty Center for the History of Art and the Humanities, 1992), 11–32.

3. This traditional version was also put forward in Daniel Boorstin's *The Discoverers* (New York: Random House, 1983), a 1983 best-seller. For the origin and persistence of the notion that Columbus proved the earth was round, see Jeffrey Russell, *Inventing the Flat Earth* (Westport, Conn.: Praeger, 1991).

4. Paolo Emilio Taviani, informal remarks given during summation of an unpublished paper, "La Figura de Colón en el Descubrimiento," presented at a conference on "Encounter of Two Worlds: Hispaniola, Threshold of America," held at Universidad Nacional Pedro Henríquez Ureña (UNPHU) under the sponsorship of UNPHU, Ohio State University, and the Dominican National Quincentenary Commission, December 6, 1988 (notes in Williams Collection, box 35).

5. Salvador de Madariaga, *Christopher Columbus, Being the Life of the Very Magnificent Lord Don Cristobal Colon* (New York: Macmillan, 1940; reprinted 1978), 1–49.

6. Paolo Emilio Taviani, *Christopher Columbus: The Grand Design*, translated from the Italian by William Weaver (London: Orbis, 1985), 22.

7. Stephen Marlowe, *The Memoirs of Christopher Columbus* (New York: Charles Scribner's Sons, 1987); Abel Posse, *The Dogs of Paradise*, translated from the Spanish edition of 1987 by Margaret Sayers Peden (New York: Atheneum, 1989).

8. Alice P. Kenney, "America Discovers Columbus: Biography as Epic, Drama, History," *Biography* 4, 1 (1981): 45–65; Terence Martin, "Three Columbiads, Three Visions of the Future," *Early American Literature* 27, 2 (1992): 128–34; Saul K. Padover, *Thomas Jefferson and the National Capital, 1785–1818* (Washington: U.S. Government Printing Office, 1946), 68–75; William H. Robinson, *Critical Essays on Phillis Wheatley* (Boston: G. K. Hall,

1982), 26–37; Charles Fred Heartman, ed., *Phillis Wheatley: Poems and Letters*, with an introduction by Arthur A. Schomburg (repr. Miami: Mnemosyne, 1969), 51–52; James L. Woodress, *A Yankee's Odyssey: The Life of Joel Barlow* (New York: Greenwood, 1969); Arthur L. Ford, *Joel Barlow* (New York: Twayne, 1971), 46–52, 65.

9. Christopher J. Kauffman, *Faith and Fraternalism: The History of the Knights of Columbus, 1882–1982* (New York: Harper and Row, 1982).

10. Taviani, "Informal Remarks."

11. Rudolph J. Vecoli, "*Contadini* in Chicago: A Critique of *the Uprooted*," *Journal of American History* 51, 3 (1964): 404–17.

12. John Alexander Williams, "The Columbus Complex," in David A. Taylor and John Alexander Williams, eds., *Old Ties and New Attachments: Italian American Folklife in the West* (Washington: Library of Congress American Folklife Center, 1992), 197–207.

13. Luis Arranz Márquez, "Comments on Taviani Paper," UNPHU–Ohio State conference on "Hispaniola, Threshold of America," December 6, 1988 (notes in Williams collection, box 35).

14. Ralph H. Orth, ed., *The Journals and Miscellaneous Notebooks of Ralph Waldo Emerson* (Cambridge, Mass.: Belknap Press of Harvard University Press, 1966), vol. 6 (1824–38), 201–2.

15. John T. Flanagan, *Theodore C. Blegen, A Memoir* (Northfield, Minn.: Norwegian-American Historical Society, 1977), 127–29.

16. Garrison Keillor, *Lake Wobegon Days* (New York: Vintage Books, 1985), 115.

17. Ivan van Sertima, *They Came before Columbus* (New York: Random House, 1976).

18. The conference proceedings are published in Vera Lawrence Hyatt and Rex Nettleford, eds., *Race, Discourse, and the Origin of the Americas: A New World View* (Washington: Smithsonian Institution Press, 1995).

19. Samuel Eliot Morison, *The European Discovery of America: The Southern Voyages, A.D. 1492–1616* (New York: Oxford University Press, 1974), 3.

20. Alfred W. Crosby, Jr., *The Columbian Exchange: Biological and Cultural Consequences of 1492* (Westport, Conn.: Greenwood, 1972), and *Ecological Imperialism: The Biological Expansion of Europe, 900–1900* (Cambridge: Cambridge University Press, 1986). These important books, which today serve as introductions to environmental history for many readers, were themselves syntheses of a generation of earlier scholarship.

21. Robert H. Power, "The Vinland Map—The World before Columbus," paper presented at the annual conference of the National Association of Private Art Foundations, Williamsburg, Virginia, October 22, 1988. The latest version of the scholarly controversy is summarized by Michael Farguhar, "Nordic or Forged? New World Map Sunders Scholars," *Washington Post*, February 26, 1996, A3.

22. Burton Benedict, "The Anthropology of World's Fairs," in Burton

Benedict, ed., *The Anthropology of World's Fairs: San Francisco's Panama Pacific Exposition of 1915* (Berkeley: Lowie Museum of Anthropology in Association with Scolar Press, 1983), 2–65.

23. Personal communication during the van Sertima conference (see note 18).

24. Christopher Columbus Quincentenary Jubilee Commission (hereafter cited as CCQJC), "Declaration of Purpose," adopted September 5, 1986 (CCQJC records in Williams Collection, box 26). After several false starts by other commissioners, Vice-Chairman William H. McNeill and Williams drafted this manifesto at McNeill's home in Colebrook, Connecticut, on July 7, 1986; it was adopted by the commission at its meeting in Chicago in September.

25. Taviani, *Columbus: The Grand Design*, 121–26.

26. In *Inventing the Flat Earth*, Jeffrey Russell argues that the enduring popularity of the story among people who should know better is due to its anti-*religious*—not just anti-Catholic—bias and was rooted in the debates over Darwinism in the nineteenth century. He adds, "Our determination to believe that Flat Error arises out of our contempt for the past and our need to believe in the superiority of the present—that is, of ourselves" ("Inventing the Flat Earth," *History Today* [August 1991]: 19).

27. *Columbus Breaking the Egg (after Hogarth)* [1805], in *Michele Felice Corne, 1752–1845, Versatile Neapolitan Painter of Salem, Boston, and Newport*, Foreword and Notes by Philip Chadwick Foster Smith, Introduction by Nina Fletcher Little (Salem, Mass.: Peabody Museum of Salem, 1972), 34–35. Cf. Austin Dobson, *William Hogarth* (New York: Dodd, Mead 1891), 140–45, 277, and Benjamin Franklin West, *Columbus Breaking the Egg* (1836), Essex Institute, Salem, Mass. (accession numbers 106 and 759).

28. A. Hyatt, *Columbus Sighting Land, by Mrs. Hyatt* (1872), Essex Institute (accession number 1796).

29. "Self-Reliance," in Ralph Waldo Emerson, *Essays, First Series* (Boston: Houghton Mifflin, The Riverside Press ed. of 1968; vol. 2 of *The Complete Works of Emerson*), 86.

30. Daniel Boorstin, *The Image: A Guide to Pseudo-Events in America*, 25th anniversary edition (New York: Atheneum, 1987).

31. *Special Events Report* 7, 16 (August 29, 1988): 1; ibid., 7, 19 (October 10, 1988): 7; ibid., 7, 20 (October 24, 1988): 2.

32. Scott Redmond, interviewed by John Alexander Williams, San Francisco, November 20, 1988; see also Events America Foundation, *The 500th Edition* 3, 1 (December 1988), 1 (notes in Williams Collection, box 21).

33. *Special Events Report* 7, 21 (November 7, 1988): 2.

34. Creative Time, Inc., Press Kit, November 30, 1988 (Williams Collection, box 21).

35. Barnett Lipton, Radio City Music Hall Productions, interview with author (Williams), New York, February 17, 1988.

2. SAILING OVER THE EDGE

1. Michael Deaver, interview with author (Williams), Washington, D.C., November 30, 1988 (notes in Williams Collection, box 45).

2. Patrick J. Sloyan, "Another Blue-Ribbon Blunder," *Washington Post*, February 12, 1989, C5.

3. When one of us made this point to a *Post* reporter, he misconstrued our comment to mean that we thought that he worked *for* the Style Section. His indignant denial of such an affiliation reinforced our conclusion that the political culture of official Washington was partly responsible for the Jubilee Commission's poverty and weakness. (Bill McAllister, telephone conversation with author [Williams], October 18, 1991; McAllister's story ran in the *Post* on November 1, 1991, 20A.)

4. "Draft minutes, meeting of the Christopher Columbus Quincentenary Jubilee Commission, Thursday, September 12, 1985," 2–8, transcript in Commission Records, copy in Williams Collection, box 26.

5. Henry Raymont to John N. Goudie, Washington, March 9, 1987, Commission Records, copy in Williams Collection, box 26; Henry Raymont, "Columbus Can Mean a Still Newer World," *New York Times*, October 12, 1983.

6. This group is discussed on pp. 139–40 of this volume.

7. Jane Lee García to Rafael Hernández Colón, March 31, 1986, copy in Commission Records, copy in Williams Collection, box 26.

8. Goudie's financial woes are conveniently summarized in the *Miami Herald*, January 6, 1991, 1B, 4B.

9. "Christopher Columbus Scholarship Program of the Christopher Columbus Quincentenary Jubilee Commission" [1988], typed copy in Williams Collection, box 26.

10. See pp. 89–91 in this volume.

11. Goudie's viewpoint on this matter may be found in U.S. House of Representatives, Subcommittee on Census and Population of the Committee on Post Office and Civil Service, "[Hearings to] Review Allegations of Misconduct or Wrongdoing on the Part of Certain Individuals Associated with the Christopher Columbus Quincentenary Commission, November 20 and 21, 1991" (Washington: U.S. Government Printing Office, 1992), serial no. 102–36, 223–24. This document will be cited hereafter as *Hearings* (November). A preliminary hearing on April 23, 1991, was also published ("Oversight Hearings to Review the Activities of the Christopher Columbus Quincentenary Jubilee Commission," serial no. 102–10), and will be cited hereafter as *Hearings* (April). Paula Jellinghaus presents her view of the matter in a letter to Rep. Thomas C. Sawyer (April 20, 1991), reprinted in the latter, 9–12.

12. *Hearings* (April), 48.

13. Typed statement, undated [September 1990], copy in Williams Collection, box 29.

14. *Special Events Report* 9, 17 (September 10, 1990): 4–5.

15. "Statement of William K. Tell, Jr., Senior Vice President, Texaco, Inc.," *Hearings* (April), 89–95.
16. *Hearings* (November), 205.
17. *New York Times,* December 18, 1990, A1, B16.
18. *Miami Herald,* January 6, 1991, 1B, 4B.
19. *Hearings* (November), 59–60.
20. Ibid., 53–54, 65–70.
21. Ibid., 224.
22. Ibid., 236.
23. Ibid., 239–40, 252–77.
24. *Hearings* (April), 85.
25. Ibid., 74–76.
26. *Washington Post,* July 14, 1989, A1, A8; September 12, 1990, A17; June 27, 1992, E1, E14; *Wall Street Journal,* May 8, 1990, A22; October 24, 1990, A8; *New York Times,* February 12, 1989, B12; April 17, 1990, A8; *World's Fair* 12: 3, 2–3. In Genoa, by contrast, the American pavilion was generously funded by Amway Corporation, whose president, Jay Van Andel, was a Grand Rapids neighbor and fellow Republican activist of then U.S. Ambassador (and former Jubilee Commission member) Peter Secchia (*World's Fair* 12, 3, 13).

3. CITIES OF GOLD

1. In Los Angeles, for example, where the rise of activism opposing the city's traditional unlimited growth policies in the name of "livability" is chronicled by Mike Davis, *City of Quartz: Excavating the Future of Los Angeles* (New York: Verso, 1990). Davis's account emphasizes skepticism about the activists' proclaimed motives and posits a racial subtext to the conflicts, both of which are also appropriate to Chicago.
2. Burton Benedict, "The Anthropology of World's Fairs," 2.
3. Ibid., passim; George Pratt, interview with author (Williams), Washington, D.C., December 15, 1988 (notes in Williams Collection, box 35).
4. Robert A. Caro, *The Power Broker: Robert Moses and the Fall of New York* (New York: Alfred A. Knopf, 1974), 1085–1113.
5. René Chalon and Marie-Hélène Defrène, interviewed by Evelyn Rivers Wilbanks, Paris, October 5, 1983, transcript, 6–7, Chicago World's Fair Collection, Chicago Historical Society. We are grateful to the society for permission to quote from this collection, which hereafter is cited CHS, preceded by the name of the person(s) interviewed and the interview date and followed by the page numbers of the interview transcript. Unless otherwise noted, all interviews cited took place in Chicago and were conducted by Evelyn Rivers Wilbanks.
6. Some months after the meeting, Chalon shot himself in a botched suicide attempt. When Petkus visited him in the hospital, Chalon told him he had bought the gun in Chicago during the Century of Progress Exposition of 1933.

7. George Burke interview, August 11, 1983, CHS, 13.
8. Pratt interview with Williams, December 15, 1988.
9. "Miami's Power Elite," six-part series in the *Miami Herald*, January 31–February 5, 1988.
10. Joan Didion, *Miami* (New York: Simon and Schuster, 1987), esp. chaps. 2 and 5. When John Williams learned of the *Herald*'s egregious omission of Goudie's name, he sent copies of the clipping and of Didion's chapter on the ethnic biases of Miami institutions to one of the coauthors, Wilcomb E. Washburn, whom he knew well and who in turn showed it to his collaborator, Joan R. Challoner. Unknown to Williams, the R. in Mrs. Challoner's name stands for Ridder, as in Knight-Ridder, the parent company of the *Herald*. Within days Goudie received an invitation to meet with the paper's editor and an apology from the publisher for the omission.
11. In fact, a "Miami World's Fair Organizing Committee" briefly mobilized for a 1995 fair effort but never made it past its initial contacts with the BIE, whose sanction went instead to a 1996 Expo in Budapest. *Miami Herald*, December 10, 1988, 2D; *World's Fair* 14, 4 (January–March 1994): 16.
12. Thomas G. Ayers interview, August 25, 1983, CHS, 4; Chalon/Defrène interview, October 5, 1983, CHS, 10.
13. Chalon/Defrène interview, ibid.
14. Ibid., 21–23.
15. Clayton Kirkpatrick interview, October 12, 1983, CHS, 12.
16. Thomas G. Ayers interview, August 25, 1983, CHS, 6–9. The paraphrases of Solti's remarks are by Ayers.
17. See chap. 6.
18. Weese's ideas are laid out in his interview, November 14, 1983, CHS, passim. The quotation is from an interview with Philip Klutznick, September 26, 1983, CHS, 5.
19. Burke interview, August 11, 1983, CHS, 22. The chronology of early planning may be followed in interviews with Ayers, Cook, Weese, Kirkpatrick, Considine, and Petkus in the CHS collection and in Catherine T. Ingraham, "Land of No Discovery," *Inland Architect* 30, 3 (May–June 1986): 46–53.
20. Cleo Messinger, "The Image of Chicago on Film," master's thesis, University of Chicago, 1990, 19–22; CHS interviews with Cook (December 5, 1987, 2), Schultz (October 27, 1983, 4), and Chalon (October 5, 1983, 10–11).
21. *Chicago Tribune*, June 28, 1985; Robert McClory, *The Fall of the Fair: Communities Struggle for Fairness* (Chicago: Chicago 1992 Committee, 1986), 1–41.
22. "The City That Almost Works," *Economist*, January 12, 1980, 31–32; "The City That Survives: Chicago—A Survey," *Economist*, March 29, 1980, supp., 1–28.
23. *Economist*, March 29, 1980, esp. 5, 9–10, 24–28.
24. *New York Times*, April 12, 1983, sec. 1, 16.

25. Maurice Thominet interview, March 8, 1984, CHS, 3, 5.
26. CHS interviews with Schultz (October 27, 1983, 5–6) and Ayers (August 25, 1983, 16).
27. Bruce Graham interview, December 2, 1983, CHS, 5.
28. Ingraham, "Land of No Discovery," 50.
29. Burke interview, CHS, August 11, 1983, 5–6.
30. *Washington Post,* July 14, 1989, A1, A8, and September 12, 1990, A17; *Wall Street Journal,* May 8, 1990, A22, and October 24, 1990, A8; *New York Times,* February 12, 1990, B12, and April 17, 1990, A8.
31. Donald A. Petkus, interview with author (Williams), Chicago, November 14, 1988; Pratt interview with Williams, December 15, 1988.
32. This account of fair politics during the crucial years 1983–84 is based on Ingraham, "Land of No Discovery"; McClory, *The Fall of the Fair;* and reports in the *Chicago Tribune* (e.g., May 7, 1982, sec. 3, 14, on Thompson's endorsement). An authoritative summing up of financial issues may be found in a *Tribune* series by R. C. Longworth, May 8–11, 1983.
33. John D. Kramer interview, July 23, 1984, CHS, 1–3.
34. Kramer interview, CHS, 3. New Orleans stories appeared in the *Chicago Tribune* on January 4, February 24, May 10, 13, 26, June 2, 14, 27, July 1, 18, August 2, 12, 31, September 9, 18, October 3, 6, 12, 25, November 11, 16, December 8, 14, 1984.
35. *Chicago Tribune,* June 27, 1985, sec. 1, 27; Lisa Uckman, interview with author (Williams), Chicago, December 23, 1988 (notes in Williams Collection, box 35).
36. *Chicago Tribune,* June 20, 1985, sec. 2, 1; June 21, 1985, sec. 1, 1; June 22, 1985, sec. 5, 5; June 23, 1985, sec. 1, 1, sec. 5, 2; McClory, *Fall of the Fair,* 38–39.
37. Lloyd Wendt and Herman Kogan, *Bosses in Lusty Chicago: The Story of Bathhouse John and Hinky Dink* (Bloomington: Indiana University Press, 1943).
38. Petkus interview with Williams, Chicago, February 5, 1990.
39. *Chicago Tribune,* March 29, 1984, sec. 1, 1, 18; April 1, sec. 5, 2; Kramer interview, July 23, 1984, CHS, 10–11.
40. The so-called East-West Canal is discussed in Ingraham, "Land of No Discovery," 49–50, and in the Graham interview, December 2, 1983, CHS, 4. See also *Chicago Tribune,* June 22, 1982, sec. 1, 3, and March 4, 1983, sec. 2, 1. On the idea of a single huge building, an "envelope of space," see Ian Gill, "Paris: New Rules for World's Fairs?" *World's Fair* 7, 3 (Winter 1987): 10. There was also some talk of a privately funded suburban location (*Chicago Tribune,* January 8, 1989, sec. 2, 1).
41. Graham interview, December 2, 1983, CHS, 4.
42. Considine interview, October 25, 1983, CHS, 7, 13.
43. *Chicago Tribune,* June 27, 1985, sec. 1, 27.
44. Petkus interviews with Williams, November 11, 1988, February 5, 1990;

on Kramer's view of Mayor Washington, see Kramer interview, July 23, 1984, CHS, 3–6.

45. *Chicago Tribune*, June 10, 1983, sec. 2, 1; World's Fair Advisory Committee, "A Report to Mayor Harold Washington" (October 1983), copy in Williams Collection, box 40.

46. *Chicago Tribune*, December 3, 1987, sec. 3, 13.

47. Petkus interview with Williams, February 5, 1990.

48. Margaret Newkirk, "Cleaning Up After Ameriflora," *Columbus Monthly* (April 1993): 24–29; *Columbus Dispatch*, September 11, 1992, B1; *New York Times*, December 20, 1993, I8.

49. Uckman interview with Williams, December 23, 1988.

50. *Los Angeles Times*, July 11, 1986, 2: 4; *New York Times*, October 29, 1986, B1.

51. *New York Times*, January 1, 1999, A18.

52. John Lloyd, "An Epic Gamble on the Gas Flats of Greenwich," *New Statesman* 126 (December 12, 1997), 20; cf. "Zero-based Celebrations," *Economist*, April 18, 1998, 18; Gaylene Carpenter, Maureen Glancy, and Christina V. Howe, "Event Planning for the Millennium," *Parks and Recreation* 33, 9 (September 1998): 132; Adam Gopnik, "What Next? The Millennium Is Over but the Melody Lingers On," *New Yorker*, October 20, 1997, 27; Paul Goldenberger, "The Big Top," *New Yorker*, April 27, May 4, 1998, 152–59; Richard Jenkyns, "Questioning the Millennium: A Rationalist's Guide to a Precisely Arbitrary Countdown," *New York Review of Books*, May 28, 1998, 4; and Hanna, *The Millennium: A Rough Guide*, 60–103, 240–42.

53. "Maryland: The Columbus Commemoration, 1492–1992," press kit, copy in Williams Collection, box 40.

54. "The Christopher Columbus Center for Marine Research and Exploration," booklet [Baltimore, 1991], copy in Williams Collection, box 40.

55. Williams telephone interview with Stanley Heuisler, February 1, 1991.

56. *Washington Post*, September 9, 1987, A1, A8; *New York Times*, March 14, 1990. A29.

57 *Washington Post*, December 2, 1988, H1.

58. Robert N. Bellah et al., *Habits of the Heart: Individualism and Commitment in American Life* (Berkeley: University of California Press, 1985).

59. Petkus interview with Williams, February 5, 1990.

4. ETHNOS, HISTORY, AND MYTH

1. *New York Times*, July 21, 1988, A22.

2. Richard D. Alba, "The Twilight of Ethnicity among Americans of European Ancestry: The Case of the Italians," *Ethnic and Racial Studies* 8, 1 (January 1985): 134–54; Alba and Mitchell Chamlin, *Italian Americans: Into the Twilight of Ethnicity* (Englewood Cliffs, N.J.: Prentice Hall, 1985).

3. Stanley Lieberson, "Unhyphenated Whites in the United States," in *Eth*-

nic and Racial Studies 8, 1 (January 1985): 159–80. Micaela di Leonardo, in *The Varieties of Ethnic Experience: Kinship, Class and Gender among California Italian-Americans* (Ithaca: Cornell University Press, 1984), argues that symbolic ethnicity among Bay Area Italian-Americans persists either through the efforts of "ethnic brokers" (organizational politicians and purveyors of ethnic foods) or the volunteer efforts of women, who undertake with declining enthusiasm the burdens of sustaining patriarchal myths about the importance of family ties among Italian-Americans and the performance of ethnic identity through the production of special foods.

4. Phyllis C. Martinelli, in *Ethnicity in the Sunbelt: Italian American Migrants in Scottsdale, Arizona* (New York: AMS Press, 1989), reviews the debate on symbolic ethnicity (14–40) and adopts a "modified pluralist" conclusion supporting the notion that symbolic ethnicity represents a valid expression of group values, even though members of the group are free to opt out if they so choose.

5. Shirley Williams, *South Italian Folkways in Europe and America* (New Haven: Yale University Press, 1938); Edward Banfield, *The Moral Order of a Backward Society* (New York: Free Press, 1958); William Foote Whyte, *Street Corner Society* (Chicago: University of Chicago Press, 1955); Herbert Gans, *Urban Villagers: Group and Class in the Life of Italian-Americans* (New York: Free Press, 1962); Nathan Glazer and Daniel Patrick Moynihan, *Beyond the Melting Pot* (Cambridge, Mass.: M.I.T. Press, 1963).

6. For the role of Joseph Cervetto and his son as Columbus impersonators, see *San Francisco Chronicle*, October 3, 1987, 5. For earlier Columbus impersonators, see Speroni, "The Development of the Columbus Day Pageant," *Western Folklore Quarterly* 7, 4 (October 1948): 334. For a similar negative assessment by community leaders of a commercial food and street fair, see Anthony T. Rauche, "Festa Italiana in Hartford, Connecticut: The Pastries, the Pizza, and the People Who 'Parlo Italiano,'" in Theodore C. Humphrey and Lin T. Humphrey, eds., *We Gather Together: Food and Festival in American Life* (Ann Arbor: UMI Research Press, 1988), 205–17.

7. *San Francisco Chronicle*, October 12, 1981, 2; October 8, 1984, 10; October 14, 1985, A3; October 5, 1986, B4.

8. Phyllis Cancilla Martinelli, "From Ethnic Enclave to Ethnic Dispersion: Residence Patterns of Italian Immigrants," paper presented to the Pacific Sociological Association Annual Conference, March 27, 1976; Alessandro Baccari, interview with author (Williams), May 17, 1989; *San Francisco Chronicle*, January 26, 1978, 6; October 4, 1981, 4; September 5, 1988, A8.

9. San Francisco Bay Columbus Quincentenary Jubilee Committee, "Mission Statement," "Registered Projects Guidelines," "CQ Committee Organization," "Executive Committee," and "San Francisco Bay Columbus Quincentenary," all statements included in a press kit provided by the executive director, Rita Barela, who also provided a copy of a letter from Mayor Art Agnos to Ms. Helen Toribil and Mr. Samuel Vásquez, Resistance 500 Committee, May 31,

1991, from which the quoted words are taken (Williams Collection, box 42).

10. *San Jose Mercury News*, May 5, 1991, 8A. Goudie acknowledged making the demand, apparently basing it on a clause in the city's proposal to the commission promising "substantial reimbursement" to the commission for its expenses in organizing the tall ships regatta; George Bush to George Jewett (chair, San Francisco Bay Columbus Quincentenary Jubilee Committee), December 14, 1989 (copy in committee press kit cited in note 9).

11. *San Francisco Chronicle*, March 4, March 17, 1992.

12. Though we recognize that the terms *Hispanic* and *Latino* are not the same, we use them in a generally interchangeable way here partly to suggest that both are recognized yet neither is really adequate. In fact, both terms are abstractions that tend to obscure the diversity of the U.S. Spanish-speaking population. The word *Hispanic* is generally more oriented to traditional understandings (i.e., those associated with Spain) while the word "Latino" has a somewhat more progressive or contemporary flavor.

13. See Candace Nelson and Marta Tienda, "The Structuring of Hispanic Ethnicity: Historical and Contemporary Perspectives," in Mary Romero, Pierrette Hondagneu-Sotelo, and Vilma Ortiz, eds., *Challenging Fronteras: Structuring Latina and Latino Lives in the U.S.* (New York: Routledge, 1997), 7–27; Antonia Darder and Rodolfo D. Torres, eds., *The Latino Studies Reader: Culture, Economy, Society* (Malden, Mass.: Blackwell, 1998).

14. *New York Times*, August 14, 1988, 1.

15. Indigenous Communications Resource Center, "500 Years: Preliminary Results of a Quincentenary Survey," in Jose Barreiro, ed., *View from the Shore: American Indian Perspectives on the Quincentenary* (Cornell University: Northeast Indian Quarterly [Fall 1990]), 12, 21–22.

16. Ibid., 19, 94.

17. Ibid., 16.

18. Jerald T. Milanich and Susan Milbrath, eds., *First Encounters: Spanish Explorations in the Caribbean and the United States, 1492–1570* (Gainesville: University of Florida Press, 1989), esp. chaps. 1, 3–10, 13.

19. *Miami Herald*, February 25, 1990; Jan Elliott, quoted in Barreiro, *View from the Shore*, 14.

20. Barreiro, *View from the Shore*, 14.

21. "In Conversation: The Myths of Columbus," *U.S. News & World Report*, October 8, 1990, 74.

22. "Response to the Quincentenary Statement of the NCSS and AHA," *History Teacher* 26, 2 (1992); Russell Kirk, "Columbus the Exemplar," *Continuity* 16 (1992): 65–74. Cf. Wilcomb E. Washburn, "Columbus: Agent of the Inevitable," *Continuity* 16 (1992): 57–63, and Bryan LeBeau, "The Rewriting of America's First Lesson in Heroism: Christopher Columbus on the Eve of the Quincentenary," *American Studies* 33, 1 (1992): 113–27.

23. David E. Stannard, *American Holocaust: Columbus and the Conquest of the New World* (New York: Oxford University Press, 1992).

24. James Axtell, "The Columbian Mosaic in Colonial America," *Humanities* (September–October 1991): 16.

25. For example, Benjamin Franklin, writing in 1771: "I contrived to disguise my hand; and writing an anonymous paper, I put it at night under the door of the printing house. . . . I wrote and sent in the same way to the press several other pieces, . . . and I kept my secret till my small fund of sense for such performances was pretty well exhausted, and then I *discovered* it" (L. Jesse Lemisch, ed., *Benjamin Franklin: The Autobiography and Other Writings* [New York: New American Library, 1961], 33; italics added); see also a similar usage on p. 179, written in 1784. The phrase *discovery of America* seems to have come into general use during Franklin's lifetime.

26. *New York Times*, August 14, 1988, 1, 2.

27. Quoted in Inga Clendinnen, *Ambivalent Conquests: Maya and Spaniard in Yucatan, 1517–1570* (Cambridge: Cambridge University Press, 1987), vi. This is one of the most interesting and important ethnohistorical studies of recent years.

28. Augusto Roa Bastos, "El Controvertido V Centenario" [The Controversial Quincentenary], *El Pais*, June 18, 1991, 17.

29. *San Francisco Chronicle*, October 12, 1992, A1, A4, B1, D1; October 11, 1992, D1, D8; *San Francisco Bay Guardian*, October 7, 1992, 15–17, 19, 20.

30. Stated in private conversation with author (Summerhill). For a survey of Indian viewpoints, see *View from the Shore*, passim.

31. "An American Indian Perspective," typescript, draft chapter for *Seeds of Change* catalog, November 2, 1990, copy in Williams Collection, box 39.

32. "NEH Conference on the Columbian Quincentenary, Santa Fe, New Mexico, November 21–22, 1983," 3, copy in Williams Collection, box 6.

33. Elgy Gillespie, "Indian Wars on Capitol Hill," *Museum and Arts Washington* (May–June 1988): 39–42; *Washington Post*, January 20, 1989, B2; January 30, 1989, B7; May 9, 1989, A1, A14; March 6, 1991, B1, B8; *New York Times*, September 13, 1992, H53.

34. James Axtell, "A Moral History of Indian-White Relations Revisited," in *After Columbus: Essays in the Ethnohistory of Colonial North America* (New York: Oxford University Press, 1988), 10. Ethnohistory has been no less important in Latin America.

35. It is difficult to mention only a few works in this immense field, but the interested reader might begin with Tzvetan Todorov, *The Conquest of America: The Question of the Other*, trans. Richard Howard (New York: Harper and Row, 1984), and Eric R. Wolf, *Europe and the People without History* (Berkeley: University of California Press, 1982). Also recommended are René Jara and Nicholas Spadaccini, eds., *1492–1992: Re-Discovering Colonial Writing* (Minneapolis: Prisma Institute, 1989), and Stephen Greenblatt, ed., *The New World* (special issue of *Representations* 33 [Winter 1991]).

5. THE QUINCENTENARY AS EXCESS

1. "Presentación" [Presentation], *Descubre el Quinto Centenario: Guía de programación* [Discover the Quincentenary: Guide to Programs], (Madrid: Sociedad Estatal para la Ejecución de Programas del Quinto Centenario, 1992), 7. This and other translations from Spanish are Summerhill's.

2. A strongly negative interpretation of Spanish Quincentenary efforts can be found in Ariana Hernández-Reguant, "The Columbus Quincentenary and the Politics of 'Encounter,'" *American Indian Culture and Research Journal* 17, 1 (1993): 17–35.

3. On the history of Spain, see Raymond Carr, *Spain, 1808–1975*, 2d ed. (Oxford: Oxford University Press, 1982); Raymond Carr and Juan Pablo Fusi, *Spain, Dictatorship to Democracy* (London: HarperCollins, 1979); and Paul Preston, *The Triumph of Democracy in Spain* (London: Methuen, 1986).

4. In his *España* (Spain) (Barcelona: Ediciones B, 1993), Ian Gibson criticizes the Latin American push of the Quincentenary as mere "sentimentalism and rhetoric" (46) because, he says, Spain's only real future lies in Europe. Also, the nation is disregarding its significant historic ties with another much more important region, the Arab world lying immediately to the south. This is a not uncommon view among Spanish intellectuals, who look to the eight centuries of Islamic presence in Spain (711–1492) as a period of tolerance and enlightenment that could be considered a beacon for the present.

5. T. D. Allman, "Barcelona, Star of the New Europe," *National Geographic* (December 1998): 42–59.

6. Penelope Harvey, *Hybrids of Modernity: Anthropology, the Nation State and the Universal Exhibition* (London: Routledge, 1996), 100.

7. Dana Facaros and Michael Pauls, *Southern Spain* (London: Cadogan, 1999), 88. See also R. Mead, *Andalucía Handbook* (Chicago, Passport Books, 1997), 274.

8. A full analysis of Expo '92 that includes the story of these tensions can be found in Richard Maddox, "The Politics of Space and Identity in a Europe 'Without Borders': Cosmopolitan Liberalism, Expo '92 and Seville," *Irish Journal of Anthropology* 4 (1998): 8–25. We would like to thank Professor Maddox for providing an advance copy of this article.

9. Maddox, "The Politics of Space," 13; Harvey, *Hybrids of Modernity*, 99–130.

10. "Seis meses que se quedaron cortos" [Six months that came up short], *El País, International Edition*, October 19, 1992, 3.

11. See the various articles in *El País*, November 1, 1997, 10, 13, 15; November 2, 1997, 15, 17; November 9, 1997, 22–23; November 13, 1997, 17.

12. Ibid., January 4, 1993, 6.

13. See Maddox, "The Politics of Space," 15–19.

14. See pp. 46–47.

15. The most recent English translation is Enrique Pupo-Walker, ed., *Cast-*

aways: The Narrative of Alvar Núñez Cabeza de Vaca, trans. Frances López-Morillas (Berkeley: University of California Press, 1993).

16. See below, p. 177.

17. Augusto Roa Bastos, "El Controvertido V Centenario" [The Controversial Quincentenary], *El País,* June 18, 1991, 17.

18. See Somerset R. Waters, *Travel Industry World Yearbook: The Big Picture,* vols. 37–40 (New York: Child and Waters, 1993–98).

19. Harvey, *Hybrids of Modernity,* 63.

6. THE SAME AND THE OTHER

1. Naila Clerici has pointed out for example how difficult it was for American indigenous issues to receive any sustained attention during the Quincentenary in Italy. Topics outside the ken of Christopher Columbus, especially controversial ones, were for the most part ignored. See "Italy Celebrates Columbus: The Indian Rediscovered," *American Indian Culture and Research Journal* 17, 1 (1993): 37–54.

2. See the various articles in the *New York Times,* March 30, 1993, A10; June 7, 1993, A8; June 8, 1993, A1.

3. "Piazza Italia," *Italy, Italy* 10, 5 (September–October 1992): 60–65.

4. *Conoscere, Genoa and the Celebrations of Columbus, L'Agenzia di Viaggi,* February 20, 1990, 16.

5. Detailed information on this project and on the eight volumes published as of 1999 can be found at the project website: http://www.humnet.ucla.edu/humnet/cmrs/publications/repertorium/rcvols.html.

6. The NIAF journal *Ambassador,* nos. 12–14 (Winter–Summer 1992), carries several articles on visiting Italy, especially Genoa.

7. A more detailed description of the site can be found in Fausto Fini, "Il nuovo volto del porto antico" [The new face of the old port], *Columbus 92* 7, 4 (April 1991): 5–7.

8. See the articles in *Il Sècolo XIX* of May 16, 1991, 12.

9. We are thinking about Edmundo O'Gorman's and Germán Arciniegas's ideas about the "invention" of America, which have been reconsidered and updated by José Rabasa in *Inventing America, Spanish Historiography and the Formation of Eurocentrism* (Norman: University of Oklahoma Press, 1993). There is also Leopoldo Zea's theory of the *encubrimiento* or covering over of the New World, which will be discussed later in the section on Mexico.

10. Mabel Moraña, "Descubrimiento, postcolonialismo y postmodernidad" [Discovery, postcolonialism, and postmodernity], *Cuadernos de Marcha* (Montevideo) 8, 76 (October 1992): 5–8.

11. The director of the bank, Enrique Iglesias, never tired of repeating the idea that the 1980s constituted the greatest economic disaster in Latin American history. A typical example would be the interview he provided Spanish Quincentenary officials in 1991, called "El derecho y la obligación de América Latina de aspirar a un desarrollo altamente tecnificado" [The right and the

obligation of Latin America to aspire to a highly technological development], in Alfredo Roca and Carlos Aznárez, eds., *La nueva Europa y el futuro de América Latina* [The new Europe and the future of Latin America] (Madrid: ICI, 1992), 173–80.

12. *New York Times*, May 1, 1985, A2.

13. Carlos Fuentes, *The Buried Mirror: Reflections on Spain and the New World* (New York: Houghton Mifflin, 1992), 9.

14. It can be mentioned that Balaguer was not new to Dominican public life, having served many years before as the crony and hand-picked president of the infamous dictator Rafael Trujillo (1930–61). Though Balaguer subsequently won three democratic elections as president from 1966 to 1978, the opposition always claimed that he manipulated the ballots. The same charges were raised when he won again in 1986, by which time he was eighty-two years old and blind. He was reelected in 1990 and again in 1994. By this last time, the engineering of ballots had become so obvious that he had no choice but to agree to early new elections in 1996 while withdrawing his candidacy. Alastair Reid has written an excellent analysis of the 1994 elections in "Urn Burial," *New York Review of Books*, June 23, 1994, 32–36. One should also consult Reid's earlier "Waiting for Columbus," *New Yorker*, February 24, 1992, 57–75. For general background on Dominican politics, see Jan Knippers Black, *The Dominican Republic: Politics and Development in an Unsovereign State* (Boston: Allen & Unwin, 1986). A good standard history is that by Howard J. Wiarda and Michael J. Kryzanek, *The Dominican Republic: A Caribbean Crucible* (Boulder, Colo.: Westview, 1982).

15. This information comes from private conversations with different members of the Dominican national commission.

16. As noted earlier, the indigenous population died out soon after the conquest, and black African slaves quickly became the workforce. Dominican society is therefore not *mestizo* but *mulato*, with all the typical contradictions and ambiguities found in most mulatto societies.

17. Reid, "Waiting for Columbus," 72.

18. As recently as January 12, 1999, the *Listín Diario* of Santo Domingo (Internet edition) reported a continuing crisis in the Dominican tourist sector because tourism again declined significantly in 1998. The reasons cited are the same as ever: poor airports, inferior roads and transportation throughout the country, questions about sanitary conditions in hotels and other locations, electrical blackouts that cause problems with air-conditioning, and so forth.

19. James Patrick Kiernan, ed., *Quinto Centenario del Descubrimiento de América: Encuentro de dos mundos; Quincentennial of the Discovery of America: Encounter of Two Worlds* (newsletter) 33 (Washington: Organization of American States, 1985–93), 1.

20. The bibliography on Mexican history is immense. The interested general reader might consult Lynn V. Foster, *A Brief History of Mexico* (New York: Facts on File, 1997); Michael C. Meyer and William L. Sherman, *The Course of*

Mexican History, 5th ed. (New York: Oxford, 1995); Charles C. Cumberland, *Mexico: The Struggle for Modernity* (London: Oxford, 1968). Also interesting is a journalist's account of modern Mexico: Alan Riding, *Distant Neighbors: A Portrait of the Mexicans* (New York: Alfred A. Knopf, 1984).

21. Leopoldo Zea, "¿Descubrimiento o encuentro?" [Discovery or encounter?], *Cuadernos Americanos*, nueva época, año 2, núm. 11, vol. 5 (September–October 1988): 147.

22. See *Cuadernos Americanos*, especially the articles by Zea, "¿Qué hacer con quinientos años" [What to do with five hundred years?]: 127–37, and by Silvio Zavala, "El nuevo mundo" [The new world]: 141–45.

23. Such ideas were not new in Zea's thinking. See his article "América: ¿descubrimiento o encubrimiento?" [America: discovery or concealment?], in *Cuadernos Americanos*, año 44, vol. 258, 1 (January–February 1985): 93–104.

24. "Rumbo a 1492" [Toward 1992], *Nexos* 14, 168 (December 1991): 43.

25. The journals we reviewed were *Vuelta, Plural, Nexos, Cuadernos Americanos, Cuadernos Hispanoamericanos,* and *Americas*, plus several bibliographies of Mexican journals. Of course, there are many more Mexican journals and newspapers, so we do not claim to have exhausted all possibilities. On the other hand, only *Cuadernos Americanos* published articles on the Quincentenary, and the others did not even mention the event prior to 1991. That is, one has to say that the Quincentenary attracted very little attention in Mexico.

7. CONCLUSION

1. Arts & Entertainment Television Network Productions, *Las Vegas: House of Cards* (film, first broadcast in 1996).

2. "The Honeymoon Project," *Neon: Artletter of the Nevada State Council on the Arts* (Winter 1990–91): 7–8; *Las Vegas Review-Journal*, February 13, 1992, 1D, 5D.

3. *New York Times*, October 10, 1991, B1, B4.

4. Spain '92 Foundation, *Imagine America: 1992 Tour of the Niña, Pinta and Santa María*, provides the official version of the tour. See also *Washington Post*, February 17, 1992, A4, A5; *New Yorker*, January 25, 1993, 31.

5. *New York Times*, July 5, 1992, passim; *OpSail 92: The Official Program of Operation Sail*, copy in Williams Collection, box 9.

6. Margaret Newkirk, "Cleaning Up After AmeriFlora," *Columbus Monthly* (April 1993): 24–28.

7. *New Yorker*, January 25, 1993, 31.

8. Bill McAllister, "Who Controls the Coins," *Washington Post*, April 24, 1992, 65; "President Bush Signs Columbus Coin Foundation Bill into Law," press release, May 13, 1992 (office of Rep. Frank Annunzio) (copy in Williams Collection, box 31); "Medals of the United States Mint Issued for Public Sale," pamphlet (copy in the Williams Collection, box 31); CCQJC, "Final Report, July 12, 1993," 5 (copy in Williams Collection, box 29). As of 1999, the director of

the Columbus Fellowships Foundation was Rep. Annunzio's former administrative assistant.

9. The predominantly revisionist thrust of Quincentenary-inspired scholarship is amply demonstrated by several bibliographical and historical assessments published soon after 1992. See note 12.

10. Edwin M. Yoder, Jr., "Columbus Discovers Pasadena," *Washington Post*, November 24, 1991, C1–C2; author's notes on television broadcast, January 1, 1992.

11. National Endowment for the Humanities, "Awards on the Columbian Quincentenary Initiative, from 1985 to November 1992" (Washington 1993), copy in the Williams Collection, box 6.

12. James Axtell, "Columbian Encounters: Beyond 1992," *William and Mary Quarterly*, 3d ser. 49 (1992): 335–60, and "Columbian Encounters: 1992–1995," ibid., 52, 4 (1995): 649–96. Further assessments of the outpouring of scholarship that the Quincentenary inspired can be found in Ida Altman and Reginald D. Butler, "The Contact of Cultures: Perspectives on the Quincentenary," *American Historical Review* 99, 2 (1994): 478–503, and Marvin Lunenfeld, "Adrift in a Sargasso Sea: Recent Books on Christopher Columbus," *History Teacher* 26, 1 (1992): 15–21.

13. Jay A. Levenson, "Circa 1492: History and Art," in Levenson, ed., *Circa 1492: Art in the Age of Exploration* (New Haven: Yale University Press, 1991), 19.

14. Herman J. Viola, "Seeds of Change," in Viola and Carolyn Margolis, eds., *Seeds of Change: Five Hundred Years since Columbus* (Washington: Smithsonian Institution Press, 1991), 14–15.

15. Not that the idea was new, for it had been developed as early as the mid-1960s in Alfred Crosby's *The Columbian Exchange*. See chap. 1, n. 20.

16. William H. Truettner, ed., *The West as America: Reinterpreting Images of the Frontier* (Washington: Published for the National Museum of American Art by the Smithsonian Institution Press, 1991), esp. vii–xii and 27–53. For novelist Larry McMurtry's take on the exhibition, see *Chronicle of Higher Education*, November 14, 1990, 3; for a selection of visitor comments, see the *New York Times*, July 7, 1991, H25. The authors are grateful to the NMAA's Office of Public Affairs for providing copies of the texts of both the original and revised labels. Interestingly, while most revisions toned down the original "politically correct" language, in one case the revision resulted in a lengthier label that quoted documents affirming the explicitly racist intent of Frederic Remington's paintings (label 54, "Cowboys, Indians, Race, and Class").

17. This exchange can be followed in the pages of *Chronicle of Higher Education* (November 20, 1991, B1; December 18, 1991, B6; January 22, 1992, B2).

18. Materials on the Quincentenary-related history of this painting and of the activities of its new owner, Japanese investor Issei Fujiwara, and his American public relations firm can be found in the Williams Collection, box 21.

Fujiwara's team had unsuccessfully sought an endorsement of these efforts from the Jubilee Commission.

19. Abel Posse, *The Dogs of Paradise* (New York: Atheneum, 1989).

20. Michael Dorris and Louise Erdich, *The Crown of Columbus* (New York: HarperCollins, 1991).

21. Carlos Fuentes, *Christopher Unborn*, translated from the Spanish by Alfred MacAdam and the author (New York: Farrar Straus Giroux, 1989), 19.

22. Ibid., 522.

23. Barbara Abrash, "The Quincentenary on Television," *Perspectives: American Historical Association Newsletter* 30, 7 (1992): 1, 4, 6; Bryan F. LeBeau, "Of Hollywood and History: The Columbus Movies of '92," *American Studies* 34, 1 (1993): 151–57.

24. The quotes are from Williams's notes on Hughes's sermon, heard in person at Grace Cathedral. These remarks roughly parallel Hughes's discussion of "multi-culti" history in his book *Culture of Complaint* (New York: Oxford University Press, 1993), 116–30.

25. Hugh H. Iltis, "From Teosinte to Maize: The Catastrophic Sexual Transmutation," *Science* 222 (November 15, 1983): 886–94.

26. Michel de Certeau, *The Practice of Everyday Life*, trans. Stephen Rendell (Berkeley: University of California Press, 1984); Andreas Huyssen, *After the Great Divide: Modernism, Mass Culture, Postmodernism* (Bloomington: Indiana University Press, 1986).

27. William H. McNeill, "1492 in World Perspective," unpublished paper delivered at the Organization of American Historians Annual Meeting, Chicago, April 2, 1992.

Index

American Indian Movement (AIM), 103, 104
American Revolution Bicentennial, 49
Ameriflora, 9, 88–90, 99, 180, 185
America's Cup, 32
Annunzio, Frank, 40
Arranz Márquez, Luis, 16–17
Art Institute of Chicago. See Chicago Art Institute
Ayers, Thomas, 69, 74, 77, 81, 86
Axtell, James, 120, 183

Balaguer, Joaquín, 102, 168–71, 209n
Baltimore: Christopher Columbus Center, 92, 134; Columbus 500, 91–92; Columbus Day Parade, 15, 92
Barcelona, 7–8, 98, 148; Exposition of 1929, 65, 68; and Miralda Honeymoon Project, 29–30; as site of 1992 Olympics, 61, 133
Barlow, Joel, 13–14, 21
Bellah, Robert, 93

Bemporad, Alberto, 161. See also Genoa Expo
Benedict, Burton, 64
Bennett, William E., 39
Biblioteca Quinto Centenario. See Quincentenary Library
Bicentennial of U.S. Constitution, 28
Blegen, Theodore, 18
Boorstin, Daniel, 27–28, 31–32
Borchard, Susan, 39, 42, 45, 47
Bureau of International Expositions (BIE), 68–73, 75, 78–79; cancels Chicago World's Fair, 88; creation and purpose of, 68
Buried Mirror, The. See Fuentes, Carlos
Burke, George, 69–70, 74, 78
Bush, George, 89, 108
Byrne, Jane, 72, 76, 85

Campbell, Ben Nighthorse, 182
Canneto, Stephen, 99
Cárdenas, Alberto, 74
Cartuja '93. See Universal Exposition of Seville

Catalonia, 17, 132–33
Catastrophic sexual transmutation, theory of (CSTT), 191–92
Cervantes Institute, 148
Cervetto, Joseph, Jr., 97, 204n
Cervetto, Joseph, Sr., 204n
Chalon, René, 69–70, 75, 200n
Checchi, Mary Jane, 57
Chicago: reputation for gangsters, 74; social geography of, 81–83; urban problems in, 75–76
Chicago Art Institute, 31–32
Chicago 1992 Committee, 84–85
Chicago 1992 World's Fair Corporation, 74–75, 77, 80, 81, 86; World's Fair Steering Committee, 74
Chicago World's Columbian Exposition (1892–93), 9, 21, 64–65, 82, 118
Chicago World's Fair, 33, 38, 39, 45; archive at Chicago Historical Society, 64; attitude of promoters, 84; BIE visit, May 1982, 72–73; collapse of plans, 88; controversy over sites, 77, 83–84; corporate involvement, 75; early organization, 73–75; initial proposal to BIE, 69–70, 71; Illinois Exposition Authority, 80–81; official U.S. candidate to BIE, 71; political problems, 79; purpose, 73–75; reasons for failure, 84, 85, 86, 88; rivals for BIE approval, 70–72; role of state government, 79–80; theme, 78, 184
Christopher Columbus (film, 1947), 18
Christopher Columbus, Genoese (exhibition), 17
Christopher Columbus Licensing Group, 58, 59. *See also* Christopher Columbus Quincentenary Jubilee Commission, sponsorships
Christopher Columbus Quincentenary Jubilee Commission, 30–31, 70, 120, 193; and Ameriflora, 88; appointment of commissioners to, 21–22, 39–40, 41, 117; "Blue Room Strategy," 50–52; and Chicago World's Fair, 83, 86–87, 88; and ethnicity, 114, 117; and Iberoamerican Conference of National Commissions, 139; Columbus Scholars Program, 53, 181; criticism of leadership of, 57–58; critics of, 28, 58; election of chairman of, 42–43; enabling legislation for, 35–38, 86; finances of, 38, 40, 56–57, 90, 91; fundraising for, 53–56; GSA audit of, 1991, 59; interpretation of Quincentenary by, 22; and 1992 events, 180–81; program of, 45, 89–90, 108, 114; reasons for failure of, 61–62; sponsorships, 55, 91, 111; sponsorships with Texaco, 56, 58; status in Washington, 40–41; swearing in (1985), 9
—meetings of: Chicago (1986), 52, 55, 83; Genoa (1987), 88; Miami (1988), 56; Miami Beach (1986), 45; Puerto Rico (1986), 47; Seville (1988), 68; Washington (1990), 57
Christopher Unborn. See Fuentes, Carlos
Circa 1492. See National Gallery of Art
Cole, King, 74
Colombo '92. See Genoa Expo
Colón, Hernando, 24
Columbia, South Carolina, Columbus statue, 9
Columbiad, The (1805). *See* Barlow, Joel
Columbian Exchange, The. See Crosby, Alfred W.
Columbian exchange, the, 189
Columbus, Christopher: achievements of, 22–23; as American hero, 2, 8–10, 13–16, 21, 25, 29, 95; as anti-hero, 2, 119, 189; and Chicago World's Fair, 64, 78; and Dominican Republic, 167–68, 170; as ethnic hero, 14–18, 107; life of, 9–11, 121; as mariner, 22, 48; representations of, 7–8, 24–25, 95, 96, 97, 190; reputation of, 1–2, 124, 183, 186–87, 189–90, 192, 194; and Seville, 71–73, 134; Spanish attitude toward, 16, 129; testament to, 10–11, 15
Columbus, Ohio, 27, 54; Replica of Santa María, 9. *See also* Ameriflora
Columbus and the Age of Discovery. See Dor-Ner, Zvi
Columbus Day, 36, 55; creation of, 9, 15; parades on, 14, 15, 42; in San Francisco, 111, 181

Columbus Fellowship Foundation, 181
Columbus Lighthouse, 102, 170–71, 172, 181
Columbus on the Deck of the Santa María. See Leutze, Emanuel
Comisión Dominicana Permanente para la Celebración del Quinto Centenario del Descubrimiento y Evangelización de América. See Dominican National Quincentenary Commission
Comisión Nacional de México Conmemorativa del Quinto Centenario del Encuentro de Dos Mundos. See Mexican National Quincentenary Commission
Comisión Quinto Centenario. See Spanish National Quincentenary Commission
Comitato Nazionale per le Celebrazzioni del V Centenario della Scoperta dell'America. See Italian National Quincentenary Commission
Conquest of Paradise, The. See Sale, Kirkpatrick
Considine, Frank, 74, 84, 93
Conte, Silvio, 35, 36
Cook, Stanton, 69
Corne, Michele Felice, 24–25
Costner, Kevin, 189
Crosby, Alfred W., 197n, 211n
Crown of Columbus, The. See Dorris, Michael, and Louise Erdrich
Cruz, Armen, 45, 47, 70
Cuomo, Mario M., 40, 41, 42, 57, 116

DACOR Bacon House, 50–51
Daley, Richard J., 75
Daley, Richard M., 76
D'Angelo, Eugene, 54
DeAngelis, Aldo, 87
Dechant, Virgil, 39, 41, 43, 54
Decio, Arthur, 40, 52, 54
Defrène, Marie-Hélène, 69, 72–73
del Junco, Tirso, 42, 47
Denver, Colorado, 103, 104, 118
Derwinski, Edward, 43
Didion, Joan, 70
Discovery. See Quincentenary, Discovery

District of Columbia, 13
Dogs of Paradise, The. See Posse, Abel
Dominican National Quincentenary Commission, 168, 171–72
Dominican Republic, 102, 167–68; as mulatto society, 209n; tourism difficulties in, 209
Donatelli, Frank, 60
Dor-Ner, Zvi, 51, 228, 188
Dorris, Michael, and Louise Erdrich, *Crown of Columbus, The,* 121, 187
Dukakis, Michael, 108–9

Ecological Imperialism: The Biological Expansion of Europe, 900–1900. See Crosby, Alfred W.
El Día de la Raza, 36. See also Columbus Day
El dorado (film, 1988). See Saura, Carlos
Emerson, Ralph Waldo, 17, 25, 187
Encounter. See Quincentenary, Encounter
Ente Colombo '92. See Genoa
Erickson, Leif, 18
Ethnicity, 36, 107, 114–15, 204n
Ethnohistory, 125–26
Evangelization, 168–69
Expo '92. See Universal Exposition of Seville
Eyes of the Goddess. See Graham, Martha.

Faro a Colón. See Columbus Lighthouse
First Encounters (exhibition). See Florida Museum of Natural History
Ferdinand (king of Spain), 9
Florescano, Enrique, 176–77, 226
Florida Museum of Natural History, *First Encounters* (exhibition), 118
1492: Conquest of Paradise (film, 1992). See Scott, Ridley
Fourth Columbian Centenary (1892–93), 4, 9, 45, 192
Franco, Francisco, 130, 133
Fuentes, Carlos, *The Buried Mirror,* 44, 142, 166, 177, 178, 227, 188; *Christopher Unborn,* 187–88
FUNDICE (Fundación Pro-Difusión del Medio-Milenio en América), 174–75

Gala, Antonio, 188
García, Jane Lee, 36–37, 40, 47, 57, 98, 114
García, Robert, 36–38, 114
Garzón, Baltasar, 137
Genoa, Italy: archives of, 10; architectural restoration projects in, 156–57, 162–63; characteristics of, 157–59; Columbus's origins in, 10–11; "Columbus Walk" project in, 163; Ente Colombos '92 (Genoa Planning Commission), 159; historic center of, 158–59; and Italian politics, 152–53; and Quincentenary goals, 157–59; as starting point of Gran Regata, 155
Genoa Expo, 101; attendance, 180; BIE permit for, 73; overview of, 159–62. *See also* Bemporad, Alberto
George Horse Capture, 124
Glass, Philip, *The Voyage*, 188
Goizueta, Robert, 54
Gonzales, Manuel, 59
González, Felipe, 127, 130, 134, 138, 144
Goudie, Jack, 59
Goudie, John, 45, 51, 61, 70, 98, 114; and Iberoamerican Conference, 139; as temporary director of Jubilee Commission, 56–57; background and accomplishments of, 45–47; bankruptcy, 47–48; difficulties of, as fundraiser, 54–55, 205n; election as chairman of Jubilee Commission, 42, 201n; financial difficulties, 54–56; investigation of, 59–60; resignation of, 58; travels in 1989–90, 57
Graham, Martha, 180
Grand Columbus Regatta. *See* "Tall Ships"
Groseclose, Barbara, 96, 196n
Guardabassi, Frederick W., 42, 43, 48–50, 60, 114
Gurr, Ted Tobert, 110

Habits of the Heart. See Bellah, Robert
Harjo, Susan Shown, 117
Harvey, Penelope, 133, 135
Hayward, Lisa, 106
Hispanics, 36–37. *See also* Latinos
Hispanidad, 37, 114, 126, 146, 149; and Carlos Fuentes, 177; and neocolonialism, 129
Hogarth, William, 24–25
Honeymoon Project. *See* Miralda, Antoni
Hughes, Robert, 190–91

Iaccoca, Lee, 45, 90, 108
Iberoamerican Conference of Commissions for the Commemoration of the Quincentenary, 47, 139–40, 168, 168, 174
Illinois Exposition Authority. *See* Chicago World's Fair
Iltis, Hugh H., 191
Indians. *See* Native Americans
Indigenism: of Mexico, 172–73; of Native Americans, 116–18
Inter-American Development Bank, 140, 166, 208–9n
Invasion. *See* Quincentenary, invasion, concept of
Irving, Washington, 11, 16, 19
Isabela (settlement), 167, 171–72
Isabella (queen of Spain), 9, 18, 95
Italian National Quincentenary Commission, 152, 154–57
Italian-Americans, 2, 17, 44, 53, 54, 146; in Baltimore, 36; *Campanilismo*, 15; ethnicity of, 15–16, 109–14, 204n; members of Jubilee Commission, 16, 42, 47, 60; in New Haven, Connecticut, 20; and origins of Jubilee Commission, 35–38; in San Francisco, 107, 111–14
Italy: Quincentenary goals and programs, 150–52, 208n. *See also* Genoa; Genoa Expo

Jellinghaus, Paula, 56
Jennings, Edward, 98
Joustra, Jana, 57, 60
Juan Carlos (king of Spain), 130, 175
Jubilee Commission. *See* Christopher Columbus Quincentenary Jubilee Commission

Keillor, Garrison, 18
Kensington Runestone, 18

Kirkpatrick, Clayton, 72
Knights of Columbus, 14, 15, 20, 104, 182. See also Dechant, Virgil
Kramer, John D., 80–81, 85
Kuhn, James, 60

La Navidad, 167
La Rábida, 8
Las Casas, Bartolomé de, 122
Las Vegas, Nevada, 106, 179–80
Latin America: and the Quincentenary, 43–44, 165–66
Latino, 112; and Columbus Day, 36; and ethnicity, 15, 53, 111; meaning of term, 205n; members of Congress, 44; members of Jubilee Commission, 16, 42, 114. See also Hispanidad
León-Portilla, Miguel, 169, 173, 175, 176, 177
Leutze, Emanuel, 186
Library of Congress, 51
Liebert, Rich, 27

Madariaga, Salvador de, 12–13, 16
Maddox, Richard, 135
Madigan, Michael, 81
Madrid, 138–39
Magnani, Rinaldo, 152
Manzano Manzano, Juan, 23
Mathias, Charles "Mac," 35–38
McNeill, William H.: and Columbus Scholars Project, 53; and interpretation of world history, 193, 194; as member of Jubilee Commission, 39, 41, 43, 51, 198n
Means, Russell, 103, 118, 121
Mega-event, 33, 64, 133, 158, 164; and 1992, 180–81; concept of, 32, 90
Mexican National Quincentenary Commission, 173–78
Mexico: and the Quincentenary, 173–78; Indigenism, 172–73. See also Mexican National Quincentenary Commission; León-Portilla, Miguel
Miami, Florida, 55, 70, 201n. See also Goudie, John, background and accomplishments
Miami Beach, Florida, 45

Milhaud, Darius, 189
Millennium, 5–6, 90
Miralda, Antoni, 29–31, 106, 179–80
Morison, Samuel Eliot, 12, 13, 22
Museum of America (Madrid), 184

National Congress of American Indians, 117
National Council of La Raza, 16
National Endowment for the Humanities (NEH), 39, 124, 192; and Quincentenary programs, 11, 119–20, 183
National Gallery of Art, Circa 1492 (exhibition), 180, 183–84, 186
National Hispanic Quincentenary Commission. See National Council of La Raza
National Italian-American Foundation (NIAF), 35, 60, 157
National Museum of American Art, The West as America (exhibition), 185–86
National Museum of American History, 185
National Museum of the American Indian, 125, 190
Native Americans, 19, 21, 97; and ethnicity, 110, 112; and the Quincentenary, 53, 116–18, 124–25, 181, 182, 183; and Dances with Wolves (film), 189–90
Neil, Andrew, 75–76
Nuova Raccolta Colombiana, 155–56

O'Connor, James, 39, 54, 86
Ohio State University, 3, 54, 98, 119–20, 156
Olivencia, Manuel, 137
Olympic Games, 32, 64, 65; in Barcelona (1992), 61, 93, 133, 144, 148; in Los Angeles (1984), 46, 89
O'Neill, Tip, 40
Organization of American States, 122, 171, 173, 226. See also Plan Carimos

Pellón, Jacinto, 137
Percy, Charles, 38, 86
Perrone, Carlo, 159
Peterson, John C., 89

INDEX 217

Petkus, Donald, 83, 93; and Chicago World's Fair, 69, 74, 81, 85; and Jubilee Commission, 87, 88
Piano, Renzo, 160, 161
Pinzón Brothers, 17
Plan Carimos, 168, 171
Polzer, Charles, 41, 43
Posse, Abel, 13, 186–87
Power, Robert, 20
Pratt, George, 69, 70, 71, 79
Public Law 98-375, 41. *See also* Christopher Columbus Quincentenary Jubilee Commission, enabling legislation
Puerto Rico, 36–37

Quesada, Radl de, 57
Quincentenary: concept of, 11, 117, 118, 122–23, 177, 178; controversies over, 2–3, 4–5, 9, 114–17, 119–20; discovery, concept of, 122; encounter, and Dominican Republic, 168–72; invasion, concept of, 116–18, 120–21, 123; and Latin America, 44, 164–67, 207n; and Mexico, 165, 169, 173, 178; and National Endowment for the Humanities, 44–45; outcomes of, 5, 125–26, 181–82, 190, 193–94; and scholarship, 211n; and Spain, 145; as special event, 27–29, 32
Quincentenary Library, 141, 146

Raymont, Henry, 41, 43–45, 50
Reagan, Ronald, 3, 35, 39, 47, 71
Reagan administration, 39–40, 73, 79
Redmond, Scott, 25–27, 29
Repertorium Columbianum, 156
Replicas of Columbus's ships, 53; American tour of (1992), 57, 92, 146, 155, 181; and Jubilee Commission, 48–49, 56, 58; in 1892, 9
Richardson, Malcolm, 44
Roa Bastos, Augusto, 123
Rodino, Peter, 35, 37
Rudd, Thomas and Judy, 195n
Russell, Jeffrey, 198n

Saint Brendan, 19
Saint Paul, Minnesota, 18
Sale, Kirkpatrick, 118–19, 186

San Diego Chicken, 27
San Francisco Bay Columbus Committee, 113–14
Santo Domingo Conference (1988), 15–16
Saura, Carlos, 142, 188
Scott, Ridley, 188
Secchia, Peter, 43, 55
Seeds of Change. *See* Smithsonian Institution
Serrano, Angel, 139
Seville, 61, 79, 141, 148; 1929 Iberoamerican Exposition, 68; and Chicago World's Fair, 71–73. *See also* Universal Exposition of Seville
Shaefer, William Donald, 92
Shultz, George, 9
Smithsonian Institution: 1892 exhibit, 65; and Jubilee Commission, 51, 70; and Native Americans, 124–25; and Quincentenary programs, 51, 122, 185–86; *Seeds of Change* (exhibition), 180, 183, 184–85, 191; Van Sertima Conference (1991), 19, 22
Solti, Sir Georg, 72–73
Spain: and Jubilee Commission, 37–38; and Latin America, 128–29; and U.S. ethnicity, 115; and impact of Quincentenary, 61, 146–49; and Quincentenary goals, 129–32. *See also* Barcelona; Iberoamerican Conference; Seville; Spanish National Quincentenary Commission; Universal Exposition of Seville
—and Quincentenary projects, 140–42; criticism of, 3, 142–46; replicas of Columbus's ships, 49, 57
Spain '92 Foundation, 146, 180
Spanish National Quincentenary Commission, 30, 54, 57, 138–39, 140
Special Events Report, 28, 30, 31, 58
State Society for the Execution of Quincentenary Programs, 139–42, 140–42
Statue of Liberty Centennial (1986), 28, 45, 49, 54, 114–15; as special event, 31, 32, 32, 89
Stella, Frank, 60
Sterud, Eugene, 44

Summerhill, Stephen J., 3, 206n
Super Bowl, 32, 90–91
Swedish Maritime Museum, 1

"Tall Ships," 49–50, 53, 114; Grand Columbus Regatta, 55, 155, 180
Tangentopoli, 152–53, 154
Taviani, Paolo Emilio, 17, 24, 29, 98; accomplishments, 155–56; as biographer of Christopher Columbus, 11–12, 13, 15–16, 17, 22; as Quincentenary spokesman for Italy, 17, 151, 152, 155–56
Teele, Arthur, 42
Texaco, 56, 58
Thompson, James, 80, 81, 83
Thurmond, J. Strom, 38, 86
Trachtenburg, Alan, 185
Truettner, William H., 186
Tuttle, Robert H., 39, 45

Ueberroth, Peter, 46, 48, 90
Universal Exposition of Seville, 78, 93, 100, 133–35, 148; attendance, 135–36; *Cartuja '93*, 134; cost, 136–37, 144–45; and Chicago World's Fair, 72–73; criticisms of, 143, 144; Italian pavilion, 155; location and construction, 134–35; objective, 72, 133–34; U.S. pavilion, 61–62, 79

University of California at Los Angeles (UCLA), 156

Vanderlyn, John, 96
Van Sertima, Ivan, 19, 22
Varela, Consuelo, 156
Vecoli, Rudolph, 15
Vinland Map, 20, 23
Viola, Herman, 185
Vision of Columbus, The (1784). *See* Barlow, Joel

Warren, Dave, 117
Washington, Harold, 76–77, 80, 84–86, 88
Webster, Noah, 13
Weese, Harry, 73–74
West as America, The (exhibition). *See* National Museum of American Art
Wheatley, Phillis, 13
Wiesenthal, Simon, 12
Williams, John Alexander, 26–27, 30, 55, 58, 59–60, 195n, 197n, 198n, 201n; and Jubilee Commission, 3, 44–45, 48–52, 55–56
World's Fairs, 64–69

Yáñez Barnuevo, Luis, 98, 128, 138–39
Yaqui Indians, 97

Zea, Leopoldo, 175–76, 177

Stephen J. Summerhill is associate professor and a former chair of the Department of Spanish and Portuguese at Ohio State University. In the years 1986–90 he served as assistant vice-provost for International Affairs and directed Ohio State's Center for International Studies. He has written scholarly articles on Miguel de Unamuno, María Zambrano, and Luis Cernuda.

John Alexander Williams, director of the Christopher Columbus Quincentenary Jubilee Commission from 1986 to 1988, is professor of history at Appalachian State University, where he holds the I. G. Greer Distinguished Professorship in History for 1999–2001. This book is his fourth.

DATE DUE

MAY 1 1 2002		
MAY 0 7 REC'D		
NOV 0 8 2002		
OCT 3 0 2002		
MAR 2 1 REC'D		
MAY 0 6 2006		
MAY 0 2 REC'D		
MAR 0 3 2010		
APR 0 2 REC'D		
MAR 0 3 2010		
APR 2 4 2013		

GAYLORD   PRINTED IN U.S.A.

E119.2 .S86 2000
cop.2
Summerhill, Stephen J.,
1944-
Sinking Columbus : contested
history, cultural politics,

DISCARD